CRIMES WITHOUT VICTIMS:

Deviance and the Criminal Law

Robert M. Rich
Criminologist

UNIVERSITY
PRESS OF
AMERICA

LANHAM • NEW YORK • LONDON

Copyright © 1978 by

University Press of America, Inc.™

P.O. Box 19101, Washington, DC 20036

ISBN: 0-8191-0618-6

Library of Congress Catalog Card Number: 78-63258

TABLE OF CONTENTS

PREFACE

This text is the logical extension of the research initiated by Edwin Schur in his pioneer work, <u>Crimes Without Victims</u>, that appeared in 1965.

This text explains the origins and problems in dealing with a variety of so-called victimless crimes following the Anglo-American legal tradition. Each form of social deviance selected for analysis deals with the legal history, definitions, criminal code and enforcement procedures, description of types of offenders, and presentation of the pros and cons of the decriminalization debate.

I would like to thank the police officers, both men and women, of the Metropolitan Police Department (District of Columbia) for their help and cooperation in making this text possible.

My thanks to May Thompson for her understanding, patience, and persistence at the task of typing the manuscript of this book. Also special thanks to Pamela J. Caldarone for her work as proof-reader, indexer, and special editor.

Robert M. Rich, Ph.D.
Alexandria, Virginia
1978

I

AN OVERVIEW OF DEVIANCE

Deviance Definitions

Deviance is behavior that is contrary to the standards of conduct or social expectations of a given group, institution, community, or society. Deviance refers to the activities described in such terms as delinquency, crime, drug abuse, alcoholism, moral insanity, and sexual perversion. These concepts imply a departure by individuals from accepted standards of conduct of the group.

The use of the term deviance can be attributed to the statistical idea of atypical behavior as compared to that which is the norm. Both atypical and normal behavior are identified in relation to the standards of the group in which they take place. Deviant behavior is evaluated in terms of the degree to which it departs from these standards. It is typical for a person to deviate to some degree, but to oversubscribe to group norms is just as deviant as to deliberately violate standards of the group.[1]

Deviance As Social Pathology

The deviancy concept first appeared in the form of the theory of social pathology. According to Spencer and other biological sociologists social pathologies were reflected by maladjustments in social relationships (i.e., events were seen as deviant when they interfered with the normal functioning of some part of society just as a disease is seen as a problem because it disrupts a person's normal biochemical processes). These maladjustments developed as society progressed and some people and social groups were unable to keep up with the growth. This theory stated that one should create and protect healthy people and societies by eliminating social pathology which constitutes a violation of societal standards (i.e., morals, norms, and laws). Deviant behavior was seen as sick and pathological. Social pathology theory in its early form felt that the sickness resided within the individual while later views held that the environment was at fault. These social Darwinian views felt that the sick became useless or died out while the strong survived and multiplied. Thus deviant behavior was labeled as inherently defective, dependent, or delinquent/criminal.[2]

1

The theory of social pathology gradually declined due to its pronounced moral and naturalistic biases explicit in its structure. This theory is still found in the definitions of deviance that feel that the individual exhibits pathological traits or that deviant behavior is a manifestation of a sick society.[3]

Deviance As Social Disorganization

In the 1920's the social pathology theory (i.e., viewing people as injurious to society) was replaced by the social disorganization theory (i.e., examining learning theory to find out why some people learn to be deviant while others learn to conform). Social disorganization theory stated that there was a position correlation between increasing social complexity of industrial society and higher rates of deviance especially in the large urban centers of the United States. Social disorganization theory is based on the assumption that social order and organization exists when there is a high degree of internal cohesion binding people and their institutions in a society closely together. This cohesion consists for the most part of consensus about the normative system (i.e., value-attitudes) that binds all groups and institutions in a common culture. When consensus concerning the normative system of society is upset and people no longer automatically apply common value-attitudes conflict, social disorganization, and deviant behavior become increasingly common. Thus the basic premise of social disorganization theory is that conflict and disorganization increase when the status quo is disturbed (i.e., dysfunctioning of the social system) during periods of rapid technological change. Therefore as rapid sociocultural change produces conflict and disorganization so the rate of deviant behavior escalates in society.[4]

Social disorganization theory especially deals with the disorganizing aspects of urban life and on the rates of deviant behavior within large urban areas. The city typified the social environment most conducive to social disorganization and the emergence of deviant behavior. The indicators of social disorganization developed by the Chicago School of Sociology were many (i.e., heterogeneity of population, normative conflicts between residential groups based on race, religion, and ethnicity, mobility of population - both socially and physically, lack of community organization, and physical deterioration of housing stock and recreational facilities). According to the theory, areas of a city which manifested most of these characteristics were viewed as disorganized and the high rates of deviance found validated the high degree of disorganization. This was especially true when comparing disorganization-deviance rates of suburban and rural areas with inner cities. Chicago School theorists concluded that only certain inner city neighborhoods were typical disorganized communities and these areas appeared to contain only lower class slum residents. Therefore social disorganization theory concluded that inner city slum lower class people tended to be deviant by nature.[5]

The Cultural Relativity of Deviance In Society

Deviant behavior can be conceived of as ranging along a continuum from extreme underconformity to extreme overconformists. Behavior patterns can be diagramed on a normal or bell-shaped curve. Most individuals fall within the range of normal conforming behavior although many may occasionally either become tolerated underconformists or tolerated overconformists. Those individuals who become extreme underconformists or extreme overconformists are considered to be deviant by conventional standards but are thought to be receptive to programs of rehabilitation. On the other hand those individuals whose behavior completely rejects the normative system of society (i.e., underconformists) or those who accept societal norms in an extreme form (i.e., overconformists) are attempting to restructure society and bring about cultural change by either violent or peaceful means.[6]

Individuals are defined as deviant as a result of having been perceived by others in their reference group as violators of group value-attitudes. This kind of behavior does not apply to outsiders who may break group rules since they are not members of a particular social group, either primary or secondary. Most individuals by adulthood belong to several groups and are expected to role play in the status hierarchy to which they fit at that particular moment (i.e., their role behavior should conform to the social system of the moment).[7]

Deviance can be looked upon by the social group or society as either harmful or beneficial. The genius and artist are examples of deviants who are positive role models for their social group and/or community. Positive deviance is rewarded because it usually is beneficial to society in one way or another. On the other hand negative deviance is punished since the behavior of these individuals is a threat to the normative system of society. Thus the drug addict, violent criminal, or sexual pervert is publicly identified as a person whose behavior will not be tolerated and who should be removed from society so that their behavior can be inhibited or modified.[8]

Variations in social deviation occur not only in terms of type of group membership but also from place to place and time to time within the same society and between societies. Such criminal statutes that govern public drunkenness, prostitution, vagrancy, obscenity, and homosexual behavior by consenting adults may be enforced in one community, rescinded in another community, and just plain ignored in a third community. These contrasting moral standards may be in adjacent communities in a single metropolitan area, counties of the same state, and neighboring states. Thus the confusion concerning normal versus deviant behavior is made more unclear by the official policy of each sovereign state and its many communities. On top of this the Federal government may take a stand that goes against the consensus of most states (i.e., prohibition, dangerous drugs, and public morals).[9]

Criticism of Deviance Theory

Deviance theory can be criticized for having implicit value judgments built into it. This can be seen in reviewing the statements concerning both the social pathology and social disorganization approaches. These approaches assume that either the individual is "no good" or "evil" or that the social system in which people live, especially lower class people, suffers from the same social problems (i.e., slums that breed corruption, vice, and encourage the activities of the devil). Finally since most lower class people are associated with slum and transitional community residential patterns, they are assumed to have higher rates of deviance because traditionally these neighborhoods are most disorganized. Thus middle and upper class people who do not live in slum and transitional communities cannot be disorganized and manifest common forms of social deviance. These middle class value judgments held by many theorists have blinded them to the facts concerning deviance theory.[10]

A second major criticism of deviance theory concerns the view that deviants are uniquely aberrant. This view is challenged as many deviants supposedly do what conventional society expects them to do (i.e., this implies that normal people to a certain extent covertly applaud the exploits of those who are unconventional). Thus many respectable individuals may be latently as deviant as those who they label as publicly deviant.[11]

The last major criticism of deviance theory is concerned with the assumptions that deviance is easy to identify and that most members of society can agree as to which acts are deviant. A basic myth is that most individuals can readily agree that deviance is simple to define and analyze because it is so obvious and evident in society. In reality in a gesellschaft society (i.e., urban, bureaucratic, and rapidly changing), most people have a difficult time agreeing on normative limits for behavior.

This makes it extremely difficult for the average person to
recognize and categorize many forms of deviance. The recent
example of political corruption such as Watergate where over
sixty high ranking appointed and elected officials were convicted
of crimes and the continuing rise and proliferation of corporate
and professional white collar crimes has the public confused as
to what is normal politics and business practices and what is
deviant behavior.[12]

Thus deviance is not only difficult to define but also
difficult to identify and describe in exact terms because of
value judgments in deviance theory itself. One problem with
deviance theory is the inability to distinguish between the
motives of persons who later become labeled as deviant. Thus
some people who are basically normal are falsely accused by the
public of deviance despite their motivation for such apparently
abnormal behavior. Deviance theory postulates that most acts
will involve either normal people or social deviants. Thus what
the public assumes to be aberrant behavior becomes aberrant
behavior over time. This means that unusual life-styles (i.e.,
dressing, speaking, and interacting with others) will be pointed
out by normal people to be avoided and those engaging in such
behavior will be voluntarily or forcefully made to conform to
accepted standards of conduct in public. Therefore deviance can
become a function of public definition, not professional diagnosis.
Finally what is considered deviant during one social order may
become the norm for another. Consider the "Hippy movement" of
the 1960's in speech, dress, and life-style which has become the
norm in many ways by the late 1970's.[13]

Deviance Theories

In 1975 George Ritzer published his book <u>Sociology: A
Multiple Paradigm Science</u> which consisted of his thoughts of what
sociological models of society should be based on his interpretation of the writings of Thomas Kuhn.[14] This section of the book
will attempt to place deviance theories in the three proposed
paradigms or models of Ritzer.

Sociological Paradigms

According to Ritzer, there are currently only three basic
paradigms in sociology. These are the social facts paradigm, the
social definition paradigm, and the social behavior paradigm.[15]
A paradigm is defined as "a fundamental image of the subject
matter within a science. It serves to define what should be
studied, what questions should be asked, and what rules should be

followed in interpreting the answers obtained. The paradigm is the broadest unit of consensus within a science and serves to differentiate one scientific community or sub-community from another. It subsumes, defines, and interrelates the exemplars, theories, and methods/tools that exist within it.[16]

Social Facts Paradigm

. The social facts paradigm is composed of two theories, structural-functional and conflict theory. Structural-functional theory states that structures and institutions can contribute to the maintenance of other social facts and can also have negative consequences for them (i.e., utilization is made of the concepts of function and dysfunction). Followers of this theory justify the status quo and tend to have a conservative societal orientation (i.e., emphasize order in society and de-emphasize conflict and social change).[17] In particular structural-functional theory is oriented toward the analysis of social structures, processes, and institutions. Concern is with the relationships between structures, between institutions, and between structures and institutions. The individual is largely controlled by social facts that are external and coercive to him. This theory views society as static or in a state of moving equilibrium. Strong emphasis is placed on the fact that society is orderly and its parts function in a predictable manner; every societal element contributes to this stability; and society is permanently kept together informally by its normative system (i.e., value-attitudes) and common morality.[18]

Conflict theory, for the most part, is simply a series of intellectual positions directly opposite to structural-functional ideas according to Ritzer. Thus conflict theory is oriented toward the study of social structures and institutions like structural-functional theory but perceives society as based on the consensus-conflict continuum and emphasizes the role of social power in the maintenance of societal order.[19]

In particular, conflict theory sees every structure, process, and institution of society as subject to change, conflict ridden, and riddled by dissension. Whatever order there is in society stems from the coercion of the powerless by those in authority or representing authority. Differential authority is an attribute of various societal position (i.e., in status hierarchies). Authority does not reside in individuals but in these positions. Thus the individual is concerned with societal institutional positions and the differential distribution of power among these positions. Hence the structural origin of conflicts must be sought in the arrangement of social roles endowed with expectations

of domination and subjection (i.e., authority implies both super-
ordination and subordination). Finally the identification of
various authority roles within society is the primary focus of
conflict theory.[20]

Social Definition Paradigm

The social definition paradigm is composed of three theories –
action, symbolic interaction, and phenomenology. Action theory
(ala Weber) views the individual as possessing a dynamic, creative,
voluntaristic mind. It sees Weber's <u>verstehen</u> concept (i.e.,
utilizes the method of participant observation and the value-free
or neutral concept) as a method for gathering data on social
institutions and social structures, not as a method for understanding the mental process. The action theorist attempts to put
himself in the place of the actor, not in order to comprehend the
person but to understand the cultural and societal milieu in which
the actor exists.[21] Social action theory examines the problem
solving process through the mind of the actor under study. The
theory examines the actor's means to ends whether both are valued
in the same manner or differently utilizing the <u>verstehen</u> concept
(i.e., empathy and reliving the experiences of the actor). The
feelings, emotions, and habits of the actor are sometimes receptive
to analysis using this concept which can also be called interpre-
tive understanding.[22]

Symbolic interaction theory deals with the covert aspects of
human behavior. This theory views behavior as a social process of
interpretation inserted between the environmental stimulus and
response of the actor. Social facts are not viewed as things
controlling or coercing the individual but only as a framework
within which symbolic interaction takes place. Individuals fit
their actions to those of others through a process of interpretation. Through this process actors form groups, the action of
the group serving as the action of all actors within it. The
world of the actor is found in the process of interpretation or
orientation of himself vis-a-vis the group. The mind is seen
as a process in which the individual interacts with himself and
others through the utilization of symbols.[23]

Phenomenological theory is more philosophical than sociological. This theory states that human beings constitute and
reconstitute what is real (i.e., objective social reality is
not independent of the individual). Thus to define a situation
as real makes it real. Phenomenological theory tries to comprehend the meaning that the actor's behavior has for him by both
studying the process through which social facts are created by

the actor rather than the social facts themselves and by examining
the ongoing process of reality construction in society as social
facts do not possess an objective existence. By uncovering the
processes through which social order emerges from the negotiative
behaviors of everyday life, phenomenologists hope to learn how
people engage in the process of creating the social facts that
are coercive on them. Order and meaning cannot have an objective
existence since people impose order and meaning on themselves
through manipulation and molding of norms. Reality is what
each person makes of it. Thus order and social reality have a
tenuous existence according to phenomenological theory.[24]

Social Behavior Paradigm

The social behavior paradigm consists of two theories,
behavioral sociology and exchange theory. Behavioral sociology
is virtually the same theory as psychological behaviorism. Thus
as a theory behavioral sociology applies psychological principles
to areas of sociological inquiry. Behavioral sociology concerns
itself with the relationship between the consequences of behavior
in the individual's environment and the behavior of the individual
(i.e., behavior is explained by the environmental consequences
that follow it). Thus behavioral sociology concerns itself with
the relationship between the past account of environmental consequences for behavior and the nature of present behavior
(i.e., past consequences of a particular behavior govern its
present state). Therefore by knowing what caused a specific past
behavior, one can predict whether the same behavior will manifest
itself in the individual at the moment.[25]

Behavioral sociology is primarily keyed upon the relationship
between the individual and his environment. Contingencies are
built into the individual/environment relationship. Thus the part
played by the concept of reinforcement/punishment is crucial to
behavioral sociology (i.e., how both positive and negative
reinforcers and punishers effect the individual and his environment). The reinforcement concept is quite complex (i.e., more
than a simple stimulus-response) and environmental conditions to
determine the probability for reinforcement of a given behavior
pattern in an individual are necessary. Thus reinforcement of
a specific response leads to a whole series of other similar
responses being rewarded at the same time. This revelation lead
behavioral sociology to the concept of behavior modification which
is utilized as a therapeutic tool.[26]

Exchange theory attempts to explain basic social behavior in
terms of rewards and costs. There are.five basic propositions

that explain exchange theory. The first proposition deals with
the relationship between past and present behavior. A rewarding
past stimulus-situation that is similar to a present stimulus-
situation will probably elicit the same behavior pattern in an
individual. The second proposition deals with the frequency
of reward and activity (i.e., concern is with the maintenance of
interpersonal relationships). If an individual's activity
rewards the activity of another, the more often the latter person
will replicate the activity for the former person. The third
proposition of exchange theory states that the value of one
person's activity may be seen in terms of his effect on another
person's activity (i.e., if one does not consider another's
activity as valuable, one will cease his activity and end the
interpersonal relationship).[27]

The fourth proposition deals with the relation of past rewards
to future rewards (i.e., if one has been rewarded for an activity
in the recent past, the amount of reward in the present will be
less valuable). Thus the more often one has been rewarded by
the activity of another over a short period of time, the less
valuable the activity becomes for the one rewarded. The final
proposition deals with the fair distribution of rewards and costs
among individuals (i.e., norm of reciprocity). The more one feels
that a relationship is to his disadvantage, the more one is likely
to disrupt the relationship (i.e., become angry).[28]

Deviancy As Social Fact

Durkheim's Anomie Theory

Durkheim's concept of anomie (i.e., aimlessness or norm-
lessness) states that during times of rapid social change the
traditional rules of a group, institution, or even a society
become less important to individuals with the result of increased
deviance among the population. According to Durkheim the
happiness of an individual depends upon a balance between desires
and the ability to fulfill one's desires. Thus people have limit-
less needs and desires which must be controlled by societal norms
or else many members of society will become anomic in their
inability to satisfy their endless wants. It is the task of
society to restrain and regulate an individual's desires through
the examples set by societal institutions such as the legal system
and the family. Through rapid technological change society
becomes unsettled institutionally with the result that normative
restrictions become confused and people find themselves dealing
with unfamiliar situations. Anomie is a result which can produce
all types of social deviance in people and their institutions.[29]

Merton's Modes of Individual Adaptation

Merton examines how some social structures exert pressure on
individuals to engage in deviant behavior. He also uses the concept of anomie but extends Durkheim's explanation of its causes
and puts forth a typology dealing with anomie on the part of
individuals (i.e, one conforming and four deviant adaptations).
Merton feels that anomie originates from an unsuitable emphasis
in a society upon the relative importance of attaining culturally
valued goals on the one hand and the availablility of legitimate,
institutionalized means to reach these goals on the other hand.
Thus the condition for anomie are present when members of society
are told in school or via the media that they can be successful
if they conform to societal norms while in reality their experience
tells them that the legitimate means for success in life are almost
impossible to utilize (i.e., the discrepancy between means and
ends). An anomic response results as people maintain their desires
to achieve the culturally approved goals but reject the traditionally legitimate means for achieving them because these means are
blocked. Merton calls this adaptation innovation. He also explains
three other adaptations which are considered deviant (ritualism,
retreatism, and rebellion.)[30]

Merton goes beyond Durkheim in analyzing the breakdown of
societal norms by examining the disparity between means and ends.
He emphasizes the reaction of individuals to anomic conditions.
Anomie is found in the disparity between culturally accepted goals
and the legitimate institutionalized means to be used by people
in achieving approved goals. Anomie is the outgrowth of an
inherent structural weakness in American society (i.e., the
overemphasis on success-oriented goals with corresponding under-
emphasis on equality of opportunity). Merton's anomie theory
assumes that there are dominant value-attitudes accepted by all
members of society and does not explain why lower class people
tend to deviate more than members of other social classes.
Merton's theory also does not utilize the concept of social
power as well as group pressure that labels a person as deviant.[31]

Cohen's Subculture Theory

Cohen's theory of deviance is also based on Durkheim but
through Merton's interpretation of anomie theory. Cohen feels
that blocked opportunities for achieving goals or an inability
to take advantage of whatever opportunities are available cause
people to become deviant. People will either reject or react
negatively toward their environment that represent sources of the
problem or barriers to solutions. At this point many will substitute goals and norms that are more suitable but will come in

conflict with the norms of conventional society. Thus these
individuals will end up defending their social deviance in order
to realize their goal in life. Thus individuals who deviate
eventually communicate with others having similar problems and
reinforce each other in their deviance. Eventually a subculture
is formed based on deviant value-attitudes whereby deviant means
to legitimate ends are supported by the social group.[32]

Deviant behavior is patterned as the deviant normative
system of the subculture is internalized and followed by group
members according to Cohen. Members of the subculture socialize
each other and thus gradually reject the culture of society.
Cohen feels that lower class members of society are particularly
susceptible to being pressured into developing negative value-
attitudes which are conducive to deviant behavior since pursuance
of culturally acceptable goals is usually out of reach to them.
Thus the deviant behavior of lower class subcultures is often
malicious and nondirectional since these people reject cultural
goals.[33]

Quinney's Conflict Theory

Quinney feels that the content of any norm violating behavior
is learned in the value-attitude systems of certain social environments. While the content of social action differs greatly for
individuals in a gesellschaft society, it all represents the
behavior patterns of certain parts of the society. On the other
hand in a gemeinschaft society, people learn a variety of group
and individual action patterns. The general content of social
behavior is shaped by the type of societal structure but each
member of society makes rational choices concerning his behavior.
Thus the individual learns about alternative behavior systems
but does not have to accept any given set of behavior patterns.
In other words, to Quinney people behave intentionally in the
pursuit of specific goals well aware of the consequences of their
choices. Finally the subcultural milieux and the reactions of
significant others influence the everyday behavior of any given
person.[34]

When those in power interact with those defined as deviant,
the latter often react more deviantly partly because they are
negatively treated by those in authority positions (i.e., people
may develop a life-style and self-concept that is deviant because
those of legitimate high status expect them to do so). These
patterns of deviance evolve as the individual experiences more
negative social reactions by those around him. Thus the deviant
acts as a deviant with others so labeled or in the presence of

those who feel he is a deviant. Therefore to Quinney deviant
behavior depends partially on the deviant or nondeviant substance of structured opportunities, learning experiences, interpersonal associations and identifications and in part, on the
continued experience of being defined as deviant and giving in
to such deviant self-concepts.[35]

Quinney perceives deviance as a result of a political process
wherein the politically powerful rely in the criminal law to
neutralize the actions of the powerless in society. There is a
definite relationship between power politics and definitions of
what is considered deviant and criminal behavior. In our
gesellschaft pluralistic society the value-attitudes of different
social group and communities are often in conflict with each other.
Thus definitions of what constitutes deviance vary from community
to community with little chance for uniformity of behavior. Therefore the criminal law is utilized as a means of establishing some
common base for all to conform to, regardless of differences in
value systems. Rules are developed and enforced by and for the
politically powerful because it is to their advantage, not because
someone's behavior is necessarily at odds with the majority of
members of a community. Specifically the powerful members of
society are able to influence and intimidate the less powerful
(i.e., elected and appointed officials) to enact and apply sanctions
against people perceived to be real threats to the vested interests
of the elite. This analysis of Quinney's makes both those who
are minority groups (i.e., race, ethnic, social class) and those
who are the elite deviant.[36]

Other Social Factists

Cloward and Ohlin utilize the theoretical foundations
presented by Durkheim and modified by Merton and Cohen (i.e., their
theory of deviance is derived from these theorists). They perceive
deviants to be individuals who have been mislead to expect opportunities because of their own felt potential ability to meet the
formal criteria for success. These people feel capable of success
but lack or are blocked from the opportunities to achieve success
and eventually feel cheated by middle class society. Thus these
lower class people respond to the lack of opportunity by becoming
deviant. Cloward and Ohlin utilize the subculture concept and
perceive three types of deviant subcultures: criminal, conflict,
and retreatist. They examine the environmental nature of deviance
and are concerned with social groups, structures, and institutions -
not individual characteristics of deviancy.[37]

13

Miller feels that lower class value-attitudes are inherently
conflictual with the middle class norms of society. Thus lower
class people are inherently prone to deviant actions. For
example gang activity of lower class youth is similar to peer
activity of middle class adolescents but the former are prone
toward delinquent actions while the latter are conformist to
the norms of society. This is explained by Miller by stating that
the gang activity of lower class youth is similar to peer activity
of middle class youth but subcultural differences in behavior
patterns leads to problems with society (i.e., seeking excitement,
being tough and smart to authority figures). Lower class value-
attitudes offer status where middle class aspirations cannot be
achieved (i.e., lower class deviant behavior offers one status
and prestige when middle class aspirations cannot be realized).[38]

Deviancy As Social Definition

Sutherland's Theory of Differential Association

Sutherland's theory of differential association stresses the
learning process involved in becoming deviant. He does not under-
estimate the importance of social structure in the evolution of
deviance theory but focuses basically on the interactional processes
involved in learning any behavior (i.e., deviant as well as conventional). Sutherland's theoretical foundations are based in
part on the writings of Gabriel Tarde who was a pioneer in the
social psychology of deviant behavior.[39]

People acquire criminal behavior patterns through the same
socialization processes by which they acquire conventional
behavior patterns according to Sutherland (i.e., criminal behavior
has much in common with conventional behavior). He perceives
deviant behavior as related to individual's interactions with
significant others (i.e., individuals in their associations with
primary group members learn value-attitudes, life-styles, and
techniques that are both oriented towards and away from breaking
the law). Thus people act in a deviant manner when the situation
is appropriate. Situations are defined by the person as favor-
able or unfavorable to deviance depending upon what one has
learned from reference group members. Therefore according to
Sutherland one learns deviant behavior patterns and is more
likely to engage in a specific form of deviance when the opportunity presents itself if one has been exposed to deviant behavior
for a long time by those with whom one has a strong emotional
attachment.[40]

Becker's Labeling Theory

Becker assumes that most individuals frequently wish to
engage in deviance but do not do so because they are afraid
that they will suffer psychologically or socially (i.e., lose
their job, cause family members to suffer at their expense, or
lose their reputation). Thus those who act in a deviant manner
are likely to lack constraints upon them (i.e., no fear of societal
mores and taboos) or are already defined by the public as deviant
(i.e., individuals labeled as deviant behave aberrantly in order
to conform to public opinion about them).[41]

Deviant behavior evolves in only two ways according to
Becker: as a result of the person being missocialized (i.e., sociopath or psychopath) or as a result of rationalizing one's deviant
behavior and associating with known deviants rather than with
conventional people. Becker states that the fastest way of being
labeled deviant is to be caught in the act and publicly given
the title of nonconformist. Public recognition of one's deviance
usually evokes the application of a negative label to all future
acts of the individual and those associating with him. Thus at
this point one is identified as deviant whether one acts in this
manner or not. The deviant is henceforth cut off from association
with normal people and pushed into association with other deviants
whether he wants to conform to community standards by public
opinion. Therefore the deveant eventually finds it more rewarding to join with other known deviants in their activities and
develop a truly deviant identity.[42]

Matza's Control Theory

Matza states that most deviants drift into deviance since
their behavior fluctuates between conventional and deviant
behavior with only a small part of their activity oriented toward
deviant (i.e., criminal) activity. Thus the deviant is "neither
compelled nor committed to deeds nor freely choosing them; neither
different in any simple or fundamental sense from the law abiding,
nor the same; conforming to certain traditions in American life
while partially unreceptive to other more conventional traditions;
and finally, an individual whose motivational system may be explored
along lines explicitly commended by classical criminology – his
peculiar relation to legal institutions."[43]

Sykes and Matza state that delinquents justify their deviant
behavior utilizing what they call "techniques of neutralization".
These techniques aid in neutralizing the cultural value-attitudes
of society and thus neutralize their responsibility for delinquent
behavior. Therefore the delinquent is in reality acting out the
"subterranean values" of society since the public really admires
his rebellious and anti-social behavior (i.e., this offers the
delinquent a defense for his behavior since society really applauds
his actions). Last Sykes and Matza list five major types of
neutralization: (1) denial or responsibility, (2) denial of injury,
(3) denial of the victim (i.e., person injured or wronged is not
a victim), (4) condemnation of the condemners, and (5) gang
loyalties are more important than loyalty to community and
society.[44]

Lemert's Societal Reaction Theory

Lemert classifies deviant behavior into three categories:
(1) the social (i.e., product of the socialization process),
(2) the cultural (i.e., environmental influences that impinge
upon and interact with one's genetic makeup), and (3) the psychological (i.e., organic problems or role problems). Lemert makes
the distinction between what he calls primary and secondary
deviance.[45]

Primary deviance according to Lemert is the action of an
individual who occasionally engages in deviant behavior for a
number of reasons and is seen by others and by himself as basically
normal since his aberrant behavior is short lived. Secondary
deviance occurs when a person is labeled by significant others
in the community as deviant and the individual accepts the label.
Thus because one is labeled deviant publicly, one has no alternative but to act deviant on a regular basis. Lemert developed an
eight step model to explain the primary-secondary deviance
continuum: (1) primary deviance; (2) social degradation; (3) further
primary deviance; (4) stronger penalties and social degradation;
(5) further deviance with hostile reactions toward those imposing
the penalties; (6) formal action taken by the community against
the deviant; (7) reaction of the deviant becomes hardened against
the community; and (8) final acceptance of one's deviant social
status and adjustment to one's new role.[46]

Other Social Definitionists

Tannenbaum elaborates on what he calls the transference from an individual committing "evil" acts to the individual considering himself to be "evil". The end result is that behavior of "evil" people is viewed with distrust. As the public's definition of the individual changes from occasional troublemaker to deviant, the person so labeled also changes his self-perception. Tannenbaum makes reference to what he calls the "dramatization of evil" (i.e., the process of making a deviant, a process of tagging, defining, identifying, segregating, describing, emphasizing, and making known to all that an individual possesses negative traits that should be shunned by all).[47]

Reckless explains deviant behavior with his theory of containment. This theory consists of five vertical factors: (1) social pressures consisting of adverse factors (i.e., low socioeconomic status, racial prejudice and discrimination, personal and social group conflicts), (2) pull factors which lead the person away from acceptable societal standards (i.e., association with deviant peers), (3) external containment which is the social situation surrounding the individual (i.e., a structure consisting of family and peer groups), (4) inner containment which is the value-attitude system of the individual (i.e., proper socialization, self-control, and strong self-concept), and (5) pushes (i.e., inner tensions, hostility, aggressiveness, inferiority). Reckless' theory utilizes the concepts of outer and inner containment to demonstrate how the individual may be pushed or pulled into or away from deviant behavior by his socialization process as well as inter-action with social groups, processes, structures, and institutions of society.[48]

Reiss utilizes three sources of social control to explain how individuals conform to societal norms: (1) community and institutional controls, (2) primary group controls, and (3) personal controls. The evolution and continuance of deviant behavior are the result of ineffective social and personal controls. Reiss states there are four conditions in which ineffective controls can result in social deviance: (1) if previously established social controls break down, (2) when group rules are not clear or absent, (3) when there is a conflict in group rules, and (4) when the person is sociopathic (i.e., not been socialized to accept societal norms).[49]

Nye states there are four mechanisms of social control, the absence of which are causal of social deviance. He also states that weak social controls may also produce the same result. Direct control (i.e., imposed from outside by means of restriction and punishment) is the first social control mechanism. Internalized control (i.e., social conscience). Third is indirect control (i.e., affective identification with family members and nondeviant peers). The fourth control mechanism is provided through a wide opportunity of means to goal attainment.[50]

Hirschi identifies four ways in which a person is socialized to conform to societal norms: (1) attachment (i.e., internalization of societal value-attitudes), (2) commitment (i.e., the extent to which an individual's reputation and/or material possessions and wealth might be threatened if one becomes labeled deviant), (3) involvement (i.e., conventional behavior prevents one from partaking of deviant behavior), and (4) belief (i.e., acceptance of societal normative systems). Thus when the social bonds that hold individuals to cultural standards are weakened or broken, the person is free to engage in deviant behavior although he may or may not do so.[51]

Deviancy as Social Behavior

Alexander and Staub's Psychoanalytic Theory

Alexander and Staub best represent the Freudian view of deviance. They feel that people are born psychodynamically deviant; that the first deviant act is committed early in childhood and is an important factor in the formation of a sense of justice; and the Oedipus Complex is causal in producing deviancy. It is felt by Alexander and Staub that a comprehension of unconscious motives of the individual will aid in deviance prevention and control.[52] Further they differentiate two broad types of deviants: chronic and accidental. The former type is recognized by the fact that his deviancy is due to his psychic structure (i.e., organic, symptomatic, neurotic acting out, normal, and genuine) while the latter type is recognized by the environmental circumstances leading to unusual pressures on his psychic functioning (i.e., mistaken and situational).[53]

Abrahamsen's Personality Trait Theory

Abrahamsen classifies deviants on the basis of unusual circumstances in their environments (i.e., momentary offenders) or those suffering from psychodynamic problems (i.e., chronic offenders). The former category consists of situational deviants (i.e., those with an opportunity to partake in deviance), accidental deviants (i.e., those who inadvertently become deviant), and associational deviants (i.e., those whose peers are deviant). The latter category consists of neurotic deviants (i.e., those who are cleptomaniacs, pyromaniacs, and those suffering from unconscious guilt), character disorder deviants (i.e., psychopaths, alcoholics, drug addicts, and homosexuals), psychotic and mentally defective deviants and faulty superego structure deviants (i.e., sociopaths and psychopaths).[54]

Trasler's Reinforcement Theory

Trasler utilizes reinforcement theory to explain how an individual learns to be a social deviant. At an early age the child must learn not to become deviant by inhibiting certain kinds of behavior. The child must be conditioned to feel anxious if he has done something wrong or thinks he has done something wrong. Thus the degree of anxiety within the individual when deviant is in direct proportion to the amount of punishment given during the early stages of the socialization process. Thus social conditioning effectiveness depends upon the strength of the anxiety state with which it is associated. There must be a strong dependence of child upon parents so that approval withdrawal will not evoke anxiety. Therefore predisposition to deviancy depends upon differences in conditioning methods, family attitudes toward deviance, and social class attitudes towards deviance.[55]

Scheff's Psychiatric Theory

Scheff perceives the origin of initial deviance in people as having diverse sources (i.e., organic, psychological, external pressures, innovative, or rebellious). The socially deviant individual is the product of labeling processes according to Scheff which fit the behavior into a public stereotype, make the person psychologically receptive to the deviant role forced on him by public reaction, and force the labeled individual to conform to the public expectations of what the specific deviant behavior should be. Scheff states seven factors which have an effect upon social deviants: (1) degree of rule-breaking, (2) amount of rule-breaking, (3) visibility of rule-breaking, (4) power of rule-breaker in relation to that of the enforcers of community standards, (5) social distance (i.e., status) of deviant and community members who are conformists, (6) community tolerance for socially deviant behavior, and (7) the degree of availability of normal roles versus deviant roles in one's reference group.[56]

Notes

1. The Dushkin Publishing Group, Encyclopedia of Sociology, Guilford, Connecticut: The Dushkin Publishing Group, 1974,79.

2. Ibid, 79, Ritchie Lowry, Social Problems: A Critical Analysis of Theories and Public Policy, Lexington, Massachusetts: DC Heath and Company, 1974, 81-82.

3. Lowry, op. cit., 82.

4. Lowry, op. cit., 93-94; The Dushkin Publishing Group, op. cit., 79; Stuart Traub and Craig Little (eds.), Theories of Deviance, Itasca, Illinois: F. E. Peacock Publishers, 1975, 31-32.

5. Traub and Little, op. cit., 33-34

6. Lowry, op. cit. 96-98; The Dushkin Publishing Group, op. cit., 81.

7. The Dushkin Publishing Group, op. cit., 81.

8. Lowry, op. cit., 94-95; The Dushkin Publishing Group, op. cit., 81.

9. The Dushkin Publishing Group, op. cit., 81.

10. Lowry, op. cit., 102-105.

11. Lowry, op. cit., 106-112.

12. Lowry, op. cit., 112-113.

13. Lowry, op. cit., 113-116.

14. Thomas Kuhn, The Structure of Scientific Revolutions, 2nd edition, Chicago: University of Chicago Press, 1970.

15. George Ritzer, Sociology: A Multiple Paradigm Science, Boston: Allyn and Bacon, 1975, 24.

16. Ibid., 189.

17. Ibid., 48-57.

18. George Ritzer, Sociology: A Multiple Paradigm Science, The American Sociologist, 10 (August, 1975), 159-160.

19. Ritzer text, op. cit., 57-67.

20. Ritzer article, op. cit., 160.

21. Ibid., 161-162.

22. Ritzer text, op. cit., 86-87; Ritzer article, op. cit., 162.

23. Ritzer text, op. cit., 96-115; Ritzer article, op. cit., 162.

24. Ritzer text, op. cit., 98-110; Ritzer article, op. cit., 161-162.

25. Ritzer text, op. cit., 145-146.

26. Ibid., 146-150.

27. Ibid., 158-162.

28. Ibid., 163-164.

29. Traub and Little, op. cit., 59-60; Charles Frazier, Theoretical Approaches to Deviance: An Evaluation, Columbus, Ohio: Charles E. Merrill Publishing Company, 1976, 50-54.

30. Traub and Little, op. cit., 60-61; Frazier, op. cit., 52-54.

31. Traub and Little, op. cit., 31.

32. Albert Cohen, Delinquent Boys: The Culture of the Gang, New York: Free Press, 1955; Cohen, Deviance and Control, New Jersey: Prentice-Hall, 1966; Frazier, op. cit., 16-17.

33. Ibid.

34. Richard Quinney, The Social Reality of Crime, Boston: Little, Brown, 1970; Richard Quinney and John Wildeman, The Problem of Crime: A Critical Introduction to Criminology, New York: Harper and Row, 1977; Quinney, Class, State, and Crime: On the Theory and Practice of Criminal Justice, New York: David McKay Company, 1977; Frazier, op. cit., 40-42.

35. Ibid.

36. Traub and Little, op. cit., 181-183, 223-225.

37. Richard Cloward and Lloyd Ohlin, Delinquency and Opportunity: A Theory of Delinquent Gangs, New York: Free Press, 1960; Frazier, op. cit., 17-19.

38. Walter Miller, Lower Class Culture as a Generating Milieu of Gang Delinquency, Journal of Social Issues, 14 (1958), 5-19; Frazier, op. cit., 19-20.

39. Edwin Sutherland and Donald Cressey, Criminology, Philadelphia: J.B. Lippincott Company, 1970, 71-91; Traub and Little, op. cit., 107-108; Frazier, op. cit., 13-14.

40. Ibid.

41. Howard S. Becker, Outsiders: Studies in the Sociology of Deviance, New York: Free Press, 1963; Becker, The Other Side: Perspectives on Deviance, New York: Free Press, 1964; Frazier, op. cit., 31-34; Traub and Little, op. cit., 159-161; Lowry, op. cit., 114-116.

42. Ibid.

43. David Matza, Delinquency and Drift, New York: John Wiley, 1964, 28, 97-98; Traub and Little, op. cit., 109-110; Frazier, op. cit., 58-61; Matza, Becoming Deviant, New Jersey: Prentice-Hall, 1969.

44. Gresham Sykes and David Matza, Techniques of Neutralization: A Theory of Delinquency, American Sociological Review, 22 (December, 1957), 665-666.

45. Edwin Lemert, Social Pathology, New York: McGraw-Hill, 1951, 77; Lemert, Human Deviance, Social Problems and Social Control, New Jersey: Prentice-Hall, 1967; Frazier, op. cit., 28-31; Traub and Little, op. cit., 160.

46. Ibid.

47. Frank Tannenbaum, Crime and the Community, New York: Columbia University Press, 1938; Frazier op. cit., 26-28; Traub and Little, op. cit., 160.

48. Walter Reckless, The Crime Problem, New York: Appleton-Century-Crofts, 1961, 355-356; Frazier, op. cit., 61-65.

49. Albert Reiss, Delinquency as the Failure of Personal and Social Controls, American Sociological Review, 16 (1951), 196-207; Frazier, op. cit., 55-56.

50. F. Ivan Nye, Family Relationships and Delinquent Behavior, New York: John Wiley, 1958; Frazier, op. cit., 56-58.

51. Travis Hirschi, <u>Causes of Delinquency</u>, Berkeley, California:
    University of California Press, 1969; Frazier, <u>op</u>. <u>cit</u>.,
    65–68.

52. Franz Alexander and Hugo Staub, <u>The Criminal, the Judge</u>,
    <u>and the Public</u>, Glencoe, Illinois: Free Press, 1956,
    52–85.

53. <u>Ibid</u>., 83–124.

54. David Abrahamsen, <u>Psychology of Crime</u>, New York: Columbia
    University Press, 1960, 123–150.

55. Gordon Trasler, <u>The Explanation of Criminality</u>, London:
    Routledge and Kegan Paul, 1962.

56. Thomas Scheff, <u>Being Mentally Ill: A Sociological Theory</u>,
    Chicago: Aldine Publishing Company, 1966; Frazier,
    <u>op</u>. <u>cit</u>., 37–40.

II

VICTIMLESS CRIMES AND SOCIAL POLICY

Prevention of Deviancy

Clinard states that deviant behavior is basically a violation of certain types of group value-attitudes (i.e., proscribed behavior). He notes that deviation depends both on the reaction of the community and of the individual to his so-called abnormal behavior. The problem faced in prevention of deviancy is the multiplicity of definitions of what constitutes deviance as defined by different groups in a complex, rapidly changing society. Since the average individual is a member of a number of primary and secondary groups, his behavior will vary according to the value-attitude system of each group. He also must attempt to conform to the cultural ideals of society which may conflict with the reality of everyday life. Thus one cannot prevent deviancy if the concept is too relative to apply uniformly to all social situations in all communities of society.[1]

Law and Morality

There has been a problem concerning the relationship of law and morality since the origins of the classical school of criminology. Jeremy Bentham developed his ethical system of social control based on utilitarianism (i.e., pleasure-pain principle). He specified several categories of social sanction (i.e., legal, political, moral, physical, and religious) in his concept of social control. Bentham stated that a legal sanction is only effective if the majority of the population adhere to it. Thus only explicit social controls can keep the average person from becoming deviant. Therefore more good would be gained by allowing people to indulge in activities that are deviant but harmless than by making such activities against the law.[2]

William Graham Sumner stated that all institutions, laws, and actions of legislation were products of the mores but the nature of the circumstances and from what mores can only be determined by historical analysis. Customs and taboos are first codified, then enacted, and finally legislated. In this last stage the mores are put into the criminal law. The taboos and customs evolve into prohibitions and punishments that are planned as deterrents rather than instruments of revenge. The mores of different societies or social orders within the same society are characterized by greater or less readiness to use enactments for societal purposes. When folkways become laws, they have changed their character and are distinguished from mores. Laws are rational, practical, mechanical, and utilitarian whereas mores are unformulated and undefined. Acts under the laws are conscious and voluntary while acts under the folkways are unconscious and involuntary. Laws supercede the mores whereas mores come into operation when laws become dysfunctional. Mores cover areas of the culture where no laws and regulations are created although new laws and regulations are created out of old mores as society changes over time.[3]

Durkheim stated that deviance is a necessary societal component and its presence allows for the evolution of the criminal law. He maintains that the kind and degree of punishment and the rationale behind sanctions for deviant behavior have varied according to societal organizational structure (i.e., homogeneous undifferentiated and advanced differentiated urban societal types). In the homogeneous undifferentiated type of society, punishment is meant to protect and preserve social solidarity. Punishment is a mechanical reaction to preserve social solidarity, and there is no concern with rehabilitation of the deviant. The individual is punished as an example to the community that deviance will not be tolerated. In the advanced and differentiated urban type of society, punishment is focused upon the deviant individual. Deviance is thought of as behavior that offends others and not the collective conscience of the community. Punishment is evaluated in terms of what is good and proper for the individual.[4]

Where the mores of society are strong, there is no need for law according to Sutherland. Sagarin feels that there are still some individuals who will disobey strong mores so the law is still necessary to protect the public. But this depends on the type of mores (i.e., wife beating and incest are abhored by most individuals publicly but police know these practices are more common than realized). Sagarin states that strong mores are sufficient to protect society without legal enactments under the following conditions: (1) whether discouragement from the act occurs through internalization of the mores or through fear of sanctions for offenders; (2) whether violation of the mores is practiced by a small percentage of the community despite strong communal disapproval; (3) whether individuals need protection against victimization; (4) whether there is interest society-wide in the enforcement of the mores; and (5) whether the enactment or repeal of legislation would greatly increase the deviance.[5]

Where the mores of society are weak, the law cannot be effective according to Sutherland. Sagarin states that the law may have negative and unanticipated effects; those in the power structure along with the majority of the population must want to change the mores; there may be political considerations that take precedence over the fact that the law cannot be effectively enforced (i.e., narcotic drug laws, gambling laws, and laws attempting to regulate alcohol manufacture and sale).[6]

Devlin states that the purpose of all legislation is to protect morality. Further it is the state's obligation to protect individual citizens against their own shortcomings and their exploitation at the hands of deviants. Devlin would probably agree that a distinction should be made between the criminalization of widely condemned deviance and criminalization of little known behavior that only zealots consider morally condemnable. An act which is universally condemned as deviant is easier to criminalize since it has public support than an act that the public is ignorant of or indifferent to since informal social controls should be satisfactory in the curtailment of such behavior.[7]

Hart feels that the state should only deal with the criminalization and control of activities that threaten the public order or the personal lives of individuals other than those willingly participating in deviant activities. He would probably agree with those wishing to decriminalize many types of social deviance but not make these deviant activities legitimate. Sagarin raises some interesting points if decriminalization is to be accomplished: (1) are deviant activities such that the community wants to discourage them but not criminally punish offenders? (2) should harmful behavior be handled by trained personnel such as doctors or be left alone? (3) has the deviant behavior caused a great deal of secondary crime which would diminish if the deviance were decriminalized? (4) will decriminalization weaken the position of elected and appointed public officials? (5) will decriminalization lead to eventual acceptance of deviant behavior and transform it into normal behavior?[8]

Schur states that criminal sanctions are not necessarily appropriate to every effort at social control. Attempts to employ criminal law to regulate morality ultimately face difficulties in society. Theorists have stated that criminal laws that do not have the support of the dominant societal social norms are limited in their effectiveness.[9] The British Governmental Committee on Homosexual Offenses and Prostitution broke ground with its conception of the role that the criminal law should play in society. The Committee placed the burden of justifying applications of the law on those who seek to impose such control over the behavior of individuals.[10]

There is a growing recognition that the criminal law is the inappropriate means to deal with deviance. These crimes without victims are unenforceable laws that attempt to legally proscribe the willing exchange of socially disapproved but demanded goods

or services. These types of crimes involve a consensual trans-
action or exchange and no direct and clear harm is inflicted by
one person against another so no complaint is lodged. Some
criminal laws that deal with victimless crimes produce more
social harm than good, cause a great deal of immorality themselves, throw the legal system into disrepute, and allow organized
crime to grow and prosper (i.e., allowing new forms of deviance to
appear).[11]

Schur feels we rely upon a criminal solution to all social
problems and thus criminalize situations that do not concern the
criminal justice system. There has been overlegislation in the
area of social deviance. Political behavior should be designated
a crime only if it constitutes a distinct threat to social order
(i.e., Nixon era abuses). Schur also feels that the present
system of juvenile justice creates social deviants out of children
and adolescents who commit status offenses which would not be
considered crimes if perpetrated by adults. Thus the law itself
is making many youth into deviants when it should be preventing
such deviance from occurring in society.[12]

Crimes Without Victims

The concept of crimes without victims is described in detail
in the writings of Schur.[13] Victimless crimes consist of several
types of behavior: (1) this type of crime is consensual among
adults (i.e., there is no complainant and any harm that occurs
is limited to the two parties); (2) the crime consists of the
voluntary exchange of a desired commodity between the willing
buyer and the equally willing seller; (3) there is considerable
controversy whether this deviant behavior should even be considered
abnormal, let alone should it have been criminalized in the first
place (i.e., there is much social conflict on the alleged wrong-
fulness of the behavior); and (4) the laws concerning victimless
crimes are virtually unenforceable since there is no complainant
and it is difficult to obtain evidence (i.e., often the police
utilize harassment tactics, make poor arrests, create an atmosphere
of public distrust, and allow those detained to bribe officers or
extort money or favors from those engaging in such activities).[14]

The fact that victimless crimes are consensual acts between
adult members of a community does not remove the stigma attached
to such behavior on the part of the public in general. This is due
in part to the misrepresentation of facts concerning these forms
of deviance (i.e., stereotyping participants such as all drug
addicts are "dope fiends" or all prostitutes come from the lower
class and are mentally retarded) and in part to some public agencies

and/or politicians looking for a "safe" issue to attack in order to justify more funding or get elected to public office (i.e., the Marijuana issue and the federal Drug Enforcement Administration and "the increase in street crime" issue used by every politician running for election).[15]

According to the Anglo-American Common Law tradition, immorality is a danger to society and a burden to the criminal justice system because the public must be protected from the offender and the latter must be reformed at public expense. Thus many members of legislative bodies (i.e., Congress, state legislatures, county councils, and city councils) feel obligated to set the formal standards of public morality for their jurisdiction. This is in spite of the fact that these public officials often know that the statutes they create in the area of public morality will be difficult if not impossible to enforce in practice by the police. Traditionally it has been comparatively easy for a legislator to introduce legislation concerning victimless crimes since no one is opposed to such a bill. Further it makes the politician look good in the public eye since he stands as protector of community morals.[16]

On the other hand it is quite difficult to rescind a statute dealing with public morality by a legislative body. Few public officials wish to be identified as supporters of victimless crimes (i.e., sexual immorality, gambling, drug addiction, homosexuality, abortion, etc.) since this would create controversy and possibly spell defeat at the next election. Even the repeal of such disregarded statutes as the Sunday blue-laws are usually rescinded by public referendum because the politicians are afraid of negative repercussions by the church and other special interests. The few victimless crimes that do disappear from the criminal codes of various states occur quietly by legislative omission without debate when the criminal code is revised.[17]

Victimless crimes are crimes against the public interest or morality (i.e., classified in most criminal codes as crimes against public decency, public order, or public justice). Crimes without victims are crimes mala prohibita (i.e., behaviors that are criminal per se since there is no consensus whether these acts are criminal of themselves). Crimes like murder and robbery are mala in se (i.e., they are evil in themselves with public agreement on the dangers of these types of deviance). Thus with no clear agreement as to the harm caused by victimless crimes, individuals more frequently commit such acts and the police are not clear as to the implementation of enforcement procedures - if any.[18]

Perceptions of Victimless Crimes

Sumner states that legislation can only be effective if it is consistent with societal mores.[19] Thus attempts to legislate victimless crimes have been less than successful when the majority of a population do not truly support the legislation. Thus the law can be used in an attempt to change community norms but not successfully unless the majority accept the ruling. This idea of the law as a tool of social engineering goes back to such legal theorists are Ehrlich and his concept of "living law", Pound's theory of interests, and the writings of the sociological jurisprudents such as Llewellyn, Stone, Hall, Allen, Hart, Fuller, and Devlin. Such conflict theorists in criminology as Hills, Turk, Chambliss, Quinney, and Reasons strongly believe that the criminal law cannot change the mores or for that matter force members of society to stop deviant practices or accept such practices on the part of others.[20]

The state has always had in interest in the preservation of public morality. Thus the law as an instrument of the state must be concerned with morality and provide moral guidance for members of society. The law must not permit certain segments of society to sway the youth and the weak away from the cultural value-attitudes concerning normal behavior and human interaction. Unfortunately the criminal law is not value-neutral nor are members of the criminal justice system. Thus the enactment of certain statutes leads to disrespect by both alleged offenders and the police since the laws are biased, are in disagreement with many who accept such behavior as acceptable and not illegal, and are status demeaning or impossible to enforce. Therefore such laws are usually not enforced, offenders are only given warnings or ignored, and such statutes become dysfunctional.[21]

On the other hand, some statutes governing victimless crimes are functional to a certain extent. First of all those labeled as deviant and criminal serve as an example to normal community members not to violate the criminal law. Second when the laws are enforced against lower class and minority group members, it allows those in power (i.e., middle as especially upper class people) to feel the law is serving a useful purpose since it preserves the myth that low status members of society account for most social deviance. Third and last, both the statutes and the great number of convictions of those perpetrating at least certain victimless crimes such as public drunkenness reinforce the feeling in the community that the police and criminal justice system in general are doing a good job protecting community moral standards.[22]

Devlin feels that the criminal law has the duty to regulate public morality. He feels that crime and deviance cannot be separated since this would be bad for the law and criminal both.

If the criminal law did not control public morals, all victimless crimes would be legal. Since the criminal law is based on morality, then the society would suffer and decline (i.e., law functions to enforce morality) if there were no victimless crimes. Finally Devlin states that there can be no private morality that is distinct from public morality. Since victimless crimes are usually carried on in private with mutual consent of the parties and involving no outsiders to the action, there is supposedly no harm done since this deviance is a matter of private morality. But a society that allows one to act deviant in private is endangering the public interest since sooner or later others will suffer or be exposed to this deviance albeit indirectly through normal interpersonal contacts.[23]

Control of Deviancy

Deviance can be seen as a mechanism of social control since the punishment of the deviant individual by the criminal justice system serves as an example to other members of society not to deviate from the accepted normative system or suffer the same end as the nonconformist to community moral standards. There are a number of means that have been used to control deviance in society (i.e., revenge, repression, rejection, restraint, rehabilitation, and reintegration). The first four concepts will be dealt with in this section while the latter two will be dealt with in the last section.[24]

Secondary Crime Problem

The criminalization of goods (i.e., drugs, alcohol, pornographic materials) or services (i.e., prostitution, gambling, abortion) makes access to these goods or services difficult and forces the prices up. Since it is a crime to sell such items or services as well as purchase such items or services, those offering these items or services are taking high risks. Thus organized crime which has access to funds, can provide its employees with protection, and has means to both pay off police and use force to collect debts enters and expands the black market for such goods and services. The fact that people want such goods and services and are willing to pay for such attracts individuals into the subterranean network of manufacturers, wholesalers, and retailers of such products since transactions are in cash with no reporting of earnings to public authorities. Thus amateurs as well as professionals enter the victimless crime field for profit.[25]

The most common reason for secondary crime is the constant need for the services or products that are offered on the black market

which continually go up in price since the risks also become greater
the more people know about the problem (i.e., mass media exposure,
church and political activism to "clean up" the problem). Thus
compulsive gamblers may borrow money from loan sharks and then
steal or embezzle funds from work to cover these debts. Hard drug
addicts may steal and/or resort to prostitution (male and female)
in order to pay for their daily habit. Prostitutes may decide to
steal from clients rather than service them since all they want
is money to pay their pimps and/or the police. Some addicts may
turn dealer in order to obtain more money and thus expose themselves
to trouble with other drug suppliers and addicts who will try to
steal from them. Thus this individual will have to arm himself
and expose himself to greater risks than those of an addict.[26]

Blackmail is a secondary crime that is usually associated with
homosexuality, adultery, prostitution (i.e., call girls), gambling
operations, abortion, and euthanasia. On the other hand individuals
are rarely blackmailed for being an alcoholic, being sexually active
outside of marriage (i.e., premarital relationships), or taking
drugs with the exception of hard drugs (i.e., heroin, morphine, etc.).
Of course the blackmailer is also open to criminal prosecution so he
usually is associated with organized crime and uses his victim for
other purposes than obtaining money. It is becoming more common for
runaway children and women to get involved in victimless crimes and
then become open to blackmail by those with whom they associate in
their activities.[27]

Overcriminalization Problem

Kadish refers to the term overcriminalization to explain the
huge number of criminal code statutes that deal with victimless
crimes in the United States on the federal, state, county, and
municipal levels. He feels that the creation of these crimes in
the area of morality creates more problems for the criminal justice
system than the statutes are worth. Kadish feels that the criminal
law is overcriminalized in the areas of: (1) public morality (i.e.,
in the declaration or enforcement of community standards on private
value-attitudes), (2) provision of social services (i.e., where
other social agencies fail or refuse to deal with the deviant
behavior), and (3) using the criminal law in extralegal fashion by
the police (i.e., in the name of protective custody of the deviant).[28]

The overcriminalization problem is most obvious in the area of
enforcement of morals. Here one finds all the statutes dealing
with sex offenses (i.e., homosexuality, heterosexuality, venereal
diseases, sex education, birth control, pornography and obscenity).
There have been and are presently more statutes dealing with sexual
behavior than in any country. The United States Code and the state
criminal codes contain statutes dealing with sodomy (i.e., bestiality

or intercourse between a human and an animal; buggery or intercourse by a male with another male or with a woman by the anus; and deviant sex acts such as oral stimulation of sexual organs). Sodomy statutes are sometimes referred to as crimes against nature.[29]

Prostitution (i.e., sexual intercourse for money or other tangible favors) statutes are found in all states with the exception of certain counties in Nevada. Other related statutes deal with solicitation of prostitutes, keeping a house of prostitution, earning an income from prostitutes (i.e., pimps and madams), and patronizing prostitutes. Almost all statutes deal with females and not males. Another statute dealing with sexual behavior is lewd and lascivious behavior (i.e., openly cohabiting and associating with an individual known not to be one's spouse under circumstances implying sexual intercourse). A third common statute deals with seduction (i.e., a man who seduces a previously chaste woman to engage in sexual intercourse under the promise of marriage).[30]

Other crimes dealing with sexuality are bigamy, adultery, and incest. Bigamy is going through the form or ceremony of marriage by one having another living spouse. Adultery is illicit sexual intercourse between individuals either of whom is married to another person. Incest is sexual intercourse between individuals who are defined by the jurisdiction as so closely related to each other that a marriage between them would be a crime. Incest also includes sexual intercourse between parent and child (i.e., mother-son or father-daughter).[31]

Finally until recently in the United States it was a criminal act to teach about sexual behavior and birth control in the public schools, write, lecture, or send through the mails material (i.e., pamphlets, books, articles) on birth control, or advertise, sell, and purchase birth control devices or supplies. These so-called criminal acts go back to the federal Comstock Law and subsequent state laws (i.e., Connecticut) which were only recently ruled unconstitutional by the United States Supreme Court.[32] These same Comstock type laws at the state level governed the definition of what constituted pornographic and obscene materials. Indirectly these laws also hampered the effective prevention and control of venereal diseases among both juveniles and adults.[33]

The overcriminalization problem is evident in the area of social services misuse. Here we find criminal statutes dealing with alcoholics, drug abusers and addicts, individuals who create family conflicts (i.e., child and spouse abusers, deserters, and divorced individuals under certain circumstances), and individuals having mental disorders or potential suicides. According to Kadish the criminal law has been utilized to provide social services to

certain types of social deviants in society. The criminal law is
not meant to deal with the rehabilitation function nor are the
police trained to deal with the types of social deviants forced
upon law enforcement personnel and facilities.[34]

As the President's Commission on Law Enforcement and Administration of Justice states, alcoholism (i.e., drunkenness) should
not be a crime.[35] From a practical point of view, public health
or social service facilities should handle this problem. If a public
drunk is of no threat to anyone or to himself, it is really dysfunctional for the police to place the individual in jail. Unfortunately in some police departments as many as half of the misdemeanor
arrests are for public drunkenness. This means that time and money
are diverted from better purposes and the drunk will be out on the
street the next day and back to the same routine in most cases
(i.e., most chronic alcoholics usually are arrested on a regular
basis, especially if they are lower class).[36]

In dealing with drug abuse and drug addiction, the problem of
whether these areas can be dealt with effectively by social services,
medical services, or the police is a very complicated question to
resolve. The criminal justice system at both the federal and state
levels have tried to deal with both abuse and addiction in the same
manner through a policy of enforcing the criminal statutes and then
dealing with the offender on the basis of type of drug abused, first
offense or chronic offender, dealer or user, and any other criminal
offenses committed in connection with the misuse of drugs. The laws
are much stricter concerning habit forming substances (i.e., opiates)
than with so-called soft drugs (i.e., barbiturates, amphetamines)
although the various state statutes are confused in dealing with
the hallucinogens, marijuana, and cocaine.[37]

The area of domestic relations deals with a variety of family
conflicts such as child and spouse abuse, desertion, and divorce
problems (i.e., refusal to pay child support and/or alimony). This
whole area of domestic relations is a very difficult one for the
police since they are not trained to deal with social work practices,
yet the criminal code and departmental operating procedures make it
mandatory for law enforcement personnel to deal with a variety of
situations that are basically torts but could escalate into criminal
acts. The welfare department should handle such problems but often
the police are called to resolve the problem since many times the
family conflict could lead to violence. Thus the police are used
as an instrument of force in an attempt to force a husband to stop
abusing members of his family or pay the money that the court has
ordered him to give to his ex-wife and/or children (i.e., the police
are called in as a last resort to reason with the family member before
he is arrested and jailed for failure to comply with a civil court
order).[38]

The last social service provision allocated to the police by
the criminal code is in dealing with people suffering from mental
disorders or potential suicides. These laws of the criminal code
are aimed at the self-protection of the individual. Again as in
the case of alcoholics and drug abuser/addicts, the police neither
have the training, the facilities, nor the time to deal with such
individuals in light of more serious problems brought to their
attention. In the case of people suffering from serious mental
problems, all the police can do is either take them to the nearest
mental hospital or general hospital or place them in a holding cell
until some social welfare authority takes over the case. The police
are not trained for such work and if a mentally ill person gets
violent have a hard time properly handling the case. People who
attempt suicide pose a problem since they are usually suffering
great mental stress and can endanger the lives of fire or police
personnel who may try to convince them not to commit suicide. This
would be especially true if the person is trying to jump off a
building or bridge. There is also the case of suicide pacts
between two parties where the end result turns into a case of one
party committing suicide and the other party not being successful
or changing his mind. The police are then dealing with a possible
murder situation and the unsuccessful suicide may attempt to complete
the act after being taken into custody. Thus the criminal law does
not consider the social service aspect when it comes to the implementation of the statutes by the police.[39]

The last area of overcriminalization deals with such minor
crimes as disorderly conduct and vagrancy. This is an area of the
criminal law that allows the police to use their discretionary
powers to deal with borderline cases of social deviance. Disorderly
conduct statutes differ from state to state and are usually enforced
when an individual's deviant behavior does not match that
behavior described in existing statutes. Thus an individual
who is allegedly swearing in public, engaged in a
family argument, and acting in a strange or sexually unusual manner
could be charged with this statute (i.e., it is used to cover new
crimes or crimes that cannot be easily classified or defined.) The
vagrancy statutes are even more vague than the disorderly conduct
statutes. They have been used to arrest and detain all sorts of
social deviants who have not committed even an act that could be
classified as disorderly. Thus the visibly unemployed, people
roaming the streets or shopping centers, loiterers, prostitutes,
drunks, gamblers, and youth who are not wanted in a particular
location or place of business are all dealt with by the police
using this statute.[40]

Costs to Society

Pursley estimates that from one-third to one-half of all
arrests made by the police fall into the crimes without victims
category. This is estimated to cost the taxpayer billions of
dollars in terms of processing these millions of people through
the criminal justice system in any given year. The cost is assum-
ing that most of those arrested will not get past the police-magis-
trate level and many will not even be jailed except for short
periods of time. A larger cost to the taxpayer is impossible to
even estimate in tax dollars. This is the area of organized crime
since the black market for goods and services would not exist if
the victimless crime statutes did not exist. Organized crime is
able to make billions of dollars per year in the areas of gambling,
narcotics, prostitution, and loan sharking because the public
demands these goods and services and the statutes that criminalize
such goods and services give organized crime a monopoly. Thus
tax dollars are lost since the goods and services are not taxed,
the police and other sectors of the criminal justice system are
clogged with victimless crime cases that bring in little money by
way of fines as compared to criminal justice system costs, and
the police often accept bribes which are estimated to run over two
billion dollars a year.[41]

The offender also suffers in a number of ways due to the
existence of victimless crimes statutes. There is obvious loss of
self-respect and status in the community due to being arrested for
such crimes. The offender may lose his job, cause his family to
suffer and be labeled as deviant, and cause the children to be
viewed with suspicion (i.e., potential delinquents) by classmates
and teachers. This labeling process could end up with the offender
and/or members of his family committing other deviant acts (i.e.,
drinking, drugs, or becoming delinquent/criminal) and thus causing
more problems for the community and the taxpayer. The offender
might also be forced to seek out and associate with other known
deviants and develop a deviant subculture. This has happened frequently with alcoholics, drug addicts, and homosexuals. This is
also the most likely way in which a juvenile becomes associated with
a street gang. Thus the ostracism of the offender can trigger the
self-fulfilling prophecy cycle that will not only degrade the deviant
but involve family and friends, lead to unemployment, and possibly
be causal in the start of a delinquent or criminal career. All
these negative results are a tremendous cost to the individual and
the taxpayer.[42]

The criminal justice system has been placed in a negative light
due to the victimless crime problem. First of all task forces have to

be created to deal with the enforcement of the statutes (i.e.,
morals or vice divisions) and officers trained. Second organized
crime units have to be created to deal with the suppliers of
goods and services. Last internal security units have to be
created to check on the police because of the constant possibility
of bribes by both offenders and organized crime. Thus the costs in
training and manpower taken away from enforcement of statutes dealing with crimes against the person and property is beyond belief.
Usually there is a point reached by public administrators in terms
of costs where it is more beneficial to the taxpayer to ignore the
victimless crime in terms of law enforcement and criminal justice
processing and concentrate tax dollars and manpower on serious
crimes. Politicians usually see this reality during election
year when asked to account for increased costs for enforcement
policies that do not work and are unpopular with many in the
community.[43]

The police have utilized both vagrancy and disorderly-conduct
type statutes in addition to the existing statutes dealing with
specific forms of deviance to arrest, search, question, or detain
individuals who appear to be undesirables in a given community.
Thus the victimless crime and related catch-all statutes have been
used in many inner city and suburban jurisdictions as a harassment
tactic by the police. Some jurisdictions such as New York, the
District of Columbia, and Ohio has instituted so-called stop and
frisk laws that allow the police more discretion in dealing with
deviants.[44]

In dealing with victimless crimes the police are often forced
to resort to the use of electronic surveillance devices and the
use of undercover officers in order to entrap the offender. This
is especially true in drug, gambling, and sexual deviance (i.e.,
prostitution, homosexuality, pornography) cases. These activities
can be dangerous to the undercover officer, are degrading and demoralizing, and can and do lead to corruption of some officers by offenders
and organized crime personnel. Thus the courts have become clogged
with entrapment cases.[45]

The United States Supreme Court has handled numerous decisions
dealing with the extralegal methods of the police in dealing with
victimless crimes. Mapp v. Ohio (1961) dealt with pornography
and obscenity (i.e., illegal search and seizure). Entrapment
decisions were reached in the areas of gambling and narcotics cases
(i.e., Sorrels v. US, 1932 and Sherman v. US, 1958). Admissi-
bility of evidence as a result of illegal arrests have come from
gambling, alcohol, and drug cases (i.e., Beck v. Ohio, 1964; Benanti
v. US, 1957; Johnson v. US, 1958; and Draper v. US, 1959). Unlawful
search and seizure cases dealing with alcohol and drugs have been

Carrol v. US (1925), Agnello v. US (1925), Marron v. US (1927),
Co-Bart Company v. US (1931), Lefkowitz v. US (1932), Johnson v.
US (1948), Rochin v. California (1952), Jones v. US (1960), Wong
Sun v. US (1963), and Ker v. California (1963). There have also
been several cases involving the illegal use of wire-tapping, bug-
ging, and other forms of electronic eavesdropping in victimless
crime cases (i.e., Olmstead v. US, 1928; Nardone v. US, 1938; Lee
v. US, 1952; Irvine v. California, 1954; Benanti v. US, 1957;
Silverman v. US, 1961).[46]

All the problems concerning the processing of offenders for
commiting victimless crimes results in a general disrespect for
the law on the part of the offenders, many of the public, and some
members of the criminal justice system - especially the police.
There is usually the differential enforcement statutes for crimes
without victims against the lower class and nonwhite segments of
the population, the young, inner city residents rather than
suburbanites. Homosexuals are more often arrested than lesbians,
street walkers than call girls, inner city gamblers and alcoholics
than suburban gamblers and drinkers, and hard drug users than
soft drug abusers. There is also differential imposition of
sentences based on social class, race, age, and place of residence
for offenders. Thus an adolescent may be a longer sentence for
possession of marijuana in Virginia than for commission of armed
robbery as a first offender.[47]

Treatment of Offenders

One could easily conclude that the creation of most victimless
crimes is dysfunctional to society in general and the criminal justice system in particular. Thus it is not hard to see why such individuals and organizations as the President's Commission on Law
Enforcement and Administration of Justice, the Police Foundation,
the National Council on Crime and Delinquency, the American Bar
Association, Edwin Schur, Norval Morris, and to a limited degree
President Carter are all calling for the decriminalization of many
crimes without victims.

Decriminalization

Decriminalization is a social process that does not automatically
lead to legitimization of social deviance. There are arguments both
for the retention of victimless crimes as well as for the decriminalization of such deviant acts. Most of the arguments for the retention
of victimless crimes revolve around the morality issue with some concern about the harm done to the individual both physically and psychologically.[48] On the other hand the decriminalization arguments state
that some acts of deviance are really normal behavior (i.e., prostitution, premarital and extramarital sex, homosexuality, abortion,
euthanasia, family conflicts, gambling, and soft drug use). Some

people do not accept that all victimless crimes are or should be
considered normal behavior. These adherents of decriminalization
want tolerance for those who practice their deviance in private
with other adults who are willing to indulge in such activities
(i.e., pornography, premarital and extramarital sex, homosexuality,
and other behavior dealing with sexuality). Finally there are
those who feel that the victimless crime is deviant and evil but
not worth the time and cost to the criminal justice system to
catch and punish the offender (i.e., prostitution, homosexuality,
pornography, gambling, drug addiction, and alcoholism). There
is obviously no consensus as to what victimless crimes should be
dealt with in which of the three suggested ways of decriminalization.[49]

According to Sagarin the decriminalization process goes through
several stages: (1) simple obsolescence, (2) new judicial interpretations, and (3) social conflict and movements to rescind legislation.[50] Enforcement of statutes against morality in a community
may become out of date because the mores of the population have
changed significantly since the statute was originally passed. This
is true of inner cities and their cosmopolitan suburbs where "X"
rated movies and adult bookstores are tolerated, laws dealing
with heterosexual behavior, divorce, massage parlors, prostitution,
gambling, public drunkenness, and certain types of mental disorders
are accepted by the public and police alike. State supreme courts
and the federal courts have made new judicial interpretations of various
victimless crimes. This is especially true in the area of abortion,
pornography and obscenity, family conflicts, gambling, and alcoholism.
To a lesser extent the courts have been reviewing the issues of
euthanasia, drug addiction, mental disorders, and homosexuality.
In the cases of abortion, pornography, alcoholism, and drug abuse
the courts have been somewhat contradictory as one Supreme Court
ruling will be definitive and other rulings will return the same
issue back to the states for their reinterpretation of community
standards. There is much conflict of law between federal and state
courts as well as within county courts in the same state on many
victimless crime issues.[51]

Finally social conflict and social movements have been quite
influential in dealing with both the criminalization and decriminalization issues. Sagarin feels that conflict will result when
public morality weakens on a victimless crime or when individuals
feel that the deviance has not diminished and/or has caused an
increase of secondary crime that is getting beyond control. This
has often happened when the criminalization process was fostered
by a well-organized minority who really did not represent the
majority view on public deviance. The Comstock laws on pornography
and obscenity, the abortion issue, venereal disease issue, prohibition

issue, marijuana and drug abuse problems, and sexual psychopath
issue are all examples of problems that have been created by a
zealous minority who had political power. Eventually these
minority statutes lead to social movements that are aired via
the mass media, public demonstrations, and political lobbying and
campaigns to replace conservative politicians. This has been the
case with homosexuality, abortion, and to a lesser extent with the
issues of prostitution, heterosexual behavior, pornography, gambling,
and alcoholism.[52]

Rehabilitation

The traditional response to criminal behavior has been
incarceration. In general this approach has been a dismal failure
in the case of offenders convicted of commiting victimless crimes.
Increasingly probation, fines, and community-based facilities are
replacing the jail sentence. To a great extent in the past and
often in the present certain categories or victimless crime
offenders have gone to prison or another total institution such as
a mental hospital or public general hospital. Drug addicts and
abusers have gone to prison or in some cases the United States
Public Health Service Hospitals in either Lexington, Kentucky or
Fort Worth, Texas. Some drug addicts and abusers as well as alcoholics have gone to state public or mental hospitals. Often
alcoholics go to county jail for a short stay. The mentally ill
have gone to public hospitals, mental institutions, and even to
prison on occasion, especially in the case of psychopaths and psy-
chotics. There are even institutions for the criminally insane in
some jurisdictions. Homosexuals are rarely incarcerated or placed
in mental institutions today although the practice was more common
in the past. Prostitutes are sometimes placed in county institutions or state facilities for women. Spouse abusers and those
guilty of nonsupport of wife and/or family are sometimes placed
in county correctional facilities.[53]

Deviants who are involuntarily committed to total institutions
(i.e., prison, mental hospital, or public hospital dealing with
alcoholics and addicts) are offered a variety of treatment programs
which vary according to the quality and case load of the staff.
Such methods as reality therapy, transactional analysis, therapeutic
community, guided group interaction, and behavior modification are
used with limited success.[54]

There is a growing number of community based treatment and
rehabilitation programs in the United States on both federal and
state levels. There are guided group interaction projects, foster
and group homes, halfway houses, intensive community treatment,
medical aftercare programs, and self-help programs (i.e., voluntary
associations) that deal with social deviants. Most of these community

based programs have been developed in response to the President's
Commission of 1967. Community based programs also utilize the
various methods of therapy already noted.

The medical aftercare programs are of special interest since
they were specifically designed to deal with drug addicts and
abusers, alcoholics, the mentally ill, and potential suicides.
The federal government has set up detoxification centers to deal
with chronic alcoholics on a short term basis. The methadone
maintenance program has also been set up by the federal government.
Both programs are controversial and appear to lack support by state
governments and local authorities in general.[55]

The self-help (i.e., voluntary associations) programs take a
great variety of form and deal with most types of victimless
crimes. Alcoholics Anonymous deals with alcoholics and their
families. Synanon, Daytop Lodge, and Narcotics Anonymous deal with
drug addicts and abusers. Recovery Inc. helps ex-mental patients.
Gamblers Anonymous deals with compulsive gamblers. The Mattachine
Society, Daughters of Bilitis, and Gay Activist League is concerned
with the problems of homosexuals and lesbians. Suicide Prevention
Centers and Suicides Anonymous deal with potential suicides. The
National Abortion Rights Action League and Pro Life deal with the
problem of abortion. The Euthanasia Education Council is concerned
with the right of the person to die with dignity. Various community
free clinics deal with the control and treatment of venereal diseases,
birth control, and abortion information. There are also programs
for battered wives and children who run away from home.[56]

40

Notes

1. Marshall Clinard, <u>Sociology of Deviant Behavior</u>, New York: Holt, Rinehart and Winston, 1974, 3-40; Dushkin Publishing Group, <u>Encyclopedia of Sociology</u>, Guilford, Connecticut: The Dushkin Publishing Group, 1974, 79-80; Taylor, Walton, and Young, <u>The New Criminology: For a Social Theory of Deviance</u>, New York: Harper and Row, 1974, 268-278.

2. Robert Rich, <u>The Sociology of Law: An Introduction to its Theorists and Theories</u>, Washington, DC: University Press of America, 1977, 59.

3. <u>Ibid.</u>, 109-110.

4. <u>Ibid.</u>, 61-62.

5. Edward Sagarin, <u>Deviants and Deviance: An Introduction to the Study of Disvalued People and Behavior</u>, New York: Praeger Publishers, 1975, 378-379.

6. <u>Ibid.</u>, 379

7. Patrick Devlin, <u>The Enforcement of Morals</u>, New York: Oxford University Press, 1965; Sagarin, <u>op. cit.</u>, 378, 380.

8. H.L.A. Hart, <u>Law, Liberty, and Morality</u>, Stanford, California: Stanford University Press, 1963; Sagarin, <u>op. cit.</u>, 378-380.

9. Edwin Schur, <u>Our Criminal Society</u>, New Jersey: Prentice-Hall, 1969, 191-194.

10. <u>Ibid.</u>, 195-201.

11. <u>Ibid.</u>, 219-223.

12. <u>Ibid</u>, 224-227.

13. Edwin Schur, <u>Crimes Without Victims: Deviant Behavior and Public Policy</u>, New Jersey: Prentice-Hall, 1965.

14. <u>Ibid.</u>, 169-171; Sagarin, <u>op. cit.</u>, 380-381.

15. Schur, <u>Crimes Without Victims</u>, <u>op. cit.</u>, 175.

16. Donald Newman, <u>Introduction to Criminal Justice</u>, Philadelphia: J.B. Lippincott, 1978, 66.

17. _Ibid._, 66-67.

18. Sue Reid, _Crime and Criminology_, Hinsdale, Illinois:
    The Dryden Press, 1976, 34; Sagarin, _op. cit._, 383.

19. William Graham Sumner, _Folkways_, New York: Dover, 1906, 55.

20. Rich, _op. cit._, 1-7, 89-99, 101-103, 69-79; Lawrence Friedman,
    Law and Society: An Introduction, New Jersey: Prentice-Hall,
    1977, 138-153.

21. Reid, _op. cit._, 42.

22. _Ibid._, 42-43.

23. Devlin, _op. cit._, 6-22.

24. Daniel Glaser, _Social Deviance_, Chicago: Markham Publishing
    Company, 1971, 55; Sagarin, _op. cit._, 370-373.

25. Schur, _Crimes Without Victims_, _op. cit._, 174-175; Sagarin,
    op. cit., 388-389.

26. _Ibid._

27. _Ibid._

28. Sanford Kadish, Overcriminalization, in Radzinowicz and
    Wolfgang (eds.), _Crime and Justice: The Criminal in Society_,
    New York: Basic Books, 1971, 57; Hart, _op. cit._; Schur,
    Crimes Without Victims, _op. cit._; Norval Morris and
    Gordon Hawkins, _The Honest Politicians Guide to Crime
    Control_, Chicago: University of Chicago Press, 1969; Norval
    Morris, Crimes Without Victims: The Law is a Busybody, _New
    York Times Magazine_, 1 (April, 1973), 10; Troy Duster,
    The Legislation of Morality, New York: Free Press, 1970;
    Herbert Packer, _The Limits of the Criminal Sanction_, Stanford,
    California: Stanford University Press, 1968.

29. Reid, _op. cit._, 35.

30. _Ibid._, 36-38.

31. Henry Black, _Black's Law Dictionary_, St. Paul, Minnesota:
    West Publishing Company, 1968, 71-72, 206, 904.

32. Robert Bell, _Social Deviance_, Homewood, Illinois: The Dorsey
    Press, 1976, 93-94, 123-126.

42

33. Ibid., 261–262.

34. Kadish, op. cit., 64.

35. President's Commission on Law Enforcement and Administration of Justice, Challenge of Crime in a Free Society, Washington, DC: US Government Printing Office, 1967, 235–237.

36. Kadish. op cit.,, 64; Reid, op. cit., 38–39.

37. Kadish, op. cit., 61–63; Reid, op. cit., 39–40.

38. Kadish, op. cit., 65.

39. Reid, op. cit., 40.

40. Kadish, op. cit., 66–68.

41. Reid, op. cit., 43–44; Robert Pursley, Introduction to Criminal Justice, Encino, California: Glencoe Press, 1977, 95–98; Kadish, op. cit., 67–68.

42. Reid, op. cit., 43–44.

43. Reid, op. cit., 44–45; Kadish, op. cit., 66–68; Pursley, op. cit., 95–97.

44. Kadish, op. cit., 44–45; Robert Rich, Essays on the Theory and Practice of Criminal Justice, Washington, DC: University Press of America, 1977, 41–74.

45. Reid, op. cit., 44–45; Kadish, op. cit., 62–63.

46. Kadish, op. cit., 62–63.

47. Reid, op. cit., 44; Pursley, op. cit., 97.

48. Pursley, op. cit., 97–98.

49. Sagarin, op. cit., 383–384; Pursley, op. cit., 98–99.

50. Sagarin, op. cit., 385–388.

51. Ibid.

52. Ibid., 387–388.

43

53. S. Dinitz, R. Dynes, and A. Clarke (eds.), <u>Deviance: Studies in Definition, Management and Treatment</u>, New York: Oxford University Press, 1975, 407–588; President's Commission on Law Enforcement and Administration of Justice, <u>Task Force Report: Corrections</u>, Washington, DC: US Government Printing Office, 1967, 51–53; Vernon Fox, <u>Introduction to Corrections</u>, New Jersey: Prentice-Hall, 1972, 239–250; Harry Allen and Clifford Simonsen, <u>Corrections in America: An Introduction</u>, Beverly Hills, California: Glencoe Press, 1975, 342–352.

54. Robert Wicks, <u>Correctional Psychology: Themes and Problems in Correcting the Offender</u>, San Francisco: Canfield Press, 1974, 13–73; Reid, <u>op</u>. <u>cit</u>., 550–561.

55. Reid, <u>op</u>. <u>cit</u>., 649–662; Wicks, <u>op</u>. <u>cit</u>., 13–73; Task Force Report: Corrections, <u>op</u>. <u>cit</u>., 38–42; Dinitz, Dynes, and Clarke, <u>op</u>. <u>cit</u>., Fox, <u>op</u>. <u>cit</u>.; Allen and Simonsen, <u>op</u>. <u>cit</u>.

56. <u>Ibid</u>.

III

PORNOGRAPHY AND OBSCENITY

Legal History

The Curl case in 1797 (i.e., Curl was prosecuted for publishing a book entitled <u>Venus in the Cloister or the Nun in her Smock</u>) set the common law crime of obscenity in England and subsequently in the United States. <u>Fanny Hill</u> was the first book prosecuted under the Curl ruling. The publisher was found guilty of obscenity in an 1821 English court. In the United States Vermont was the first state to legislate against obscenity followed by Massachusetts in 1835 which initiated the so-called obscenity test (i.e., a book or writing which corrupts youthful morality). New York passed a statute in 1868 banning obscene literature.[1]

The first federal legislation called the Comstock law (i.e., banning the sale and distribution of obscene materials through the mail) was passed by Congress in 1873. The first Federal court case was the novel, <u>Ulysses</u> by Joyce. The Court of Appeals rejected the Massachusetts test and established a new test of obscenity. This test stated that obscenity must be examined on the basis of its effect on the average individual, not on its effects upon certain types of individuals (i.e., adolescents).[2]

A number of cases were adjudicated based on this test between 1933 and 1957 when the U.S. Supreme Court examined the obscenity issue. Most notable cases were Thornhill v. Alabama (1940), Prince v. Massachusetts (1944), Kovacs v. Cooper (1949), Breard v. Alexandria (1951), Joseph Burstyn Inc. v. Wilson (1952), and Butler v. Michigan (1957). The Supreme Court in 1957 heard Roth v. United States in order to examine the relationship between obscenity and the guarantees of the First and Fourteenth Amendments of the Constitution (i.e., freedom of speech and due process respectively). The Court reaffirmed the <u>Ulysses</u> decision (i.e., average individual test) and added two more tests (i.e., whether the dominant theme of the material appeals to prurient interests and whether the material is without redeeming social importance). The Court also ruled that obscenity was not protected by First Amendment guarantees.[3]

Manual Enterprises v. Day in 1961 resulted in the expansion of the tests of obscenity as determined in <u>Roth</u> to include the concept of patent offensiveness of the material.[4] Jocobellis v. Ohio decided the issue of whether obscenity can be determined by national or community standards. The Court decided that national standards should determine whether a work is obscene or not.[5]

44

In 1966 the Supreme Court heard three cases: Ginzberg v. United States, Mishkin v. New York, and Memoirs v. Massachusetts. These cases moved away from the Roth decision. The new test of obscenity was that the dominant theme of the material taken as a whole appeals to a prurient interest in sex; the material is patently offensive because it affronts contemporary community standards relating to the description or representation of sexual matters; and the material is utterly without redeeming social value. This new test of obscenity called on the prosecution to prove something that is almost impossible to do (i.e., a work has no redeeming social value). Thus the Court at this point in time was unable to agree on a standard to determine what constituted in a clear manner obscene/pornographic material that was subject to regulation under each state's police power.[6]

A whole series of cases rapidly followed Ginzberg, Mishkin, and Memoirs. There was Redrup v. New York (1967); Interstate Circuit Inc. v. Dallas (1968); Stanley v. Georgia (1969). Stanley was convicted for owning at home some pornographic films. The Supreme Court held that it is not criminal to privately own obscene material (i.e., read or view this type of material in the privacy of one's home); U.S. v. Thirty-Seven Photographs (1971); In 1971 the Court also ruled that postal authorities can not prohibit the mailing of obscene materials since consenting adults have the right to choose their own moral standards as long as they do not directly offend other members of the community; Kois v. Wisconsin; U.S. v. Reidel; Rabe v. Washington; Paris Adult Theatre v. Slaton (1973); U.S. v. 12-200 Foot Reels Film (1973); and Miller v. California (1973).[7]

Miller reaffirms Roth that obscene material is not protected by the First Amendment. It also rejects the test of utterly without redeeming social value that was stated in Memoirs. Miller v. California states that a work may be subject to state regulation where that work, taken as a whole, appeals to the prurient interest in sex, portrays, in a patently offensive way, sexual conduct specifically defined by the applicable state law; and taken as a whole, does not have serious literary, artistic, political, or scientific value. The basic guidelines are whether the average person, applying contemporary community standards would find that the work, taken as a whole, appeals to the prurient interest, etc.[8] Thus the Court has apparently given up on a national standard for obscenity and returned the decision of what constitutes obscenity to the local communities. The Court does make the attempt to offer brief guidelines but the issue today is quite confused to say the least as to the legal standard of obscenity in America.

Legal Definitions

Webster defines obscene as disgusting to the senses; grossly
repugnant to the generally accepted notions of what is appropriate;
offensive or revolting as countering or violating some ideal or
principle. The Oxford English Dictionary defines obscene as
offensive to the senses, or to taste or refinement; disgusting,
repulsive, filthy, foul, abominable, loathsome.[9] Black defines
obscene as offensive to chastity of mind or to modesty, expressing
or presenting to the mind or view something that delicacy, purity,
and decency forbids to be exposed; calculated to corrupt, deprave,
and debauch the morals of the people, and promote violation of law;
licentious and libidinous and tending to excite feelings of an
impure or unchaste character; tending to stir the sex impulses or
to lead to sexually impure and lustful thoughts; tending to corrupt
the morals of youth or to lower the standards as to sexual relations.[10]

Webster defines pronography as a written depiction of licen-
tiousness or lewdness; a portrayal of erotic behavior designed to
cause sexual excitement. Black defines pornographic as that which
is of or pertaining to obscene literature.[11] Thus the two terms
obscenity and pornography are used interchangeably in the criminal
law and are synonymous in popular usage.

Obscenity Statute and Enforcement Policy

The D.C. code (i.e., section 22-2001) is a typical example of
the statute enacted against the crime of obscenity in the United
States. The obscenity statute states that it is unlawful to sell,
deliver, distribute, or provide any obscene, indecent, or filthy
writing, picture, sound recording, or other article or representation. It is unlawful to present, direct, act in, or otherwise
participate in the preparation or presentation of any obscene,
indecent, or filthy play, dance, motion picture, or other performance. It is unlawful to pose for, model for, print, record, com-
pose, edit, write, publish, or otherwise participate in preparing
for publication, exhibition, or sale, any obscene, indecent, or
filthy writing picture, sound recording, or other article or
representation. It is unlawful to sell, deliver, distribute, or
provide, or offer or agree to sell, deliver, distribute, or provide
any article, thing, or device which is intended for or represented
as being for indecent or immoral use. It is unlawful to create,
buy, procure, or possess any matter described with intent to
disseminate such matter. It is unlawful to advertise or otherwise
promote the sale of any matter described. It is unlawful to
advertise or otherwise promote the sale of material represented
or held out by such person to be obscene.[12]

The D.C. Code defines the various terms described. Nudity includes the showing of the human male or female genitals, pubic area or buttocks with less than a full opaque covering, or the showing of the female breast with less than a full opaque covering of any portion thereof below the top of the nipple, or the depiction of covered male genitals in a discernibly turgid state. Sexual conduct includes acts of sodomy, masturbation, homosexuality, sexual intercourse, or physical contact with a person's clothed or unclothed genitals, pubic area, buttocks, or if such person be a female, breasts. Sexual excitement is the condition of human male or female genitals when in a state of sexual stimulation or arousal. Sado-masochistic abuse includes flagellation or torture by or upon a person clad in undergarments or a mask or bizarre costume, or the condition of being fettered, bound, or otherwise physically restrained on the part of one so clothed.[13]

It is a valid defense to the charge of obscenity according to the D.C. Code if the violation of the code was for scientific, educational, or other special justification for the possession of such material by a person or institution. A person convicted of obscene behavior as a first offender shall be fined not more than $3000.00 or imprisoned not more than one year, or both. An individual convicted a second time or more shall be fined not less than $1000.00 nor more than $5000.00 or imprisoned not less than six months or more than three years, or both.[14]

The Obscenity Squad of the Morals Division of the Metropolitan Police Department (Washington, D.C.) is assigned the task of enforcing the obscenity statute described. The squad is composed of a sergeant and four detectives. Their task is to watch the many bookstores, movie theatres, topless and bottomless dancer establishments, and burlesque houses. In addition all complaints concerning obscene material and/or performances are investigated as well as routine checks of all night clubs, restaurants, and movie theatres that do not normally feature X-rated movies and/or performances.[15]

The law enforcement process consists of the continuous systematic checking of various theatres, bookstores, nightclubs, and bars to see that the obscenity statute is not violated. Taking the X-rated movie theatres and adult bookstores as an example, members of the obscenity squad regularly check the theatres and bookstores viewing the new films and books. After each check a resume of the contents of the book or film is made by the officer. In the case of indecent publications (i.e., those portraying sadistic sex scenes or those featuring juveniles in explicit sex scenes). In the case of X-rated films, only those displaying sex scenes between humans and animals (i.e., bestiality), homosexuality, urination, defacation, sodomy, sadism, the use of juveniles in sexual activity are written up by the officer.

Each case is reviewed by the sergeant and then given to a special United States Attorney of the United States Department of Justice to review. If the U.S. Attorney feels the material is unacceptable in terms of the obscenity statute, a search warrent is issued for the seizure of the material. In some situations films and books are purchased by the detective and presented with the resume to the U.S. Attorney. In these cases an arrest warrent is issued for the person selling the material. After the warrent is served and the person arrested or material seized, the evidence and testimony of the detective are presented to a grand jury which determines whether or not to indict the person responsible for selling or showing the material. Then follows a trial where the detective again must testify followed by an acquittal or conviction in the case.[16]

Description of Pornography and Obscenity

There appears to be a historical concern with what one might call erotica from ancient Greece and Rome to present-day traditional societies.[17] The League of Nations in 1929 established the International Convention for the Suppression of the Circulation and Traffic in Obscene Publications which was concerned with suppression of obscene material. The United States Congress established a Commission on Noxious Printed and Pictured Material in 1960. In 1967 Congress established the President's Commission on Pornography and Obscenity which reported its findings in 1970.[18]

The Commission report stated that the pornography industry has estimated sales in excess of two billion dollars a year (i.e., sales of films, books, journals, tapes, records, photos, and assorted equipment). Also reported by the Commission were the facts that eighty-five percent of adult men and seventy percent of adult women have been exposed to such material on a voluntary basis. Depictions of nudity with exposed sex organs and of heterosexual intercourse are quite common while homosexual activities and oral sex are less common but increasing in interest. The Commission estimates that 20-25 percent of males have regular experiences with such materials although only 10-12 percent actually purchase the materials on a regular basis. First experience with such erotica usually occurs during adolescence as eighty percent of adolescent males and seventy percent of adolescent females reported seeing visual or textual descriptions of sexual intercourse by the time they reached eighteen. Last the Commission reported that the typical customer of adult bookstores and X-rated theatres were usually middle class, middle aged, white married men.[19]

A number of studies have been conducted by social scientists for the Commission to determine the effects of exposure to sexually explicit (i.e., erotic) materials. The Commission concluded that

exposure to sexually explicit material does produce sexual arousal
in many men and women although the extent of sexual excitement
depends upon the particular characteristics of those viewing and
the type of material. Younger individuals are more readily aroused
than older people; college educated, non-religious, and sexually
active individuals are more likely to become sexually excited than
less educated, religiously active persons, and those who think sex
is "dirty". Erotic materials generally cause an increase of
heterosexual rather than homosexual activity. Viewers of sexual
intercourse are more excited than viewers of oral sex. Finally
older, less educated, puritanical, and sexually confused individuals
more often label erotic material as obscene than more educated,
sexually active, and liberal individuals.[20]

Commission research showed that most individuals exposed to
erotic material had no change in their sexual behavior although
some people did report short term increase in masturbation and
frequency of sexual relations. This increase of sexual activity
usually occurred with available sex partners who were known to the
individual. Couples who viewed erotic materials noted an increase
in sexual intercourse for a 24-hour period after seeing X-rated
films. This sample also reported an increase of erotic dreams and
conversations about sex after seeing such films. Most importantly
the Commission research concluded that exposure to sexually explicit
material has little or no effect on established value-attitudes
concerning sexuality or sexual standards (i.e., those with liberal
value-attitudes towards sex are more tolerant of erotic materials
while those who are negative toward sex are repulsed; those who are
unfamiliar with erotic materials are usually confused emotionally).[21]

Sexually explicit material has often been cited by theorists
and social critics as a contributing factor towards the creation
of social deviance (i.e., criminal and delinquent behavior).
Commission studies state that there is no evidence that erotic
material plays a major role in the causation of delinquent or
criminal behavior. Delinquent and nondelinquent adolescents state
similar experiences with erotic material. In fact most youth have
had widespread exposure to such material despite the criminal laws.
Thus the age of first exposure, the type of material seen, the
quantity and circumstances of exposure to materials are about equal
for both delinquents and nondelinquents when social class and
community are held constant. Peer pressures do play an important
part in an adolescent's exposure to erotic materials.[22]

The Commission states that pornographic and obscene material
is not associated as a cause of sex offenses. Studies in the United
States show that during periods of increased availability of erotic
material, some specific rates of arrest for sex crimes have increased
(i.e., forceable rape) while others have declined (i.e., juvenile

arrests for sex crimes). A Danish study of sexual assaults against
females shows that there has been a substantial decline in certain
offenses since pornographic material was legalized and available
to the public (i.e., exhibitionism declined 58 percent; voyeurism
declined 80 percent; exposure to women 56 percent; child molesting
69 percent). Part of the decline in sex crimes is explained by
more public tolerance (i.e., less reporting to police) and more
police tolerance (i.e., less arrests for offenses).[23]

A study of typical community members and those convicted of
sex offenses (i.e., rapists, child molesters, homosexuals, trans-
sexuals, and those convicted under obscenity laws) was undertaken
by Goldstein and Kant. The typical community members were exposed
to explicit acts of sexual intercourse during adolescence while
the sex offenders were not. The offenders felt more guilty when
thinking about sex or exposed to erotic material when growing up.
The research concluded that abnormal development of sexuality can
lead to either an absence or excessive interest in pornographic
material by sex offenders. Finally the study reported that pornography does not tend to incite deviant behavior (i.e., delinquent
or criminal) in most cases.[24]

Decriminalization of Pornography and Obscenity Statutes

The Commission concluded that the majority of American adults
want to read or see any erotic materials they wish to examine.
There is agreement among adults that children and juveniles should
not be permitted to see such erotic materials but most felt that
it would be virtually impossible to enforce the statutes against
obscene material.[25] For example Fairfax County, Virginia
(suburban area of D.C.) requires that such magazines as Playboy,
Penthouse, and Hustler be placed behind the counter or in back of
hardboard covers so youth cannot see such material. Ordinances
have been passed in several Northern Virginia jurisdictions keeping
adult bookstores a certain distance from schools, churches, and
residential areas.

The Commission recommended in 1970 the repeal of all federal,
state, and local legislation prohibiting the commercial distribution,
exhibition, and sale of erotic materials to consenting adults. The
Commission also recommended special legislation prohibiting the
same materials sale, display, or distribution to children and
adolescents. The Commission thus advocated the decriminalization
of the possession, sale, and display of erotic materials among
adults and pointed to the need for free discussion of sexual
behavior in American society. Thus the Commission recommended
an open sex education program in the public schools.

Much of the problem regarding materials which depict explicit sexual activity stems from the inability or reluctance of people in our society to be open and direct in dealing with sexual matters. This often manifests itself in the inhibition of talking openly and directly about sex. Professionals use highly technical language when they discuss sex; others escape by using euphemisms or by not talking about sex at all. Direct and open conversation about sex between parent and child is too rare in our society. Failure to talk openly and directly about sex has several consequences. It overemphasizes sex, gives it a magical, nonnatural quality, making it more attractive and fascinating. It diverts the expression of sexual interest out of more legitimate channels. Such failure makes teaching children and adolescents to become fully and adequately functioning sexual adults a more difficult task. And it clogs legitimate channels for transmitting sexual information and forces people to use clandestine and unreliable sources.[26]

Justice Douglas in his dissenting opinion in Miller v. California states that the sovereign states in their criminal codes and the Supreme Court in Miller are interfering with the Constitution in its guarantees as stated in both First and Fourteenth amendments. Thus society's attempts to legislate for adults in the area of obscenity have not been successful. Present laws prohibiting the consensual sale or distribution of explicit sexual materials to adults are extremely unsatisfactory in their application. The Constitution permits material to be deemed obscene for adults only if as a whole it appeals to the prurient interest of the average person, is patently offensive in light of community standards, and lacks redeeming social value. These vague and highly subjective aesthetic, psychological and moral tests do not provide meaningful guidance for law enforcement officials, juries or courts. As a result law is inconsistently and sometimes erroneously applied and the distinctions made by courts between prohibited and permissible materials often appear indefensible. Errors in the application of the law and uncertainty about its scope also cause interference with the communication of constitutionally protected materials.[27]

Unfortunately President Nixon totally rejected the recommendations of his own Commission and one of his appointees to the Supreme Court, Justice Rehnquist in California v. LaRue stated that indecent exposure and sexual assaults result from adult males viewing nude female ladies and certain sexual acts in California bars.[28] Thus both the executive and judicial branches of the federal government have not accepted the social policy formulated by the Commission on Pornography and Obscenity and all the research done to support its recommendations.

Those who are opposed to the decriminalization of pornography and obscenity are those who tend to be against freedom of expression (i.e., those who campaigned against the TV program "Soap" even before it went on the ABC network and those who feel that sex education is a communist plot). Those opposing decriminalization tend to be female, older, less educated, more religious, and less open to social change in society.[29] Thus the so-called anti-pornographic or public decency crusades that go back to the time of Comstock and the YMCA in New York state are likely to get their support from rural and suburban areas of the country rather than the inner cities. These groups are fundamentalist in religious outlook, politically conservative, and usually lower middle class. The leadership for such groups comes from the ranks of those who have already been active in religious or patriotic voluntary organization. These people often have the support of wealthy members of the community. They use the obscenity issue as a way to attempt to stop change in other aspects of our daily lives. These people do not want to lose their way of life but attempt to stop others from freely changing their way of life.[30]

Notes

1. Robert Pursley, Introduction to Criminal Justice, Encino, California: Glenco Press, 1977, 110-112; Marshall Clinard, Sociology of Deviant Behavior, New York: Holt, Rinehart and Winston, 1974, 532-533; The President's Commission on Pornography and Obscenity, Report of the Commission on Pornography and Obscenity, New York: New York Times Book by Bantam Books, 1970.

2. United States v. One Book Called "Ulysses", 5F, Supp. 182 (1933).

3. United States Reports, Miller v. California, Washington, D.C.: Supreme Court of the United States, 1973; 354, U.S. 476 (1956).

4. 370, U.S. 478 (1962).

5. 378, U.S. 184 (1964).

6. 383, U.S. 412 (1966); 383, U.S. 463 (1966); 383, U.S. 413 (1966).

7. Miller v. California, op. cit.; 394, U.S. 557, 567 (1969).

8. 413, U.S. 15 (1973).

9. Webster's New International Dictionary, 3rd edition, Unabridged, 1969; The Oxford English Dictionary, 1933.

10. Henry Black, Black's Law Dictionary, St. Paul, Minnesota: West Publishing Company, 1968, 1227.

11. Webster, op. cit.; Black, op. cit., 1322.

12. District of Columbia Code, 1973, supplement iv, 1977, 1437-1438.

13. Ibid., 1438.

14. Ibid., 1438.

15. Interviews with sergeant Abbott and detective Benigas of the Metropolitan Police Department (D.C.) Obscenity Squad, 1977.

16. Ibid.

17. Bronislaw Malinowski, The Sexual Life of Savages, New York: Harcourt, Brace and World, 1929.

18. The President's Commission, op. cit.

19. Ibid., 25-30.

20. Ibid.

21. Ibid., 30-32.

22. Ibid., 25-27.

23. Ibid., 27; Berl Kutchinsky, The Effect of Easy Availability of Pornography on the Incidence of Sex Crimes: The Danish Experience, Journal of Social Issues, 1974.

24. Michael Goldstein and Harold Kant, Pornography and Sexual Deviance, Los Angeles: University of California Press, 1973.

25. The President's Commission, op. cit., 49.

26. Ibid., 53.

27. Miller v. California, dissenting opinion of Justice Douglas, op. cit.; The President's Commission, op. cit., 59; Harry Clor, Obscenity and Public Morality, Chicago: University of Chicago Press, 1969; John Gagnon and William Simon, Pornography - Raging Menace or Paper Tiger?, Trans-Action, (July, 1967), 41-48; Arthur Knight and Hollis Alpert, The History of Sex in Cinema: the Stag Film, Playboy (November, 1967); David Loth, The Erotic in Literature, New York: Julian Messner, 1961; Ned Polsky, Hustlers, Beats, and Others, Chicago: Aldine Publishing Company, 1967; Polsky, Pornography, in Sagarin and MacNamera, Problems of Sex Behavior, New York: Thomas Y. Crowell, 1968, 268-284.

28. 409, U.S. 109 (1972).

29. The President's Commission, op. cit., 49.

30. L. Zurcher, G. Kirkpatrick, R. Cushing, and C. Bowman, The Anti-Pornography Campaign: A Symbolic Crusade, Social Problems, 19 (Fall, 1971), 217-238; John Gagnon and William Simon, The Sexual Scene, Chicago: Aldine Publishing Company, 1970, 149-150.

IV

PROSTITUTION

Legal History

Prostitution was not regarded as a criminal offense in England
but as a vice that was under the jurisdiction of the ecclesiastical
court. The English common law does not mention prostitution until
after 1640 and it was regarded as a tort rather than a crime.[1] The
New England colonies that were under puritan rule passed statutes
against nightwalkers and bawdyhouses as early as 1648.[2] This type
of statute was in force in England in 1707 as it refers to the
Ann Dekins case where she was detained on suspicion of solicitation
for prostitution as a nightwalker.[3] According to Holmes many early
state statutes contained statements concerning prostitutes or
nightwalkers who loitered on the street or in a public place for
the purpose of prostitution.[4]

Taking New York state as an example, prostitution was legal,
unregulated, and operating openly even to the extent of advertising
in the newspapers. Thus the New York Penal Law of the period
1864-1881 did not make prostitution per se a crime. But the New
York State Supreme Court in 1893 did rule that the profession of
prostitution is a deplorable vice productive of disorder and disease
even though the prostitute is not committing a crime.[5]

By the early twentieth century many state criminal codes
allowed for the arrest of prostitutes, not on charges of prostitution, but for disorderly conduct. This lead to the creation of
so-called red light districts in the larger metropolitan areas
where prostitutes and their employers were segregated from the rest
of the community. Thus houses of prostitution were tolerated under
the watchful eyes of the police but streetwalkers were arrested
under the disorderly conduct statute.[6]

Just prior to World War I the problem of white slavery (i.e.,
girls kidnaped and used for prostitution) became a public issue.
During and after World War I it was commonly thought that the
prostitute was a victim of a white slaver who induced young women
into the life. In 1919 the American Social Health Association
drafted a model statute which later became incorporated into both
federal and state legislation that was opposed to prostitution
(i.e., customers as well as prostitutes were considered as criminals
in nineteen states). Laws were also passed prohibiting the
establishment or maintenance of houses of prostitution in every
state during the 1920's.[7] On the federal level the White-Slave-
Traffic Act (i.e., Mann Act) made it illegal to transport women

across state lines for the purpose of prostitution or other immoral
acts. In the 1930's no significant anti-prostitution laws were
enacted. In the 1950's efforts were made to break up organized
prostitution, especially that linked to organized crime.[8]

The final report of the Committee on Homosexual Offenses and
Prostitution (i.e., the Wolfenden Committee) in England in 1957
favored removal of the criminal statutes on prostitution per se
but wanted stiff penalties for repeated street prostitution, rental
of premises for purposes of prostitution, and living off the
earnings of prostitutes. The Committee recommendations were enacted
in the Street Offenses Act of 1959. The result was that the
prostitutes became more mobile so that they would not be charged
with a second infraction in the same police district and cars and
vans were used in place of apartment rentals. Thus the law was
circumvented.[9]

By 1970 prostitution and related crimes were totally illegal
in the United States. The particular wording of the statutes
vary as twenty-seven states do not specifically mention prostitution
but legally place such behavior under their vagrancy laws. Most
states have statutes governing such individuals as procurers, pimps,
and madams. Only eight states make it a crime to be a prostitute's
customer or participate in sexual intercourse with a prostitute.[10]
Today only five states still have prostitution statutes that only
apply to women since male prostitutes are now a recognized
phenomenon (i.e., both heterosexual and homosexual prostitutes).[11]
Nevada in 1971 allowed the legalization of prostitution on a county
basis. There is legalized prostitution in thirteen of Nevada's
seventeen counties today. Other than the state of Nevada, prostitution is prohibited and prostitutes are considered criminals.[12]

The 1970's has witnessed a challenge to the laws governing
prostitution. The Woman's Liberation movement has looked upon
prostitution as a form of sex discrimination. A number of suits
have been filed in federal court dealing with the solicitation
statutes under the First Amendment of the Constitution (i.e.,
freedom of speech). There has been concern that women's rights to
privacy have been violated by the wording of the various prostitution laws. The prostitution statutes have been attacked as sexist.
The statutes have also been attacked as not allowing the prostitute
to control her bodily functions without unreasonable interference
from the state.[13]

The Supreme Court held in Cherry v. Maryland and United States
v. Moses that solicitation can be declared criminal by the states
since it is a commercial proposal. Solicitation to commit a crime
had already been established as a criminal act at common law. In

57

the cases of United States v. Cesear and Whitt v. United States,
the Court stated that immoral conduct includes not only prostitution
but also sodomy, fornication, adultery, and related crimes. Prostitutes are sometimes charged under these adultery, fornication, or
sodomy statutes. This was upheld in Doe v. Commonwealth of
Virginia.[14]

Legal Definitions

According to Black, prostitution is defined as common lewdness
of a woman for gain; whoredom; the act or practice of a woman who
permits any man who will pay her price to have sexual intercourse
with her. A prostitute is a woman who indiscriminantly consorts
with men for hire.[15] A pimp is defined as an individual who provides for others the means of gratifying lust; a procurer, a
panderer; one who solicits trade for a prostitute. A procurer is
one who procures the seduction or prostitution of young women. A
madam is one who operates a house of prostitution and who may or
may not herself be a prostitute.[16]

Prostitution Statutes and Enforcement Policies

District of Columbia Criminal Code defines prostitution as the
unlawful process of inviting, enticing, persuading, or addressing
for the purpose of inviting, enticing, or persuading any person or
persons sixteen years of age or over for the purpose of prostitution,
or any other immoral act or lewd purpose under the penalty of not
more than 250 dollars or imprisonment for not more than ninety days,
or both.[17] Virginia Code states that any person who for money or
its equivalent, commits adultery or fornication and thereafter does
any substantial act in furtherance thereof, shall be guilty of being
a prostitute, or prostitution, which shall be punishable as a class
one misdemeanor.[18]

The D.C. Code defines pandering as any person who shall place
or cause, induce, procure, or compel the placing of any female in
the charge or custody of any other person, or in a house of prostitution, with intent that she shall engage in prostitution, or who
shall compel, induce, entice, or procure or attempt to compel,
induce, entice, or procure any female to reside with any other
person for immoral purposes or for the purpose of prostitution, or
who shall compel, induce, entice, or procure or attempt to compel,
induce, entice, or procure any such female to reside or continue to
reside in a house of prostitution, or compel, induce, entice, or
procure, or attempt to compel, induce, entice, or procure her to
engage in prostitution, or who takes or detains a female against
her will, with intent to compel her by force, threats, menace, or
duress to marry him or to marry any other person; or any parent,
guardian, or other person having legal custody of the person of a

female who consents to her taking or detention by any such person, for the purpose of prostitution or sexual intercourse, shall be guilty of a felony and upon conviction shall be punished by imprisonment for not more than five years and by a fine of not more than one thousand dollars.[19]

A procurer is any person who shall receive any money or other valuable thing for or on account of arranging for or causing any female to have sexual intercourse with any other person or to engage in prostitution, debauchery, or any other immoral act, shall be guilty of a felony and upon conviction shall be punished by imprisonment for not more than five years and a fine of not more than a thousand dollars.[20] A procurer for a house of prostitution is any person who shall pay or receive any money or other valuable thing for or on account of the procuring for, or placing in, a house of prostitution, for purposes of sexual intercourse, prostitution, debauchery, or other immoral act, any female shall be guilty of a felony and punished by imprisonment of not more than five years and a fine of not more than one thousand dollars.[21] A procurer for third person is any person who shall receive any money or other valuable thing for or on account of procuring and placing in the charge or custody of another person for sexual intercourse, prostitution, debauchery, or other immoral purposes any female shall be guilty of a felony and shall be punished by imprisonment for not more than five years and by a fine of not more than a thousand dollars.[22]

An individual who runs a house of prostitution is one who knowingly accepts, receives, levies, or appropriates any money or other valuable thing, without consideration other than the furnishing of a place for prostitution or the servicing of a place for prostitution from the proceeds or earnings of any female engaged in prostitution shall be guilty of a felony and shall be punished by imprisonment for not more than five years and by a fine of not more than one thousand dollars.[23] Whoever is convicted of keeping a bawdy or disorderly house shall be fined not more than five hundred dollars or imprisoned not more than one year, or both.[24]

Any person who for purposes of prostitution persuades, entices, or forcibly abducts, from her home or usual abode, or from the custody or control of her parents or guardian, any female under sixteen years of age shall be punished by imprisonment for not less than two nor more than twenty years; and whoever knowingly secretes or harbors any such female so persuaded, enticed, or abducted shall suffer imprisonment for not more than eight years.[25] Any person who by threats of duress, detains any female against her will, for the purpose of prostitution or sexual intercourse, or any person who shall compel any female against her will to reside with him or with any other person for the purpose of prostitution or sexual

intercourse will be guilty of a felony and shall be punished by
imprisonment for not more than five years and a fine of not more
than one thousand dollars.[26] Any person who by force, fraud,
intimidation, or threats, places or leaves, or procures any other
person or persons to place or leave, his wife in a house of prostitution, or to lead a life of prostitution shall be guilty of a
felony and shall be imprisoned not less than one nor more than ten
years.[27] Any person or persons who attempt to detain any girl or
woman in a disorderly house or a house of prostitution because of
any debt or debts she has contracted, or is said to have contracted
while living in said house of prostitution or disorderly house shall
be guilty of a felony, and be imprisoned for a term not less than
one nor more than five years.[28]

Some states such as New York make it a crime to participate in
a sexual act with a prostitute or to solicit a prostitute for her
services.[29] Georgia and Hawaii require the forfeiture of an
individual's driver's license if convicted of soliciting for the
purpose of prostitution. Wisconsin has a statute that provides a
penalty of one hundred dollars fine and or a three months jail term
if a male enters a house of prostitution for the purposes of engaging
in nonmarital sex.[30]

The Mann Act (i.e., White-Slave-Traffic-Act) deals with the
interstate transportation of females for purposes of prostitution.
The United States Code states that whoever knowingly transports in
interstate or foreign commerce, or in the District of Columbia, any
girl or woman for the purpose of prostitution or debauchery, or for
any other immoral purpose, or with the intent and purpose to induce,
entice, or compel such girl or woman to become a prostitute or to
give herself up to debauchery, or to engage in any other immoral
practice, shall be fined not more than five thousand dollars or
imprisoned not more than five years, or both.[31]

The Metropolitan Police Department of D.C. (i.e., MPD) has two
units which handle solicitation violations, the Prostitution Enforcement Detail and the Youth Division Prostitution and Perversion
Squad. All pandering and procuring violations are handled by the
Vice Squad.[32]

Prostitution arrests usually come under one of three headings:
(1) solicitation, (2) disorderly conduct or vagrancy, or (3) violation of jurisdictional health regulations. Depending on the political pressures applied by elected officials, mass media coverage,
and citizen's complaints, the police enforce the laws against
prostitution in a somewhat inconsistent fashion. Enforcement policy
also depends on whether the prostitute is a streetwalker, bar-girl,
massage parlor girl, or call girl (i.e., the more visible the deviant
behavior, the more likely an arrest will be made). Most prostitutes

who are arrested tend to be either juveniles, those who are drunk,
or high on drugs. The police department has to be careful concerning the relationships between police and prostitutes as graft and
free access to services become a problem for every large police
department.[33]

There is also the ever present problem of entrapment. Entrapment is the persuasion or influence of a person who otherwise would
not have committed the criminal act by a law enforcement officer.
Metropolitan Police Departments utilize police women as decoys so
that they can arrest potential male customers on charges of solicitation. Sometimes officers will knowingly use entrapment of a
prostitute so that she will become an informer on her pimp, keeper
or a bawdy house, or give information on other criminal types such
as narcotics pushers and other street criminals.[34]

Street prostitution presents the most common problems for
police officers. The most common and most dangerous crime committed
by prostitutes is robbery. For example a customer met a prostitute
and they agreed upon a price. The prostitute led him to a room in
a vacant building where her accomplice hit the customer over the
head and then beat him up. The prostitute and her accomplice proceeded to steal the man's wallet and watch and left him. Larceny is
another common crime committed against customers. In this case a
customer   will be trusting enough to leave his wallet where the
woman can get access to its contents during or after sexual relations when the client is preoccupied.

A third common offense is being pickpocketed. This usually
involves two or more prostitutes who are dealing with a potential
client. They usually approach the victim and one prostitute will
proposition him and fondle him to divert his attention from the
other girl who will take his wallet. Assault and assault and
battery are another common type of crime. This may occur when a
customer becomes angered with the prostitute about the service
rendered, the customer may be the type that can only obtain sexual
gratification if he beats the woman, two prostitutes fight over a
customer, or the prostitute's pimp assaults her for a variety of
reasons. Murder of a prostitute or client is not very common but
does occur. Prostitutes have been murdered by insane customers so
many will refuse to perform certain types of sexual requests since
by experience trouble may occur. There was one incident in
Washington, DC where a client was murdered by a pimp after the
customer had severely beaten the prostitute.

A prostitute may claim she is a rape victim especially if the
customer refuses to pay or when he forces her to perform some act
that she is totally opposed to. The police have a difficult time
handling such cases since the prostitute only wants to harass

her client and knows that the police will not arrest the customer
on the charge of rape since they can easily arrest both parties on
a variety of other charges.

There are also several crimes that are not related directly to
prostitution but are secondary crimes considered to be part of the
illicit sex problem. The most common crime is a con game known as
"the Murphy Game". In this game, the con man frequents the same
area as the prostitutes. He usually approaches his victim and tells
him that he can take him to a place where there are prostitutes.
He takes the person to a hotel lobby and then informs him that it
would be best to leave his extra money with him while the customer
looks for a suitable woman. While the customer is looking for the
woman or a room number, the con man leaves with the remainder of
the victim's money and/or watch. A variation of this con game ends
with the victim arriving at the hotel and going into a room where
several of the con man's associates rob him and flee.

Finally there is normal street crime associated with the influx
of potential clients for prostitutes in a neighborhood who park
their cars outside of motels and hotels where prostitutes are known
to frequent. In these cases the cars are often broken into and
wallets, c.b. radios, spare tires, tape decks, etc. are taken at
will.[35]

Massage parlor crimes are less common than those connected with
street prostitution. Many times investigating officers with warrants
will find juveniles working in a parlor with falsified work papers
or IDs. Sometimes routine checks of employees would reveal that
they were wanted for prostitution in another jurisdiction. Massage
parlors also have been noted as places that sell or give away a
variety of drugs to clients or are used by the girls. The police
then arrest the users or suppliers on drug charges but not on
prostitution charges. Two types of crimes that are associated with
massage parlors are bilking and blackmail. Bilking occurs when the
customer pays for services rendered by use of a credit card. The
girls would either use his card for filling out two copies or raise
the cost after he signed the statement. Obviously when the customer
receives two bills or a higher charge he is not going to call the
police for that would admit that he was engaged in criminal activity
and/or ruin his standing with family and community. Some wealthy
clients write out personal checks with which to pay the girls and
leave themselves wide open to blackmail. Sometimes the girls will
inform on other prostitutes or other massage parlors so as to eliminate
their personal or business competition. This is especially true
when a girl or parlor cuts prices below the agreed on rates for all
parlors.[36]

The largest problem in dealing with crimes associated with prostitution is deliberate nonreporting of the crime by the victim. This in itself can be a criminal offense. Usually crimes that involve violence are reported by prostitute and client alike. Robberies involving threat of force or use of force are also often reported. Theft of money or wallet is not usually reported because of the circumstances under which the theft occurred since the victim does not want the adverse publicity. Several United States Congressmen have been victims of secondary crimes associated with prostitution on the streets of Washington, DC but have been able to keep the information out of the press in recent years.[37]

Unfortunately the attitude of some law enforcement officers, prosecuting attorneys, judges, and jury members have been negative toward the victims of secondary crime associated with prostitution. These members of the criminal justice system along with the mass media feel that the customer is acting in a deviant manner and they deserve what happens to them at the hands of prostitutes and other criminals. The typical prostitute usually gets her case thrown out by the judge or magistrate, is fined under fifty dollars for a first offense, or given less than fifteen days in a municipal or county jail. Thus rehabilitation is not the goal of the criminal court but keeping the girls off the streets as long as possible.[38]

Description of Prostitution

It is estimated that prostitution is a billion dollar industry and involves as many as 500 thousand full and parttime women in the United States with the exception of the counties in Nevada where the profession is legal and taxed by both state and federal agencies.[39] In 1976, out of 58,000 arrested for prostitution and commercialized vice, 71 percent were women and 29 percent were men. But only 22 percent of women were arrested for vagrancy and only 16 of women were arrested for disorderly conduct.[40] Since 1976 in the District of Columbia, twenty-four hundred cases of prostitution have been handled. This figure breaks down to 1507 females (1212 blacks and 295 whites) and 1821 males (928 blacks and 893 whites) arrested for soliciting prostitution. There have also been 167 juvenile prostitution cases involving mostly females from the ages between ten and seventeen.[41]

There are several types of prostitutes, both female and male in society today. There are the streetwalkers, bar-girls, massage parlor girls, women working in houses of prostitution, call girls, and call service/escort service girls. Male prostitutes are not very numerous. Some specialize in female clientele while the majority deal with homosexual clients.

The common prostitute or streetwalker gets her trade on the
streets or at public places such as bars, hotel lobbies, and other
places of recreation although she does not work in such places.
Streetwalkers usually do not have direct connections with organized
crime but usually have to pay protection to members of organized
crime and/or corrupt police officers to save themselves from
robbery or arrest. Bar girls, strippers, and other women associated
with commercial night life are legitimately employed but may select
clients and split the fees with their employer. These prostitutes
are safer from the influence of organized criminals and corrupt
police officers. Prostitutes who work in houses of prostitution
are fairly rare in the United States except in the state of Nevada.
House girls are supervised by a manager or madam who provides
protection from the police and unruly patrons, offers room and
board for the girls, and pays for police protection. Most often
the house of prostitution either is run by organized crime or pays
it for the privilege of existence.[42]

The call girl is becoming quite common today since she is safer
from the dangers and expenses of organized criminals, pimps, madams,
the police, and health officials. This type of prostitute may
operate from her own apartment or go to meet a client. She usually
has an answering service and may work loosely in conjunction with
other call girls who give each other their extra clients for a split
of the fee for services rendered. The call girl may work for a
large corporation and cater to special clients of the firm, be a
housewife, a model, or any number of legitimate occupations. She
usually is protected by the secrecy of her approach to prostitution
although if she works conventions may become known to hotel detectives or the manager of the residential hotel she uses for her work.
In these cases she may have to split fees with hotel staff or the
police for protection.[43]

The massage parlor is a recent innovation as far as a haven
for prostitutes. A customer can get a legitimate massage from a
masseuse or for a substantial fee obtain a number of sexual services
(i.e., masturbation, normal sexual intercourse, anal intercourse,
fellatio). He can also receive special services (i.e., flagellation,
voyeurism, exhibitionism, triolism, koprolognia, urolagnia,
transvestism). One must be a steady customer to receive special
services from a massage parlor girl since the owners want to make
sure that their clients are not undercover police officers. Thus
the masseuse will only provide a massage unless the client requests
some sexual service. In this way she can use the defense of entrapment if the client turns out to be a law enforcement officer and the
massage parlor operator can claim the client was at fault since his
establishment is legitimate.

Massage parlors have become fashionable since they do offer
legitimate services as well as cater to those wanting to endulge in
acts of sexual deviance. Most massage parlors that are fronts for
prostitution are operated by organized crime or those who pay it for
protection against the police and politicians who might legislate
the parlor out of existence. The typical massage parlor has a
manager and a male bouncer to keep abusive or dissatisfied customers
from bothering the girls. Since this is a "legitimate" business
operation, the police must also respond if a customer tries to
assault a girl. Girls must notify the manager if a customer wants
sexual services and fraternization with customers outside the parlor
is grounds for firing since the management would not get its share
of the profits.[44]

The massage parlor masseuse is much safer than the streetwalker or house girl since she is legitimately employed and protected by both the management and the police from abusive clients. She
can set her own hours of work, refuse certain kinds of sexual
services, and earn a steady income with no fear of robbery or lack
of medical insurance. On the other hand the streetwalker has to
worry about being robbed, beaten up by clients or her pimp, has to
work long hours to support herself and her pimp or pay protection
to organized crime, is harrassed by the police and vulnerable to
arrest or bribery, and has to pay her own doctor's bills for
checkups. Only the call girl has a safer and securer vocation and
income than the massage parlor girl.

The massage parlor business has recently moved into the call
service/escort service business in response to legislation closing
down some operations or making licensing of masseuses required. The
customer in this case places a call from an advertisement. The
masseuse calls the number back to check its legitimacy (i.e.,
hotel, motel, or private residence). The girl or girls are transported to the location by the bouncer who talks to the prospective
client (i.e., quotes price, amount of time allowed for the service,
and takes payment). Then the girl(s) go in and perform their
service. The bouncer serves as protection and makes sure that the
girl(s) do not stay longer than the agreed time. This is similar
to the call girl but provides protection against a potentially
difficult client or one who demands services not agreed upon.[45]

Male prostitutes usually service homosexual clients and frequent
homosexual bars, theatres, and public baths. Some statutes requiring
that massage parlors employ only same sex employees have resulted in
an increase of male prostitution rather than the elimination of
prostitution altogether. Male prostitutes who cater to female
clientele are quite rare and are found at resort locations, bars,
and residential hotels catering to wealthier middle class women who
are usually middle-aged and looking for paid male companions.[46]

Characteristics of Prostitutes, Clients, and Pimps

Most prostitutes are between the ages of seventeen and twenty-four although girls have been picked up as young as ten. Juvenile prostitution is becoming an increasingly troublesome problem since runaway girls and some boys turn to prostitution (i.e., hetero-sexual and homosexual respectively) as the only way of support. This area of prostitution is hard to deal with since most police department youth divisions do not have the staff to handle such cases. Further those who procure, harbor, and request the services of juveniles are open to harsh penalties so are particularly careful as to the public exposure of the girl or boy. Finally since the juvenile is a runaway who does not want to either return home or be taken to a juvenile justice facility, she is unlikely to be coopera-tive with the police or social services personnel about her contacts and associates.[47]

Bell states four basic reasons why men seek out prostitutes: (1) avoid competition (i.e., those who are emotionally insecure, physically or mentally limited, ugly, or old); (2) impersonal sex (i.e., those who want sexual release with no commitment); (3) sexual deviance or peculiarities (i.e., those who want to take part in sadomasochistic or other fetishes, or kinds of sexual activities that wives or girl friends would not normally want to take part); and (4) uncomplicated sex (i.e., no worries about one's partner, freedom to choose any woman for sexual variety without dating, need for companionship and intimacy without obligation to sexual partner).[48]

The pimp is a man who lives off the earnings of the prostitutes who work for him. He is particularly susceptible for arrest since the procuring of women for prostitution or the solicitation of customers for prostitutes is a felony while prostitutes who solicit clients directly are charged only with a misdeamor. Thus most pimps do not procure or pander but attract vulnerable young women by overtures of love and protection in return for their prostituting themselves for money which the pimp takes for their mutual benefit. According to Goode the pimp provides the prostitute with protection against clients and police; takes his girls to expensive restaurants, resorts, and other places in order to attract better clientele; gives her expensive clothes and a sumptuous place to live; provides her with psychological support and a father figure; manages her finances and daily routine; and paints a picture of future security, both financial and emotional for himself and his girl(s).[49]

Decriminalization of Prostitution

Decriminalization of prostitution in the United States has been a topic of discussion for many years. With the exception of the state of Nevada which decriminalized prostitution in 1971 and claims that it has been able to control this activity and related secondary crimes state wide, the debate on the legalization of prostitution persists today.

The major points in favor of decriminalization state that the state should not impose its morality upon consenting adults who with to endulge in sexual relations as a business transaction. There are many women who are prosecuted for solicitation who have been entraped by the police. Proponents of decriminalization feel that it is virtually impossible to arrest a prostitute without first entraping her because the average prostitute usually does not openly solicit her clients. Decriminalization of prostitution would allow the police to deal with more important matters rather than having detectives pose as prostitutes and pimps to catch both streetwalker and client. The prostitute who is convicted for solicitation and institutionalized does not benefit from her incarceration since recidivism rates are almost one hundred percent and the costs of maintaining separate facilities for women are not justified. Many experts feel that prostitutes are not mentally ill so being placed in a mental institution does not serve any useful purpose.[50]

Decriminalization of prostitution would help lower the number of sex crimes (i.e., rape, incest, procuring, and pandering) in society. There would also be less interest by organized crime in providing this service. Venereal disease control would be easier since medical authorities would know where prostitutes and their customers were located. Legalization would also allow houses of prostitution to be located in areas of the community that would not be offensive to adults in general. Finally decriminalization of prostitution would allow local, state, and federal governments to benefit from the tax revenues and license fees collected from clients, prostitutes, and the managers of houses of prostitution rather than go to organized crime, corrupt police officers, and public officials.[51]

The opponents of decriminalization state that prostitution leads to all sorts of secondary crime (i.e., drug addiction and abuse, assaults, robberies, blackmail, and even murder). Decriminalization would not eliminate the need for pimps but would encourage more males to become pimps. Thus such crimes as seduction, procuring, and pandering would lead to more violent crimes among pimps and prostitutes who would compete with each other to maximize their profits. Prostitution leads to the spread of venereal disease, corrupts the morals of youth, and involves the police in degrading

and compromising situations that may lead to taking bribes or even
setting up their own vice operations from the knowledge gained in
dealing with prostitutes. Some adherents to strict enforcement of
prostitution statutes feel that the police can use prostitutes as
informants on robbery, drug, and gambling problems in the community
in return for not arresting girls who cooperate. Last many people
feel that the decriminalization or legalization of prostitution will
lead to the decline of societal norms and encourage people not to
marry, to engage in acts of sexual deviance, and lead young girls
and women into this way of life as a career rather than engage in
legitimate occupations and roles better suited to women.[52]

68

Notes

1. Harold Greenwald, The Elegant Prostitute: A Social and Psychoanalytic Study, New York: Walker, 1970; Susan Hall, Ladies of the Night, New York: Simon and Schuster, 1973; Bruce Jackson, In the Life: Versions of the Criminal Experience, New York: New American Library, 1974; Larry Kleinman, Sex Parlor,New York: New American Library, 1973; Gail Sheehy, Hustling, New York: Delacorte Press, 1973; John Wells, Tricks of the Trade, New York: New American Library, 1970; Wayland Young, Eros Denied: Sex in Western Society, New York: Grove Press, 1966; Fernando Henriques, Prostitution and Society, New York: Grove Press, 1962; Harry Benjamin and R.E.L. Masters, Prostitution and Morality, New York: The Julian Press, 1964; Norman St. John-Stevas, Law and Morals, London: Burns and Oastes, 1964.

2. William McDonald, Stop and Frisk: An Historical and Empirical Assessment, in Robert Rich (ed.), Essays on the Theory and Practice of Criminal Justice, Washington, DC: University Press of America, 1977, 51-52, 81-83.

3. Ibid., 81-82.

4. Kay Ann Holmes, Reflections by Gaslight: Prostitution in Another Age, Issues in Criminology, 7 (Winter, 1972).

5. Ibid.

6. Ibid.

7. Charles Winick and Paul Kinsie, The Lively Commerce, Chicago: Quadrangle Books, 1971, 212; Marshall Clinard, Sociology of Deviant Behavior, New York: Holt, Rinehart and Winston, 1974, 513-514.

8. Clinard, op. cit., 514; Freda Adler, Sisters in Crime: the Rise of the New Female Criminal, New York: McGraw-Hill, 1975, 223, 55-83.

9. Report of the Committee on Homosexual Offenses and Prostitution, London: Her Majesty's Stationery Office, Cmnd. 247, 1957; Gilbert Geis, Not the Law's Business, Washington, DC: US Government Printing Office, 1972, 187-189.

10. Robert Bell, Social Deviance, Homewood, Illinois: The Dorsey Press, 1971, 229; T.C. Esselstyn, Prostitution in the United States, The Annals, (March, 1968), 123-135.

11.   Edwin Schur and Hugo Bedau, <u>Victimless Crimes</u>, New Jersey:
      Prentice-Hall, 1974.

12.   Bell, <u>op</u>. <u>cit</u>., 229.

13.   Adler, <u>op</u>. <u>cit</u>., 220-221.

14.   Charles Rosenbleet and Barbara Pariente, The Prostitution of
      the Criminal Law, <u>The American Criminal Law Review</u>, 11 (1973),
      373-427.

15.   Henry Black, <u>Black's Law Dictionary</u>, St. Paul, Minnesota:
      West Publishing Company, 1968, 1386.

16.   <u>Ibid</u>., 1306, 1373.

17.   District of Columbia Code, <u>District of Columbia Code Annotated</u>,
      Washington, DC: US Government Printing Office, 1973, 22-2701,
      1177.

18.   Virginia State Criminal Code, <u>Virginia State Criminal Code</u>,
      1975, 18.2-346.

19.   District Code, <u>op</u>. <u>cit</u>., 1178.

20.   <u>Ibid</u>., 1179.

21.   <u>Ibid</u>., 1180.

22.   <u>Ibid</u>., 1180-1181.

23.   <u>Ibid</u>., 1181.

24.   <u>Ibid</u>., 1182.

25.   <u>Ibid</u>., 1178.

26.   <u>Ibid</u>., 1179.

27.   <u>Ibid</u>., 1180.

28.   <u>Ibid</u>., 1180.

29.   <u>The Consolidated Laws of New York Annotated</u>, 1968, sections
      230.08, 230.05, 230.10.

30.   <u>Code of Georgia Annotated</u>, X, 522-523; <u>Hawaii Revised Statutes</u>,
      VII, 886; <u>West's Wisconsin Statutes Annotated</u>, XLI, 356-357.

70

31. United States Code, 18, 2421–2423.

32. Interviews with Judge Norman of D.C. Superior Court, Assistant
     United States Attorney (D.C.) Rhea, Detective Grace, and
     Sergeant Ware of Vice Squad (Metropolitan Police Department,
     D.C.), Lt. Casey of Prostitution Detail (MPD, D.C.), Detective
     Robertson, Youth Division Prostitution and Perversion Squad
     (MPD, D.C.), 1977.

33. International Association of Chiefs of Police, Research
     Division, Prostitution II–Enforcement of Prostitution Laws,
     Gaithersburg, Maryland: IACP, 1976; Denny Pace, Handbook of
     Vice Control, New Jersey: Prentice-Hall, 1971, 65–72;
     Wayne LaFave, Arrest: The Decision to Take a Suspect into
     Custody, Boston: Little, Brown and Company, 1956, 457–463;
     Paul Chevigny, Police Power: Police Abuses in New York City,
     New York: Random House, 1969; Jerome Skolnick, Justice Without
     Trial: Law Enforcement in Democratic Society, New York: John
     Wiley, 1966, 103–112; The President's Commission on Law
     Enforcement and Administration of Justice, Task Force Report:
     The Police, Washington, DC: US Government Printing Office,
     1967, 187.

34. Hazel Kerper, Introduction to the Criminal Justice System,
     St. Paul, Minnesota: West Publishing Company, 1972, 82;
     Clinard, op. cit., 522.

35. Interviews with officers Ware, Casey, Robertson, and White of
     Metropolitan Police Department (D.C.), 1977.

36. Ibid.

37. Ibid.

38. Ibid.

39. Winick and Kinsie, op. cit.

40. Uniform Crime Reports of FBI, Crime in the United States–1976
     Washington, DC: US Government Printing Office, 1977, 184.

41. Interviews, op. cit.

42. Clinard, op. cit., 512; Bell, op. cit., 232–233, Erich Goode,
     Deviant Behavior: An Interactionist Approach, New Jersey:
     Prentice-Hall, 1978, 333–340.

43. Clinard, op. cit., 512-513; Bell, op. cit., 233-234; Goode, op. cit., 333-340.

44. Interviews with anonymous members of the Alexandria, Virginia Police Department Vice Squad, 1977-1978; Goode, op. cit., 340-342.

45. Ibid.; Albert Velarde and Mark Warlick, Massage Parlors: the Sensuality Business, Society, 11 (1973), 63-74.

46. Goode, op. cit., 324-325.

47. Interview with Captain George Henry, Watch Commander, Youth Division, MPD (D.C.), 1977; Clinard, op. cit., 513; Diana Gray, Turning Out: A Study of Teenage Prostitution, Urban Life and Culture, 1 (1973), 401-425.

48. Bell, op. cit., 231; Goode, op. cit., 331-333.

49. Goode, op. cit., 350-354; Bell, op. cit., 242-243; Robert Adelman and Susan Hall, Gentlemen of Leisure, New York: New American Library, 1972; Christina Milner and Richard Milner, Black Players: The Secret World of Black Pimps, Boston: Little, Brown, 1973.

50. Robert Pursley, Introduction to Criminal Justice, Encino, California: Glencoe Press, 1977, 113-115; Edwin Schur and Hugo Bedau, op. cit.; Prostitution: A Non-Victim Crime? Issues in Criminology, 8 (1973); Robert Boruchowitz, Victimless Crimes: a Proposal for the Courts, Judicature, 1973, 69-78; Alexander Smith and Harriet Pollack, Crimes Without Victims, Saturday Review, December 4, 1971, 27-29; Edward Davis, Victimless Crimes- the Case for Continued Enforcement, Journal of Police Science and Administration, Gaithersburg, Maryland: ICAP, 1976.

51. Ibid.

52. Ibid.

V

HETEROSEXUAL DEVIANCE

Legal History

According to the Common Law, all heterosexual deviance with
the exception of adultery were torts. Adultery was specially
handled by ecclesiastical law in England. The various forms of
sexual deviance were considered in general to be wrongs directed
against community norms or standards of conduct rather than crimes
for centuries. Colonial America, especially Puritan New England,
accepted the various sexual restrictions placed on adult behavior
as passed down from the English Common Law intact.[1] After independence the various states made all forms of sexual expression
outside marriage and even some sexual behavior within the marital
context criminal offenses. Thus the United States has the most
moralistic criminal law in recent history.[2] For example, Connecticut
passed statutes which prohibited kissing in public, adultery,
fornication, and lascivious carriage (i.e., conduct that is wanton,
lewd, or lustful and tends to arouse sexual emotions).[3] These
statutes were challenged in the federal courts and since 1970, all
sexual behavior between two consenting adults is now legal in that
state.[4]

Bigamy was not a crime until it was made a felony by the time
of King James I.[5] Adultery was handled by the ecclesiastical court
in England under the Common Law. Sodomy, whether buggery or
bestiality, was considered a crime under the Common Law. Seduction
was made a criminal offense under the reign of William and Mary.[6]
Illicit co-habitation was not a crime under the Common Law. Fornication that was practiced in private was not a crime at the Common
Law. On the other hand indecent public exposure and notorious
lewdness were crimes at the Common Law.[7] The United States accepted
and strengthened the criminal law concerning premarital, marital,
and extramarital sexual relations since 1776 so that until very
recently most states had statutes governing sexual behavior.[8]

Legal Definitions

There are three categories of heterosexual deviance which are
defined by legal authorities: premarital, extramarital, and comarital. Some forms of sexual deviance are not criminal offenses
while others are classified as crimes. There is also overlap
between some forms of sexual deviance which can be classified as
premarital and marital deviance or premarital and extramarital
deviance, while other forms of sexual deviance are strictly premarital or extramarital.

Premarital heterosexual deviance consists of statutory rape, sodomy (i.e., also known as "crimes against nature" or bestiality and buggery), seduction, fornication, and cohabitation. Statutory rape is the unlawful carnal knowledge of a female under statutory age with or without the consent of the girl.[9] Sodomy is a carnal copulation by human beings with each other against nature or with an animal. The terms are often referred to in criminal statutes as "crimes against nature".[10] According to Black, sodomy is the sexual act as performed by a male upon the person of a female by penetration of the anus.[11] Buggery is a rarely used term that is equivalent to sodomy. Bestiality is the carnal copulation of a human with an animal of the opposite sex. The term according to Black is not identical with sodomy but is confused with it in some criminal codes.[12] Fellatio or fellation (i.e., the offense of placing the male sex organ in the mouth of a female human being) is not a form of sodomy but is also confused by statute with it.[13] Finally cunnilingus is an act committed with the mouth of the male in contact with the female sex organ but is not identical with sodomy.[14]

Seduction is defined as the act of a male enticing a female to have unlawful sexual intercourse with him by means of persuasion, solicitation, promises, bribes, or any other means that does not imply the use of force.[15] Cohabitation is the living together of a couple as man and wife in a state of fornication or adultery (i.e., living together as husband and wife for the purpose of sexual relations).[16] Fornication is illegal sexual intercourse between two unmarried individuals. If one of the couple is married that party is guilty of adultery while the unmarried party is guilty of fornication. Some jurisdictions consider the act adultery on the part of both parties if only the woman is married.[17]

Extramarital deviance consists of adultery and bigamy although a married party can also be guilty of statutory rape, sodomy and related crimes, seduction, and cohabitation. Adultery is defined as voluntary sexual intercourse of a married individual with a person other than the offender's spouse.[18] Adultery can be open and notorious where it is common knowledge to members of the community or it can be secretive. Bigamy is the crime of deliberately and knowingly taking a second spouse through marriage or going through the form of second marriage while knowing that the first marriage still is in legal existence.[19]

Comarital sex relations (i.e., also known as swinging, group sex, mate swapping, or wife swapping) consists of sexual relations involving two couples or single individuals in a threesome. In both situations (i.e., among married couples and singles in threesomes) the spouses or partners are exchanged. Thus swinging is in reality a mass form of adultery and fornication.[20]

There are also a number of other sexually deviant behavior patterns that are found in the criminal codes of various jurisdictions. A sexual psychopath is one who is not insane but who by a course of repeated misconduct in sexual matters has evidenced such lack of power to control his sexual impulses as to be dangerous to other persons because he is likely to attack or otherwise inflict injury, loss, pain, or other evil on a member of the opposite sex.[21]

Lewd and lascivious behavior is gross and wanton indecency in sexual relations. The term includes both illicit sexual intercourse and irregular indulgences of lust, whether public or private.[22] Within the term can be found the sexual social deviance known as exhibitionism and voyeurism. Exhibitionism or indecent exposure is exposure to sight of the sex organs in a lewd or indecent manner in a public place.[23] Voyeurism is the act of watching persons who are nude, in the act of sexual intercourse, or in the act of other sexual deviance.[24] This includes sadomasochism, koprolagnia (i.e., sexual excitement watching a person defecate), and urolagnia (i.e., sexual excitement produced by watching a person urinate).[25]

Sadism is sexual deviance in which satisfaction is derived from the infliction of cruelty upon another. This may be in the form of anal erotism or oral erotism.[26] Masochism is a form of sexual deviance in which cruel treatment gives sexual gratification to the individual.[27] Sadomasochism is a combination of being sexually aroused by the fantasies of being beaten, tortured, flogged, etc. by a member of the opposite sex. A person who obtains sexual gratification from an object of unnatural adoration is a fetishist.[28] Transvestism is the overwhelming desire to wear the clothing, shoes, etc. of the opposite sex which brings about sexual excitement.[29]

Heterosexual Deviance Statutes and Enforcement Policy

Statutory rape is the carnal knowledge of a female child under sixteen years of age and the perpetrator of this crime shall be imprisoned for any term of years and for life.[30] A person is guilty of sodomy if one takes into his or her mouth or anus the sexual organ of any other person or animal, or who shall place his or her sexual organ in the mouth or anus of any other person or animal, or who shall have carnal copulation in an opening of the body except suxual parts with another person. Said person shall be fined not more than one thousand dollars or be imprisoned for a period not exceeding ten years. Any person committing such act with a person under the age of sixteen years shall be fined not more than one thousand dollars or be imprisoned for a period not exceeding twenty years. In any indictment for the commission of any of the acts declared to be offenses, it shall not be necessary to set forth the particular unnatural or perverted sexual practice with the commission

of which the defendant may be charged, nor to set forth the particular manner in which said unnatural or perverted sexual practice
was committed, but it shall be sufficient if the indictment set
forth that the defendant committed a certain unnatural and perverted
sexual practice with a person or animal, as the case may be. Any
penetration however slight if sufficient to complete the crime
specified and proof of emission is not necessary.[31]

If any person shall seduce and carnally know any female of
previous chaste character, between the ages of sixteen and twenty-
one years, out of wedlock, such seduction and carnal knowledge shall
be deemed a misdemeanor and the offender being convicted shall be
punished by imprisonment for a term not exceeding three years, or
fined not exceeding two hundred dollars, or both fined and
imprisoned.[32] If any unmarried man or woman commits fornication,
each shall be fined not more than three hundred dollars or imprisoned not more than six months, or both.[33] Any person or persons who
make any obscene or indecent exposure of his or her person, or make
any lewd, obscene, or indecent sexual proposal, or commit any other
lewd, obscene, or indecent act is under penalty of not more than
three hundred dollar fine, or imprisonment of not more than ninety
days, or both, for each and every such offense. Any person or
persons who commit an offense of lewd, indecent, or obscene acts
knowingly in the presence of a child under the age of sixteen years
shall be punished by imprisonment of not more than one year, or
fined in an amount not to exceed one thousand dollars, or both for
each and every such offense.[34]

Any person who shall take or attempt to take any immoral,
improper, or indecent liberties with any child of either sex, under
the age of sixteen years with the intent of arousing, appealing to,
or gratifying the lust or passions or sexual desires, either of said
person or of such child, or of both such person and such child, or
who shall commit or attempt to commit, any lewd or lascivious act
upon or with the body, or any part or member thereof, of such child,
with the intent of arousing, appealing to, gratifying the lust or
passions or sexual desires, either of such person or of such child,
or of both such person and such child shall be imprisoned in
penitentiary not more than ten years. Any person who takes any such
child or shall entice, allure, or persuade any such child, to any
place whatever for the purpose either of taking any such immoral,
improper, or indecent liberties with such child, with said intent
or of committing any such lewd, or lascivious act upon or with the
body, or any part or member thereof, of such child with said intent,
shall be imprisoned not more than five years.[35]

Whoever commits adultery shall on conviction be punished by a
fine not exceeding five hundred dollars, or by imprisonment not
exceeding one year, or both; and when the act is committed between
a married woman and unmarried man, both parties to such act shall
be found guilty of adultery; and when such act is committed between
a married man and an unmarried woman, the man shall only be guilty
of adultery.[36] A person who has a living husband or wife and who
marries another shall be guilty of bigamy, and on conviction shall
be imprisoned for not less than two nor more than seven years. This
statute shall not apply to any person whose spouse has been
continually absent for five successive years next before such marriage
without being known to such person to be living within that time, or
whose marriage to said living spouse shall have been dissolved by a
valid decree of a competent court, or shall have been pronounced
void by a valid decree of a competent court on the ground of the
nullity of the marriage contract.[37]

The police and other members of the criminal justice system have
a difficult time in dealing with heterosexual deviance in most
instances. This is due to the fact that the police have a difficult
time getting at the deviant behavior since most of it is conducted
in private. Further the public tends to be rather indifferent to
the enforcement of the statutes unless the behavior is open and
notorious.[38] In general the public is tolerant of cohabitation,
fornication, adultery, swinging, and bigamy. It is much less
tolerant of statutory rape, seduction, sodomy, and lewd and indecent
behavior. The public has mixed feelings about voyeurism, transvestism, and fetishism while generally disapproving sadomasochism.
The sexual psychopath laws especially the sections dealing with
sexual abuse of children are strongly supported by public opinion.[39]

Less than one percent of the arrests made by the police are sex
offenses that exclude forcible rape and prostitution. Just what
percentage of this figure constitutes heterosexual sex offense is
impossible to know by the police reports.[40] A study of the disposition of persons formally charged by the police with such sex
offenses shows that nearly half of those arrested plead guilty to
the original charge against them, five percent plead guilty to a
lesser offense, twenty-eight percent were either acquitted or had
the charges dropped against them, and seventeen percent were referred
to juvenile court.[41] From the official statistics, one can see that
the police rarely enforce the statutes against heterosexual deviance
which creates the problems of arbitrary police and prosecutorial
discretion. This is due to the fact that there is extreme difficulty
in detecting sexual deviance by normal police practices. Thus many
law enforcement officers overlook many acts that come to their
attention via third parties; many prosecutors will not process a

great number of cases; many judges will dismiss the charges if
brought before them or refer the defendants to private community
agencies for treatment, and juries will readily acquit persons
charged with some heterosexual offenses out of a feeling that the
crime does not merit punishment of any sort.[42]

Description of Heterosexual Deviance

It appears that premarital, extramarital, and comarital deviance
are becoming more and more common in American society with each
passing year.[43] Previous studies have shown that heterosexual
deviance varied with race, ethnicity, religion, region, race, social
class, and inner city-suburb-rural areas.[44]

Premarital sexuality is becoming the norm in American society
although Reiss feels that it is still deviant.[45] Premarital sexual
behavior of all types is becoming increasingly the standard for high
school students to the elderly in our society.[46] The sexual revolution has along with women's liberation movement created an atmosphere
where both sexes are increasingly engaging in sexual expression of
all sorts outside the marital context for the pleasure of indulging
in sexual behaviors.[47]

Individuals who engage in premarital deviance come from all age
groups, but it appears that those becoming sexually active since the
1960's have the most varied of sexual experiences, both males and
females. Premarital sexuality tends to center around both physical
attraction and emotional attachment. More individuals appear to feel
less guilty about sexual experimentation every year regardless of
religion or social class. The age of first sexual experience has
been steadily declining so that it is not uncommon to see junior high
school aged youth engaged in all sorts of sexual activities. Thus
many critics of the sex laws are calling for the lowering of the age
for statutory rape from sixteen to fourteen.[48]

Premarital sexual deviance covers quite a collection of sexual
practices (i.e., crimes against nature, seducers, rapists, exhibitionists, voyeurs, transvestites, sadomasochists, and fornicators). The
general public and criminal justice system consider all of these
forms of sexual deviance clearly criminal when a juvenile is involved
with an adult. On the other hand there is a great deal of confusion
on the part of the public and those involved in the criminal justice
system when only consenting adults of the opposite sex are involved
in these practices.[49]

The statutory rapist is a male who knowingly or unknowingly has
consensual relations with a girl under the age set by the statute of
the particular jurisdiction. Most studies show that this male is not

the same type of individual as the rapist of adult women who uses force or threat of force.[50] It appears that the young men convicted of statutory rape for the most part are the least deviant of all categories of sex offenders.[51]

Crimes against nature and sodomy generally come under the sexual psychopath statutes in many jurisdictions yet the behavior of these heterosexual individuals is not usually dangerous to the other party engaged in these deviant activities. Sutherland states that the sexual psychopath laws are impossible to enforce because it is virtually impossible to identify such an individual.[52] Yet all kinds of overtly normal people engage in such activities as fellatio, anal intercourse, voyeurism (i.e., triolism, koprolagnia, urolagnia), transvestism, and sadomasochism. It appears that only those who are exhibitionists and indulge in bestiality are dealt with negatively by both the public and criminal justice system. Court cases have even found husbands guilty of soliciting their wives to commit sodomy with them. Even Kinsey was opposed to sodomy laws as they related to voluntary behavior among adult heterosexual couples.[53]

Voyeurism constitutes a criminal act that comes under lewd and indecent behavior. There are all types of voyeurs, some of whom can not be prosecuted for their behavior is not seemed illegal. The classic peeping tom type can be dealt with by the criminal justice system but this type of offender is usually a teenager or young but immature adult. This activity is usually considered as a public nuisance in this particular instance.[54] On the other hand those individuals who take and get sexual pleasure from seeing individuals engaged in sexual intercourse, triolism, koprolagnia, and urolagnia are usually prosecuted on charges of lewd conduct or related statutes.[55] Another form of voyeurism is nudism. Unfortunately many nudists find that their right to display their bodies absent of clothes with no sexual purpose is often considered to be criminal even if done in the privacy of one's roof garden or back yard.[56] Finally going to see a striptease act, topless or bottomless dancers at a bar or restaurant is an obvious form of legitimate voyeurism although the female performers are viewed as deviant in this social situation.[57]

Exhibitionists are usually considered as relatively harmless individuals, usually male. They are usually charged with lewd and indecent behavior but the general public and members of the criminal justice system usually regard this form of social deviance are relatively harmless. Exhibitionists are usually young adults, very timid, and very conscientious persons who no one would expect to behave in such deviant manner.[58]

Extramarital sexual deviance consists of adultery and its offshoot, swinging, and bigamy. Adultery is a crime in all jurisdictions but is very rarely enforced. In the past in jurisdictions with strict divorce laws (i.e., New York) adultery was very common grounds given for divorce yet almost no one admitting to it was tried and found guilty of the crime. It is estimated that both husbands and wives engage in this type of sexual deviance in almost equal numbers.[59] Various reasons are given why spouses engage in adultery (i.e., variation in partners, retaliation against spouse, rebellion against spouse, emotional attachment with another person, encouragement of spouse, fear of losing one's youth, and pleasure from a variety of sexual partners).[60]

Swinging is a variation of adultery but in this case both husband and wife exchange sexual partners in the presence of each other and with mutual approval. This group sex is conducted in private with contacts made through magazines, word of mouth, and attendance of socalled swingers bars. Comarital sex allows both spouses to endulge in partner encouraged adultery, sodomy, fellatio, triolism, and homosexuality in a truly voyeuristic atmosphere with supposedly no guilt toward one's spouse who is also engaged in the same practices. In fact this allows each spouse to see just how popular and expert his or her spouse is with other individuals. It appears that most swingers are metropolitan area residents, young to middle aged, and usually upper middle class.[61]

Decriminalization of Heterosexual Deviance

Proponents of decriminalization of the sex laws feel that these statutes go too far and only those sexual behaviors that use or threaten to use force or are applied to juveniles should retain their criminal status. There is also agreement that sex acts performed in public places should not be decriminalized. Thus the criminal laws affecting voluntary sexual relations between consenting adults should be rescinded from the state criminal codes.[62]

Packer feels that the existence of statutes governing heterosexual deviance creates more deviance (i.e., subcultures); creates a disregard for the criminal law since most of these statutes are not enforced; no harm results from heterosexual deviance if between consenting adults; the fear of detection and arrest can allow for the growth of secondary crimes such as blackmail or police bribery; most members of the community tend to be acceptant of most types of heterosexual deviance; and the criminal sanction serves no useful purpose since no harm has been done by consenting adults.[63]

Those opposed to decriminalization feel that heterosexual sex crimes should not be decriminalized since they are against the normative system of society, against basic religious tenets, are a negative influence upon the next generation, and are a destructive force upon the socio-psychological functioning of the family. The author agrees that such crimes as incest, bigamy, and such behaviors as sadism and masochism should be controlled by the criminal justice system. One also must exclude such behavior from the youth of society. This is a most difficult task to accomplish since sexual behavior is becoming more public (i.e., mass media) with the coming of each new generation.

81

Notes

1. Morton Hunt, <u>The Natural History of Love</u>, New York: Alfred A.
    Knopf, 1959; G.R. Taylor, <u>Sex in History</u>, New York: The
    Vanguard Press, 1954; Isabel Drummand, <u>The Sex Paradox</u>,
    New York: G.P. Putnam's Sons, 1953; Morris Ploscowe, <u>Sex and
    the Law</u>, New Jersey: Prentice Hall, 1951; John Gagnon and
    William Simon, <u>Sexual Deviance</u>, New York: Harper and Row,
    1967.

2. Norval Morris and Gordon Hawkins, <u>The Honest Politician's
    Guide to Crime Control</u>, Chicago: University of Chicago Press,
    1969, 15.

3. <u>Connecticut General Statutes, Annotated</u>, 1958, 28, 266–267.

4. Sue Reid, <u>Crime and Criminology</u>, Hinsdale, Illinois: The
    Dryden Press, 1976, 35.

5. 1 James I, c. 11.

6. 4 and 5 William and Mary, c. 8.

7. Reid, <u>op</u>. <u>cit</u>., 35–37.

8. Robert Bell, <u>Social Deviance</u>, Homewood, Illinois: The Dorsey
    Press, 1971, 45.

9. Henry Black, <u>Black's Law Dictionary</u>, St. Paul, Minnesota:
    West Publishing Company, 1968, 1427.

10. <u>Ibid</u>., 1563.

11. <u>Ibid</u>., 1563.

12. <u>Ibid</u>., 1563.

13. <u>Ibid</u>., 743, 1563.

14. <u>Ibid</u>., 456.

15. <u>Ibid</u>., 1523.

16. <u>Ibid</u>., 326.

17. <u>Ibid</u>., 781.

18. <u>Ibid</u>., 71–72.

19. _Ibid._, 206.

20. Marshall Clinard, _Sociology of Deviant Behavior_, New York: Holt, Rinehart, and Winston, 1974, 523.

21. _District of Columbia Code_, Annotated, Washington, DC: US Government Printing Office, 1973, 2, 22-3503, 1571.

22. Black, _op. cit._, 1052.

23. _Ibid._, 909; Clinard, _op. cit._, 499.

24. Clinard, _op. cit._, 499.

25. _Dorland's Illustrated Medical Dictionary_, Philadelphia: W.B. Saunders Company, 1957, 1502.

26. Black, _op. cit._, 1501; Dorland, _op. cit._, 1202.

27. Black, _op. cit._, 1126; Dorland, _op. cit._, 798.

28. Dorland, _op. cit._, 500.

29. _Ibid._, 1455.

30. District of Columbia Code, _op. cit._, 22-2801, 1499.

31. _Ibid._, 22-3502, 1570.

32. _Ibid._, 22-3001, 1524.

33. _Ibid._, 22-1002, 1376.

34. _Ibid._, 22-1112, 1381.

35. _Ibid._, 22-3501, 1567.

36. _Ibid._, 22-301, 1345.

37. _Ibid._, 22-601, 1368.

38. Ploscowe, _op. cit._; Ploscowe, Sex Offenses: The American Legal Context, _Law and Contemporary Problems_, 25 (1960), 217-225.

39. Herbert Bloch and Gilbert Geis, _Man, Crime, and Society_, New York: Random House, 1970, 255-269.

83

40. Uniform Crime Reports of the FBI, Crime in the United States—
1976, Washington, DC: US Government Printing Office, 1977, 184.

41. Ibid., 217.

42. Herbert Packer, The Limits of the Criminal Sanction, Stanford,
California: Stanford University Press, 1968, 304.

43. P. Gebhard, J. Gagnon, W. Pomeroy, and C. Christenson, Sex
Offenders: An Analysis of Types, New York: Harper and Row,
1965; Sex Offenses, in Law and Contemporary Problems, 25 (1960),
215-375; Bell, op. cit., 39-62; Clinard, op. cit., 503;
Ploscowe, op. cit.; Clellan Ford and Frank Beach, Patterns of
Sexual Behavior, New York: Harper Colophon, 1972; Gagnon and
Simon, Sexual Deviance, op. cit.; Gagnon and Simon (eds.),
The Sexual Scene, Chicago: Aldine Publishing Company, 1970;
Edward Sagarin and Donal MacNamera (eds.), Problems of Sex
Behavior, New York: Thomas Y. Crowell Company, 1968.

44. John Gagnon and William Simon, Sexual Conduct: The Social
Sources of Human Sexuality, Chicago: Aldine-Atherton, 1973;
Morton Hunt, Sexual Behavior in the 1970's, New York: Dell,
1975; Robert Sorensen, Adolescent Sexuality in Contemporary
America, New York: World Publishing Company, 1973; Leslie
Westoff, The Second Time Around: Remarriage in America,
New York: Viking Press, 1977.

45. Ira Reiss, Premarital Sex as Deviant Behavior: An Application
of Current Approaches to Deviance, American Sociological Review,
35 (1970), 78-88.

46. Hunt, op. cit.

47. John Kanter and Melvin Zelnick, Sexual Experiences of Young
Unmarried Women in the United States, Family Planning
Perspectives, 4 (1972), 9-18; Charles Westoff and Norman Ryder,
The Contraceptive Revolution, Princeton, New Jersey: Princeton
University Press, 1976; Erich Goode, Deviant Behavior: An
Interactionist Approach, New Jersey: Prentice-Hall, 1978,
317-321; Robert Bell, Premarital Sex in a Changing Society,
New Jersey: Prentice-Hall, 1966.

48. Bell, Premarital Sex in a Changing Society, op. cit.;
Bell, Social Deviance, op. cit., 50-62; Ira Reiss, Premarital
Sexual Standards in America, New York: Free Press, 1960;
Reiss, The Social Context of Premarital Sexual Permissiveness,
New York: Holt, Rinehart, and Winston, 1967; Clinard,
op. cit., 537.

49. Block and Geis, op. cit.; Gebhard et al., op. cit.; Law and Contemporary Problems, op. cit.; Gagnon and Simon, Sexual Deviance, op. cit.; Ploscowe, op. cit.

50. John MacDonald, Rape: Offenders and Their Victims, Springfield, Illinois: Charles C. Thomas, 1971; Gebhard et al., op. cit.; Clinard, op. cit., 302-304.

51. R. W. Bowling, The Sex Offender and the Law, Federal Probation, 14 (1950), 11-16; H.W. Dunham, Crucial Issues in the Treatment and Control of Sexual Deviation in the Community, East Lansing, Michigan: Michigan Department of Mental Health, 1951; Albert Ellis and Ralph Brancale, The Psychology of Sex Offenders, Springfield, Illinois: Charles C. Thomas, 1956; Graham Hughes, Consent in Sexual Offenses, Modern Law Review, 25 (1962), 672-686; Benjamin Karpman, The Sexual Offender and His Offenses, New York: Julian, 1954; Larry Myers, Reasonable Mistake of Age: A Needed Defense to Statutory Rape, Michigan Law Review, 64 (1965), 105-135; Robert Sherwin, Sex and Statutory Law, New York: Oceana, 1949; Sherwin, The Law and Sexual Relationships, Journal of Social Issues, 22 (1966), 109-122.

52. Edwin Sutherland and Donald Cressey, Criminology, Philadelphia: J.B. Lippincott, 1970, 161; Karl Schuessler (ed.), Edwin H. Sutherland: On Analyzing Crime, Chicago: University of Chicago Press, 1973, 185-199.

53. Bloch and Geis, op. cit., 261-262; Alfred Kinsey, C.W. Pomeroy, and Clyde Martin, Sexual Behavior in the Human Male, Philadelphia: W. B. Saunders, 1948, 370.

54. Bloch and Geis, op. cit., 257-259.

55. Ibid.

56. Lewd: the Inquisition of Seth and Carolyn, Boston: Beacon Press, 1972; Fred Ilfeld and Roger Lauer, Social Nudism in America, New Haven, Connecticut: College and University Press, 1966.

57. Libby Jones, Striptease, New York: Simon and Schuster, 1967; James Skipper and Charles McCaghy, Stripteasers: the Anatomy and Career Contingencies of a Deviant Occupation, Social Problems, 17 (1970), 391-405.

85

58. Ford and Beach, op. cit.; Ploscowe, op. cit.; Bloch and Geis, op. cit., 259-261; Nathan Rickles, Exhibitionism, Philadelphia, J.B. Lippincott, 1950; Robert Smith et al., Exhibitionism, North Carolina Medical Journal, 22 (1961), 261-267.

59. Bell, op. cit., 64-74; Ford and Beach, op. cit., 114-115; Reid, op. cit., 36-37; Gagnon and Simon, op. cit.; Sagarin and MacNamera, op. cit.

60. Bell, op. cit.

61. Ibid., 74-83; Clinard, op. cit., 523-529; Mary Walshok, The Emergence of Middle-Class Deviant Subcultures: the Case of Swingers, Social Problems, 18 (1971), 488-495; Charles and Rebecca Palson, Swinging in Wedlock, Society, 9 (1972), 28-37; Gilbert Bartell, Group Sex, New York: Peter H. Wyden Inc., 1971; Bartell, Group Sex among the Mid-Americans, Journal of Sex Research, 6 (1970), 113-130; James and Lynn Smith, Co-Marital Sex and the Sexual Freedom Movement, Journal of Sex Research, 6 (1970), 131-142; Duane Denfield and Michael Gordon, The Sociology of Mate Swapping: On the Family that Swings Together Clings Together, Journal of Sex Research, 6 (1970), 85-100.

62. Clinard, op. cit., 536-538; Gagnon and Simon, op. cit.; Morris and Hawkins, op. cit.

63. Packer, op. cit., 304.

VI

HOMOSEXUALITY

Legal History

According to Bailey, the origin of eccesiastical laws dealing
with homosexuality date back to Jewish laws that were eventually
incorporated into Christian Church rulings. The Code of Justinian
(538 AD) punished homosexuals with the death penalty.[1] English
ecclesiastical courts dealt with homosexuals through the use of
torture or the death penalty. The Common Law defined homosexuality
as a crime, an obvious reflection of the early Church's influence.
Under Henry VIII in 1553, the English parliament made homosexuality
(i.e., buggery) a secular offense punishable by death.[2]

Historically both the ecclesiastical and criminal laws have
applied to male homosexuals, not females.[3] From 1696 until 1952,
there was not a single conviction of a female in the United States
for homosexual practices.[4] Most of the states do not have laws
against lesbians, and in the states that do prosecute women for
homosexual practices, most receive minor punishments (i.e., misdemeanor charges with fines, short jail sentences, suspended
sentences, or probation).[5]

It was not until 1861 in England that the Offenses Against the
Person Act of Parliament reduced the penalty for homosexuality from
death to life imprisonment. This act remained in effect until 1956
and dealt with sodomy between two adult males as well as between
husband and wife. An act of parliament in 1956 stated that sodomy
with a child or juvenile was a crime punishable by life imprisonment
but the prison sentence for acts of sodomy between adults was
reduced. Certain types of homosexual behaviors in public were
considered misdemeanor offenses in this statute.[6]

The Wolfenden Report (i.e., Report of the Committee on Homosexual Offenses and Prostitution) stated that homosexuality was a
moral issue and not a criminal law matter when adults who consent
engage in these practices. The committee concluded that it found
no facts supporting the common view that homosexuality lead to the
decline of society. Parliament acting on the recommendations of the
committee passed the Sexual Offenses Act of 1967 which removed the
criminal penalties for homosexual practices between consenting
adults in private. The Act retains the penalty of life imprisonment
for homosexual offenses against males under age sixteen; that acts
of gross indecency against juveniles (i.e., ages 16-21) is a criminal
offense with a five year sentence; and that public homosexual acts
that are indecent are punishable by a two year sentence in prison.[7]

The history of criminal sanctions against homosexual behavior in the United States closely follow the English Common Law and British criminal law practices. For example in an Illinois case of 1897, the defendant was convicted of crimes against nature. The Court defined various acts (i.e., fellation, anal intercourse, bestiality) as sinful and applied the statute to the homosexual act of the defendant.[8] In 1961 the Illinois legislature accepting the suggestions of the Model Penal Code revised its crimes against nature statute. The new statute followed the recommendations made by the Wolfenden Report. The Illinois statute defines deviant sexual conduct as any act of sexual gratification involving the sex organs of one person in the mouth or anus of another, but does not prohibit such acts if they are entered into by consenting adults. The statute does prohibit sexual assault and contributing to the sexual delinquency of a child.[9]

Thus Illinois typifies both the old criminal law reaction to homosexuality as well as the modern enlightened view as long as the homosexual practices are between consenting adults and are in private. Since 1961 a number of other states have joined Illinois in the decriminalization of homosexual practices between consenting adults in private (i.e., California, Colorado, Connecticut, Idaho, Oregon, Hawaii, Delaware, Texas, North Dakota, Georgia, Arkansas, Nevada, and Wisconsin).[10]

The Uniform Code of Military Justice still calls for a less than honorable discharge from the armed forces if a person admits to or is found to be a practicing homosexual. Further the military will not consider a homosexual suitable for military service. We have the cases of Air Force sergeant Leonard Matlovich, PFC Barbara Randolph, and PVT Deborah Watson who were all given general discharges for revealing that they were practicing homosexuals according to article 125 of the UCMJ.[11]

In 1969 the National Institute of Mental Health of the United States Department of Health, Education, and Welfare created a Task Force on Homosexuality. The task force concluded that the federal and state criminal codes should follow the recommendations of the Wolfenden Report of Great Britain and decriminalize homosexual behavior between consenting adults.[12] The District of Columbia in the Human Rights Act of 1973 bars discrimination on the basis of sexual orientation (i.e., homosexuality).[13]

The United States Supreme Court in a number of recent rulings has upheld the constitutionality of existing state laws (i.e., Virginia, Washington, and Missouri) that criminally penalize or civilly discriminate against practicing homosexuals, both male and female. The Virginia case dealt with banning the homosexual behavior of consenting adults. The Washington state case dealt with

firing a teacher who admitted to being a homosexual, and the
Missouri case dealt with the right of gay liberation groups to meet
and organize on college campuses. This latter case was settled by
the Court in favor of homosexual organizations to be allowed to
form campus organizations.[14]

Legal Definitions

According to Black, pederasty is the crime against nature which
involves the carnal copulation of male with male, usually a man with
a boy.[15] Black states that pederasty is a form of sodomy (i.e.,
sexual intercourse as performed by a man upon another male by
penetration of the anus).[16] Buggery is sexual intercourse of a man
with another man and is equivalent to sodomy.[17] Fellatio or
fellation is the offense of placing the male organ in the mouth of
another male human being.[18] Cunnilingus is an act committed with
the mouth of one female in contact with the female organ of another
woman.[19]

All the crimes against nature defined by Black are terms used
to describe some aspect of homosexuality. Homosexuality is defined
as a compulsive sexual interest in another person of the same sex
(i.e., male) while the same deviant behavior manifested by two
females in each other is termed lesbianism.[20] Goode describes the
bisexual as a male or female who is sexually interested in both
members of one's own sex as well as members of the opposite gender.[21]
Transvestites are males who dress like women and have feelings of
eroticism when wearing feminine attire. Although the concept should
not be confused with homosexuality or bisexuality, some transvestites
are homosexuals and engage in acts of sodomy and fellatio with
unsuspecting males who mistake these "female impersonators" as
women.[22]

Homosexuality Statutes and Enforcement Policies

Homosexuality per se is not a crime in the United States. With
the exception of the states previously mentioned that have decriminalized homosexual acts between consenting adults, a number of
deviant sexual behaviors are considered criminal as applied to
homosexuals (i.e., sodomy, fellatio, cunnilingus, and mutual
masturbation), whether in public or in private. All homosexual
deviance between adults and juveniles is considered criminal. Most
statutes governing homosexual behavior are usually enforced against
males as female homosexuals (i.e., lesbians) are rarely mentioned in
statutes or arrested by the police.[23]

Homosexual practices come under the sexual psychopaths chapter
(i.e., 35) of the D.C. Code. A person shall be guilty of sodomy if
one takes into his or her mouth or anus the sexual organ of any
other person, or who shall place his or her sexual organ in the

mouth or anus of any other person, or who shall have carnal
copulation in an opening of the body except sexual parts with
another person. Said person shall be fined not more than one
thousand dollars or be imprisoned for a period not exceeding ten
years. Any person committing such act with a person under the age
of sixteen years shall be fined not more than one thousand dollars
or be imprisoned for a period not exceeding twenty years. In any
indictment for the commission of any of the acts declared to be
offenses, it shall not be necessary to set forth the particular
unnatural or perverted sexual practice with the commission of which
the defendant may be charged, nor to set forth the particular manner
in which said unnatural or perverted sexual practice was committed,
but it shall be sufficient if the indictment set forth that the
defendant committed a certain unnatural and perverted sexual
practice with a person. Any penetration however slight if sufficient
to complete the crime specified and proof of emission is not necessary.[24]

Any person who shall take or attempt to take any immoral,
improper, or indecent liberties with any child of either sex, under
the age of sixteen years with the intent of arousing, appealing to,
or gratifying the lust or passions or sexual desires, either of
said person or of such child, or of both such person and such child,
or who shall commit or attempt to commit, any lewd or lascivious
act upon or with the body, or any part or member thereof, of such
child, with the intent of arousing, appealing to, gratifying the
lust or passions or sexual desires, either of such person or of
such child, or of both such person and such child shall be imprisoned
not more than ten years. Any person who takes any such child or
shall entice, allure, or persuade any such child, to any place
whatever for the purpose either of taking any such immoral, improper,
or indecent liberties with such child, with said intent or of
committing any such lewd, or lascivious act upon or with the body, or
any part or member thereof, of such child with said intent, shall be
imprisoned not more than five years.[25]

The police generally do not arrest homosexuals unless the sexual
deviance is flagrant or involves juveniles. On occasions when there
is ample police manpower available and not needed elsewhere to deal
with serious crimes, the police will entrap homosexuals in such
places as public toilets, public meeting places such as parks, and
bars and restaurants catering to homosexual trade. The entrapment
issue has placed the police in a negative situation since the
detectives have to involve themselves with homosexuals and the
experience is demoralizing at the least and has lead to bribery and
violence on the part of certain officers. Thus most police policy
today is away from entrapment.[26]

The discretionary power of the police in terms of who gets
arrested in homosexual activities is biased in favor of the individual who is engaging in the act of sodomy fellatio. According to
the criminal law both parties engaging in homosexual activities
should be arrested. Thus many officers reason that the active
participant is the "true" homosexual while the receiver of this
deviant sex activity is not truly as perverted and need not be
arrested.[27] The police tend to arrest three types of individuals
for their involvement in homosexual acts. The active homosexual is
one who actively seeks out homosexual encounters at gay bars, public
toilets, and parks. The second type of homosexual arrested is one
who frequents known homosexual hangouts and accepts invitations from
the active type or "cruiser". The third type of person arrested is
one who seeks out active or passive homosexuals as a way of getting
kicks, is drunk, curious, and is intent on robbing or beating the
homosexual. This situational offender under normal conditions would
not have anything to do with homosexuals.[28]

The Los Angeles County study of the effects of the criminal
justice system on homosexuals shows that most arrests were made in
public or semipublic places rather than in a private residence.
Most arrests were made in public toilets, in automobiles, in jails,
in parks, in public baths, and on public beaches, in felony cases.
Most misdemeanor arrests occurred in public toilets, autos, parks,
theaters, bars, on the street, and in public baths. Most of the
charges against those arrested were for fellation. Most offenders
asked for a trial before a judge to avoid public exposure with most
convictions being fines, suspended sentences, or charges reduced in
most felony cases.[29]

The police rarely arrest the lesbian since she is typically
not public in her expression of criminal deviance (i.e., most
lesbian activity is in private, not public toilets, parked cars,
parks, and beaches). Female homosexuals generally are not as
aggressive as males in the solicitation process nor as in need of
new partners so most law enforcement agencies do not have a special
policy involving entrapment or harassment. Most lesbian bars are
left alone and undercover policewomen are rarely used in any
entrapment process.[30]

Description of Homosexual Deviance

It would appear that males and females who take part in homosexual activities come from a cross section of American society
(i.e., all social classes, races, ethnic groups, religions, regions,
and marital statuses). There appears to be a concentration of
homosexuals in the largest metropolitan areas which also contain
the most open and militant of individuals.[31]

The gay or homosexual subculture allows these social deviants to create a community in which to establish their sexually deviant relations. The homosexual community consists of a variety of social networks according to Clinard (i.e., pairs of homosexually marrieds or singles; larger secondary groups; and individuals who are members of both primary and secondary groups). Members of these cliques, groups, and networks have all types of parties together and celebrate special events (i.e., anniversaries, birthdays, other special events).[32]

The homosexual or gay bar is another special institution which serves as a place for sexual exchange for short term sexual affairs, where friends can gather free of the prying eyes of "straights", where one can be socialized into homosexual value-attitudes, and where one can learn how to improve his life-style.[33] There are also voluntary organizations that cater to homosexuals such as Gay Activists Alliance, Mattachine Society, One Institute, Society for Individual Rights, and Metropolitan Community Church which enter into settlement of disputes concerning civil rights, employment discrimination, police harassment, and criminal law reform.[34]

The lesbian subculture differs in some important ways from that of homosexual subculture. Lesbians are more interested in personalized relationships rather than the promiscuous encounters of the typical gay. Most homosexuals consider that sex is the most important aspect of their interpersonal relationships while lesbians consider their companions personality and commitment to them more important than the sexual aspect of their relationship. Lesbians are more private in their relationships while gays are quite public in comparison for their quest for homosexual companionship. Lesbian bars serve the purpose of meeting friends and as a place for socialization compared to the overt search for sexual encounters in gay bars. Gays begin their sexual encounters at an earlier age than lesbians. The latter have much more heterosexual contacts including marriages with offspring than the former who may have had little sexual contact with women and do not want children.[35]

The bisexual is both heterosexual and homosexual depending on the type of sexual relationship they refer at the moment. Thus a bisexual can be a single or married male or female and have supposedly satisfactory relationships with members of both sexes on the level of sexual encounters. Relatively few people are bisexuals and many homosexuals are convinced that a professed bisexual is really a latent homosexual but will not really admit their true sexual preferences.[36]

The homosexual prostitute is a young man who offers his services for a fee to older homosexuals who cannot attract younger men, offer services to homosexuals from another community who do not have the

time to establish contacts since they are on a business trip,
juveniles who are runaways and need the money, and those males who
want to be supported by a wealthy individual on a regular basis
(i.e., akin to a mistress). These male prostitutes are either
hustlers who consider their deviance as a temporary source of money
and those who consider themselves as professionals (i.e., career-
oriented).[37]

Prostitutes and strippers supposedly are oriented toward
homosexuality because they are faced with contacts with men that are
negative and exploitative. Thus these women spend much of their
leisure time in the company of other exploited females and conclude
that lesbianism is a warm and non-threatening relationship. Supposedly some strippers and prostitutes do not like men so their
occupations are natural for the formation of affectional relationships with other women.[38]

Decriminalization of Homosexual Deviance

The debate in favor of decriminalization of the criminal laws
against homosexual practices of consenting adults began in 1957 with
the results of the Wolfenden Committee in Great Britain. The
committee report concluded that adult consensual homosexual practices
do not threaten the family, church, or even stability of the society;
that adult homosexuality does not lower community standards of
decency nor does it create a law enforcement problem; and finally
that this adult example of private sexual deviance does not interfere
with the normal socialization process concerning heterosexuality of
the next generation of youth in society.[39]

Since 1952 the American Law Institute, based on its view that
homosexuality should not be a crime per se, has advocated the repeal
of state criminal statutes. The Model Penal Code accepted the
decriminalization concept based on the British example but it was
the Task Force on Homosexuality of the National Institute of Mental
Health that recommended that all criminal statutes dealing with adult
consensual homosexual practices be rescinded.[40]

The Task Force on Homosexuality concluded in particular that
special training for all police officers who deal with morals issues
be provided. Although many members of society still regard homosexuality with negativism, there is evidence that public attitudes
are changing, especially in the large metropolitan areas. Discreet
homosexual practices are recognized by many heterosexuals to be a
private matter that should not be regulated by statute. The Task
Force also noted that criminal sanctions are not effective in

preventing or reducing homosexual practices between consenting
adults who conduct their activities in private. The mental health
of adult homosexuals would improve and decriminalization would
encourage them to be more positive and open about their life-
style.[41]

The main arguments for decriminalization state that: (1) the
police are indiscriminate in dealing with lesbian behavior but
discriminate against private gay activities; (2) law enforcement
policies lead to suicides, blackmail, and increased public deviancy
as acts of defiance of the law; (3) homosexuals would make better
adjustments to living in the community; (4) the criminal justice
system makes it difficult for those who are stigmatized by an
incident involving homosexuality to become heterosexuals if they
wish to make that decision; and (5) there should be clear distinctions between what constitutes public and private homosexual behavior for consenting adults.[42]

Those who favor the continued enforcement of the criminal
statutes against adult consensual homosexual private practices state
that the criminal law keeps homosexual behavior in the closet where
it belongs. Overt actions of various gay liberation groups only
encourage teenagers to consider experimenting with homosexual life-
styles. The openness of homosexuality in large metropolitan areas
encourages homosexual prostitution and the gay/lesbian bar that
caters to all sorts of sexual deviance. Homosexuality leads to the
moral decay of the family, church, and school which will ultimately
destroy the very fabric of society. Finally homosexuals are in
need of psychiatric treatment and the continuance of the sexual
psychopath laws are a necessity to protect the lives of decent
members of society.[43]

1. David Bailey, <u>Homosexuality and the Western Christian Tradition</u>, New York: David McKay Company, 1955; Roger Mitchell, <u>The Homosexual and the Law</u>, New York: Arco Publishing, 1969; A.L. Rowse, <u>Homosexuals in History</u>, New York: Macmillan Company, 1977; Robert Katz, Notes on Religious History, Attitudes, and Laws Pertaining to Homosexuality, <u>National Institute of Mental Health Task Force on Homosexuality</u>, Rockville, Maryland: NIMH, 1972, 58.

2. H.M. Hyde, <u>The Love that Dare not Speak its Name: A Candid History of Homosexuality</u> in Britain, Boston: Little, Brown, 1970.

3. Robert Bell, <u>Social Deviance</u>, Homewood, Illinois: The Dorsey Press, 1971, 288-289; Donald Cory, <u>The Lesbian in America</u>, New York: The Citadel Press, 1964; Marshall Clinard, <u>Sociology of Deviant Behavior</u>, New York: Holt, Rinehart and Winston, 1974, 563-565; William Simon and John Gagnon, The Lesbians: A Preliminary Overview, in Gagnon and Simon (eds.), <u>Sexual Deviance</u>, New York: Harper and Row, 1967, 251-276; <u>Report of the Committee on Homosexual Offenses and Prostitution</u> (Wolfenden Report), London: Her Majesty's Stationery Office, Cmnd. 247, 1957.

4. Alfred Kinsey et al., <u>Sexual Behavior in the Human Female</u>, Philadelphia: W.B. Saunders, 1953, 484.

5. The Constitutionality of Laws Forbidding Private Homosexual Conduct, <u>Michigan Law Review</u>, 72 (1974), 1613; Morris Ploscowe, <u>Sex and the Law</u>, New York: Ace Books, 1962; Mitchell, <u>op. cit.</u>; John Livingood (ed.), <u>National Institute of Mental Health Task Force on Homosexuality: Final Report and Background Papers</u>, Rockville, Maryland: National Institute of Mental Health, 1972; John Gallo et al., The Consenting Adult Homosexual and the Law, <u>UCLA Law Review</u>, 13 (1966), 643-832; Gilbert Cantor, The Need for Homosexual Law Reform, in Ralph Weltge (ed.), <u>The Same Sex: An Appraisal of Homosexuality</u>, Philadelphia: Pilgram Books, 1969, 83-88.

6. Clinard, <u>op. cit.</u>, 546; Katz, <u>op. cit.</u>

7. Wolfenden Report, <u>op. cit.</u>, 25-26; Michael Buckley, <u>Morality and the Homosexual</u>, Westminster, Maryland: Newman Press, 1960; Bailey, <u>op. cit.</u>; Bailey (ed.), <u>Sexual Offenders and Social Punishment</u>, London: Church of England Moral Welfare Council, 1956, 1-28; A.J. Ayer, Homosexuals and the Law, <u>New Statesman</u>, 1960, 941; J.F. Wolfenden, Ahead of Public Opinion, <u>New Statesman</u>, 1960, 941; J.E.H. Williams, Sex Offenses: The

95

British Experience, Law and Contemporary Problems, 25 (1960),
334-360; Edwin Schur, The Wolfenden Report, American Sociolo-
gical Review, 28 (1963), 1055; Schur, Crimes Without Victims:
Deviant Behavior and Public Policy, New Jersey: Prentice-Hall,
1965, 107-114; Gilbert Geis, Not the Law's Business, Washington,
DC: NIMH, US Government Printing Office, 1972; Bloch and
Geis, op. cit., 269; Robert Pursley, Introduction to Criminal
Justice, Encino, California: Glencoe Press, 1977, 115-116.

8.   Honselman v. Illinois, 48 N.E. 304, 305 (1897).

9.   American Law Institute, Modal Penal Code, proposed official
draft, Philadelphia: American Law Institute, 1962; Illinois
Criminal Code, 1961, 38, section 11-2.

10.   Pursley, op. cit., 115; Michigan Law Review, op. cit.; Gallo,
op. cit.

11.   Colin Williams and Martin Weinberg, Homosexuals and the
Military, New York: Harper and Row, 1971; D.J. West,
Homosexuality, Chicago: Aldine Publishing Company, 1967;
Schur, Crimes Without Victims, op. cit., 83-84; Erich Goode,
Deviant Behavior: An Interactionist Approach, New Jersey:
Prentice-Hall, 1978, 360; Washington Post, March, 1975.

12.   Livingwood, op. cit.; Pursley, op. cit., 116.

13.   District of Columbia Human Rights Act, title 34, 10, 1973.

14.   Goode, op. cit., 360.

15.   Henry Black, Black's Law Dictionary, St. Paul, Minnesota:
West Publishing Company, 1968, 1288.

16.   Ibid., 1563.

17.   Ibid., 243.

18.   Ibid., 743.

19.   Ibid., 456.

20.   Thomas Hoult, Dictionary of Modern Sociology, Totowa, New
Jersey: Littlefield, Adams and Company, 1969, 152, 185; The
Dushkin Publishing Group, Encyclopedia of Sociology, Guilford,
Connecticut: Dushkin Publishing Group, 1974, 128; Schur,
Crimes Without Victims, op. cit., 69-70; Bell, op. cit., 262.

21.   Goode, op. cit., 382-387.

96

22. The Dushkin Publishing Group, op. cit., 297.

23. Clinard, op. cit., 546-547; Schur, Crimes Without Victims, op. cit., 77-79; Bell, op. cit., 250-251, 288-290; Ploscowe, op. cit., 188.

24. District of Columbia Code, Annotated, Washington, DC: US Government Printing Office, 1973, 2, 22-3502, 1570.

25. Ibid., 22-3501, 1567.

26. Schur, Crimes Without Victims, op. cit., 74-82; Laud Humphreys, Tearoom Trade: Impersonal Sex in Public Places, Chicago: Aldine Publishing Company, 1975, 84-88; Bloch and Geis, op. cit., 267-268; Benjamin Karpman, The Sexual Offender and His Offenses, New York: Julian, 1954; Bell, op. cit., 252-253.

27. Paul Gebhard et al., Sex Offenders, New York: Harper and Row, 1965, 324-325; Humphreys, op. cit.

28. Gallo et al., op. cit., 690.

29. Ibid., 707-708.

30. Ibid., 693, 740.

31. Clinard, op. cit., 541; Bell, op. cit., 260, 299-305; Schur, Crimes Without Victims, op. cit., 91-94; William Helmer, New York's Middle-Class Homosexuals, Harpers, (1963), 87; Marcel Saghir and Eli Robins, Male and Female Homosexuality, Baltimore: Williams and Wilkins, 1973; Michael Schofield, Sociological Aspects of Homosexuality: A Comparative Study of Three Types of Homosexuals, Boston: Little, Brown and Company, 1965; D.J. West, Homosexuality, Chicago: Aldine Publishing Company, 1967; Bryan Magee, One in Twenty: A Study of Homosexuality in Men and Women, New York: Stein and Day, 1966; Karla Jay and Alan Young (eds.), After You're Out: Personal Experience of Gay Men and Lesbian Women, New York: Links Books, 1975.

32. Clinard, op. cit., 559; Bell, op. cit., 260-278; Schofield, op. cit.; Martin Hoffman, The Gay World: Male Homosexuality and the Social Creation of Evil, New York: Basic Books, 1968; Donald Cory and John LeRoy, The Homosexual and His Society: A View From Within, New York: The Citadel Press, 1963; Barry Dank, The Homosexuals, in Don and Patricia Spiegel (eds.), The Outsiders, New York: Rinehart Press, 1973; Donald Cory, The Homosexual in America, New York: Greenberg Publisher, 1951; Gordon Westwood, Society and the Homosexual, New York: E.P. Dutton, 1953; Wainwright Churchill, Homosexual Behavior Among

97

Males, New Jersey: Prentice-Hall, 1971; Martin Hoffman, The Gay World, New York: Basic Books, 1968; Arno Karlen, Sexuality and Homosexuality, New York: Norton, 1971; C.A. Tripp, The Homosexual Matrix, New York: New American Library, 1976; Martin Weinberg and Colin Williams, Male Homosexuals, New York: Oxford University Press, 1974; Evelyn Hooker, The Homosexual Community, in John Gagnon and William Simon (eds.), Sexual Deviance, New York: Harper and Row, 1967; Edwin Schur, Crimes Without Victims, op. cit., 85-86, 88-89; Maurice Leznoff and William Westley, The Homosexual Community, Social Problems, 3 (1956), 257-263; James McCaffrey (ed.), The Homosexual Dialectic, New Jersey: Prentice-Hall, 1972.

33. Nancy Achilles, The Development of the Homosexual Bar as an Institution, in Gagnon and Simon, op. cit.; Schur, Crimes Without Victims, op. cit., 86-88.

34. Edward Sagarin, Odd Man In: Societies of Deviants in America, Chicago: Quadrangle Books, 1969.

35. Clinard, op. cit., 567-568; Bell, op. cit., 294-300; Goode, op. cit., 387-392; Jack Hedblom, The Female Homosexual: Social and Attitudinal Dimensions, in McCaffrey, op. cit.; Magee, op. cit.; William Simon and John Gagnon, The Lesbians: A Preliminary Overview, in Gagnon and Simon, op. cit.; Frank Caprio, Female Homosexuality, New York: Grove Press, 1962; Philip Blumstein and Pepper Schwartz, Lesbianism and Bisexuality, in Erich Goode and Richard Troiden (eds.), Sexual Deviance and Sexual Deviants, New York: William Morrow, 1974; Saghir and Robins, op. cit.; Siegrid Schafer, Sexual and Problems of Lesbians, The Journal of Sex Research, 12 (1976), 50-69; Charlotte Wolff, Love Between Women, New York: Harper Colophon, 1973; Donald Cory, The Lesbian in America, New York: The Citadel Press, 1964.

36. Blumstein and Schwartz, op. cit.; Martin Duberman, The Bisexual Debate, New Times, (June, 1974), 34-41; Louise Knox, The Bisexual Phenomenon, Viva (July, 1974), 42-45, 88, 94; Robert Stoller, The Bedrock of Masculinity and Femininity: Bisexuality, Annals of General Psychiatry, 26 (1972), 207-212.

37. Schur, Crimes Without Victims, op. cit., 89-91; Cory and LeRoy, op. cit., 96; Albert Reiss, The Social Integration of Queers and Peers, Social Problems, 9 (1961), 102-120; H.L. Ross, The Hustler in Chicago, Journal of Student Research, 1 (1959), 13-14; Simon Raven, Boys Will Be Boys: The Male Prostitute in London, in Hendrik Ruitenbeek (ed.), The Problem of Homosexuality in Modern Society, New York: E.P. Dutton, 1963.

38. Charles McCaghy and James Skipper, Lesbian Behavior as an Adaptation to the Occupation of Stripping, Social Problems (1969), 262–270; Gebhard et al., op. cit., 30; Bell, op. cit., 244.

39. Wolfenden Report, op. cit., 40; Schur, Crimes Without Victims, op. cit., 107–110; Edwin Schur and Hugo Bedau, Crimes Without Victims, New Jersey: Prentice-Hall, 1975, 83.

40. Livingood, op. cit., 5–6.

41. Ibid.

42. Schofield, op. cit., 193; R.O.D. Benson, In Defense of Homosexuality: Male and Female, New York: Julian Press, 1965; Schur, Crimes Without Victims, op. cit., 110–113.

43. Bloch and Geis, op. cit., 268; Schur, Crimes Without Victims, op. cit., 110–111.

VII

VENEREAL DISEASES

Legal History

The London Act of 1161 is the first recorded statute in England
which forbade brothel keepers to employ prostitutes who had contracted gonorrhea (i.e., women suffering from the perilous infermity
of burning).[1] A London order of 1430 ordered brothel keepers to keep
men suffering from gonorrhea (i.e., the so-called hidden disease)
from visiting their prostitutes.[2] An ordinance of 1497 of Aberdeen,
Scotland ordered all prostitutes to desist from their behavior or
be branded since they were assumed to be the source of venereal
disease.[3] The same city in 1507 passed a second regulation inform-
ing those persons infected with venereal disease to keep to themselves and stay at home until they are cured of the "Naples disease".[4]

Up until the nineteenth century a double standard prevailed
concerning the punishment of those contracting venereal diseases.
Males were at most looked upon as deviant while females were considered criminals. Prostitutes who contracted venereal diseases
were placed in the public workhouses and made to wear yellow dresses
to show how disgraceful they were to the community.[5] The Contagious
Diseases Act of 1864 dealt with military personnel who contracted
venereal diseases and the prostitutes who gave it to them. The
women were given manditory examinations by the court and detained in
specified hospitals.[6] A Ladies' National Association was formed in
1869 to try to help these lower class women accused of spreading
the diseases and a Royal Commission was appointed in 1870 to investigate the alleged breach of constitutional guarantees of these
unfortunate females. Finally a select committee of the House of
Commons studied the issue and parliament repealed the Act in 1886.[7]

Another Royal Commission was appointed in 1913 to study the
problem of venereal diseases. It studied the issue until 1916 and
based on its findings, parliament passed the Venereal Disease Regulations the same year which set up public treatment centers that
kept the identity of the patient confidential. Patients were
advised to seek treatment on a voluntary basis but during and shortly
after World War II public health authorities could force individuals
through the use of the courts into manditory treatment.[8] The
Matrimonial Causes Act of 1937 states that a marriage is null and void
if a spouse knows that he or she has venereal disease at the time of
marriage. The other spouse must be unaware that the other marriage
partner was infected, to stop sexual intercourse at the time of
discovery, and institute divorce proceedings within a year of the
wedding date.[9]

99

Venereal disease clinics were set up in 1948 under National
Health Service in Great Britain.[10] In 1951 the British Federation
against the Venereal Diseases was established as a private organization to educate the public concerning the prevention of the
diseases. It worked closely with the Venereal Diseases and
Treponematosis Division of the World Health Organization of the
United Nations.[11] The Pharmaceutical Substances Act of 1956 made
it manditory for all blood donors to have a blood test for syphilis.[12]
Finally the Street Offenses Act of 1959 was in part an attempt to
control the spread of venereal diseases from prostitution.[13]

The United States accepted the British practices without question concerning the prevention and control of venereal diseases from
colonial times. The first indirect legislation dealing with the
problem began with the legislation of Congress known as the Comstock
Law in 1873 which banned the mailing of contraceptives and information about them. Such information was deemed obscene by this federal
statute.[14] The condom was such a birth control device and also
effective at the prevention of venereal diseases. A congressional
act of Congress banned prostitutes from entering this country as
immigrants in 1875, thus indirectly stating that they were carriers
of venereal diseases.[15] It was not until the Immigration Act of
1917 that Congress stated that persons who were infected with
"loathsome or contagious diseases" should be denied entrance to the
United States.[16]

The United States Court of Appeals in 1936 stated that contraceptives imported for a lawful purpose (i.e., prevention of venereal
diseases) did not come under the Comstock Law. Connecticut passed
the first statute requiring both prospective marriage partners to
have blood tests for venereal disease in 1935.[18] Rhode Island in
1938 required that all pregnant women be required to take prenatal
blood tests to determine if they have contracted venereal disease.[19]
Since 1968 several states have enacted laws allowing juveniles to be
diagnosed and treated for venereal disease without the consent of
their parents.[20] Finally in Carey v. Population Services International, the Supreme Court ruled that the New York statute forbidding the sale of contraceptives to those under age sixteen, forbidding advertisement and display of same is unconstitutional. This
1977 ruling indirectly allows juveniles access to condoms which can
be used as a preventative for venereal disease.[21]

Legal Definitions

Black defines venereal disease as one of several diseases identified with sexual intercourse.[22] Only the three most common diseases
capable of being spread by the sex act are defined in law as venereal

(i.e., gonorrhea, syphilis, and chancroid).[23] Other venereal
diseases or medical conditions associated with sexual intercourse
are lymphogranuloma venereum, granuloma inguinale, non-specific
urethritis, trichomonas vaginalis, scabies, genital warts, and
lice.[24]

Venereal Disease Statutes and Enforcement Policies

The District of Columbia Code does not define specific venereal
diseases but only states that communicable diseases shall be defined
by the D.C. Council regulation.[25] The Director of Public Health is
empowered to remove persons believed to be carriers of communicable
diseases (i.e., venereal) if he has probable cause to believe that
the person is affected with the disease or is a carrier and that the
continuance of such person in the place where he may be is likely to
be dangerous to the lives or health of other persons, or that by
reason of the uncooperation or carelessness of such person the public
health is likely to be endangered. Further the Director may by
written order have the police detain such person in any place or
institution so designated by the Director of Public Health.[26]

Detention of a person suspected of being affected or carrier of
venereal disease shall not exceed forty-eight hours unless a judge
orders a continuance. A judge will set a hearing to determine
whether the person detained is affected with venereal disease or is
a carrier of communicable disease. If so ruled that the individual's
release would be likely to endanger the lives or health of any other
person, said person will be held in an institution designated by
the Director of Public Health. If the detained person is not affected
or a carrier, or is affected or a carrier but not likely to endanger
the lives or health of others, that person shall be released by
court order.[27]

It is unlawful for a person detained to leave a designated
institution unless properly discharged by the authority of the
Director of Public Health.[28] The Director of Public Health is
empowered to seek a warrent from a judge for the arrest of any person who is affected by or a carrier of a communicable disease. The
police under such warrent may break into the abode of the person in
order to execute the warrent if the person refuses to admit the
police.[29] It shall be unlawful for any person knowingly to obstruct,
resist, oppose, or interfere with any person performing any duty or
function under the authority of this statute.[30]

Any person who violates any of the provisions of the statute
shall be fined not more than three hundred dollars or by imprisonment for not longer than ninety days, or both. The Court may also
impose conditions upon any person found guilty. Such conditions may

include submission to medical and mental examination, diagnosis, and treatment by proper health authorities or any licensed physician approved by the court.[31]

Any juvenile who appears in any clinic, hospital, or other facility of the Department of Public Health who is affected with a venereal disease or is a carrier of a venereal disease shall be detained by authority of the Director of Public Health. The juvenile will be allowed to consent to treatment and so treated if he agrees. Otherwise no treatment will be provided if said juvenile refuses such treatment. In such instance the Director of Public Health will search out said juvenile's parents or person standing in loco parentis to such minor in order to notify them that the juvenile is affected with a venereal disease or is a carrier of a venereal disease and whether said youth has received or refused to receive treatment.[32]

The Virginia Criminal Code states that persons of "ill fame", if found guilty of fornication, adultery, lewd and lascivious conduct, illicit cohabitation, sodomy are to be considered and declared to be reasonably suspected of having a venereal disease. No individual convicted of any such charges shall be released from custody until examined for venereal diseases. The state of Virginia also makes it a crime (i.e., one hundred dollar fine and/or six months in jail) for an individual who knows he or she has a venereal disease to spread it to other persons.[33]

The United States government under the National Venereal Disease Prevention and Control Act assists states to prevent and control venereal diseases. The United States Public Health Service aids the states in this matter and PHS personnel are empowered with the aid of federal law enforcement agents to deal with problems of venereal disease which are interstate in nature.[34]

Description of Specific Deviance

Several types of deviant individuals tend to have higher rates of venereal disease than the general population: (1) prostitutes (both heterosexual and homosexual); (2) homosexuals; (3) promiscuous persons (i.e., adulterers and fornicators); (4) juveniles (i.e., those who run away and engage in prostitution, both homo and heterosexual, and those who engage in sexual intercourse); and (5) those who sexually assault or abuse children and/or adults and their victims (i.e., rapists, child molesters, and sexual abusers of children).[35]

The few studies dealing with the social background of individuals coming in for treatment of venereal disease indicates that there are essentially no differences in rates of infection between religious and ethnic groups, but differences between racial groups and social classes, although the diseases are not rare in any subculture within society.[36] The studies show a higher rate of venereal disease for the lower classes and Blacks than for middle/upper classes and whites. This may reflect the reporting techniques to a certain degree since most well to do persons go to a private doctor for treatment who may not report the case or all the social background data to the authorities while lower class and nonwhites generally seek out treatment at public facilities that report all the data to the proper authorities.[37] Venereal disease rates vary by age but appears to be highest among adolescents and young adults.[38] Morton states that venereal disease rates have increased faster for young women since the early 1960's than for young men. This finding also appears to be true in the United States.[39] The fact that the birth control pill gives no protection against venereal disease while the condom does plus the fact that young women are more sexually mature than previously and allowed more freedom of movement due to the effect of the woman's liberation ideology explains the raise of the venereal disease rate.[40]

It is estimated that the prevalence of venereal disease in the United States is about six million which is probably a conservative estimate. The rate of cases of gonorrhea is approximately four times greater than the rate of cases of syphilis. The U.S. Public Health Service estimates it cost six million dollars per year to maintain the syphilitic blind institutionally and another fifty million dollars to maintain the syphilitic insane. Thousands of babies and adults die each year due to the disease.[41]

Prostitution has long been considered the source of venereal diseases, since the women have contact with a number of clients on a daily basis, most of whom they never see again. It appears that streetwalkers have higher rates of venereal disease than massage parlor and house girls, while call girls have the lowest rate. The disease rates appear to be fairly low for prostitutes compared to females of the general population who are promiscuous.[42]

Homosexuals appear to have much higher rates of venereal diseases than heterosexuals. This is especially true of gays than lesbians who tend not to be as promiscuous. Gays tend to have twice as many sexual contacts as heterosexual males. Further it appears that anal intercourse hinders the early detection of the diseases and this is the preference of most homosexuals.[43]

Individuals who engage in indiscriminate premarital or extra-marital sexual intercourse usually have a higher rate of venereal disease than those who tend to seek out a long lasting relationship with one person. Thus those who are involved in the swinging singles scene as well as group sex (i.e., wife-swapping) appear to be

maximizing their chances to contract venereal disease. The increased
interest in experimentation with sexuality (i.e., oral sex, cunnilingus,
and anal sex) coupled with the use of oral contraceptives increases the
chances of contracting and spreading venereal disease. This new
sexual freedom is accompanied with a lack of knowledge concerning the
nature of venereal diseases since it is thought by many supposedly
educated prople that only immoral, dirty, or lower class individuals
have venereal diseases.[44]

It appears that the greatest incidence of problems with venereal
disease is among juveniles. Studies in Great Britain and the United
States show that both males and females have greater freedom to do
as they please. Despite the increased amount of sex education
courses offered in the public schools, the establishment of free
clinics that offer advice concerning birth control, and the creation
of V.D. hotlines in the larger metropolitan areas, more and more
adolescents contract a spectrum of venereal diseases each year.
Many are afraid to inform their parents or seek out medical help
so the disease gets worse. Often the infected youth is labeled as
a delinquent and sent to training school where the problem of
disease control is even more difficult to deal with by the authorities.[45]

Finally there are those who are the victims of sexual assaults
by strangers, friends, or relatives. In the case of children who
contract venereal disease, most do not know how they contracted the
disease and are quite confused concerning the deviance surrounding
the incident. Most adolescents are ashamed, afraid, and angry
about the forced sexual relationship and resulting contraction of
disease. Victims of incest are usually quite reluctant to admit
what happened to them since they are afraid that the parent or
relative will convince the police and/or juvenile authorities that
they are promiscuous and be sent to a training school. Rape victims
who contract venereal disease are already suffering from the trauma
of the sexual assault and often do not report this problem to the
public health authorities or police since they do not want further
involvement with the criminal justice system.[46]

Decriminalization

As Bell States, venereal diseases are usually a covert aspect
of some form of social deviance which may be a crime (i.e., fornication, sodomy, homosexuality, adultery, incest, and prostitution).
As long as society considers the individual who has venereal disease
to be immoral, there will be a problem in dealing with the topic in
a direct manner. Thus one who contracts venereal disease is a
violator of the sexual mores of society and should be punished. This
makes the person suffering from the disease hide his or her medical

problem so that he or she will not be ostracized by the community. This is difficult enough for the single person but worse for the husband or wife who infects an innocent spouse.[47]

As long as states like Virginia treat individuals who contract and spread venereal diseases as criminals, it is most unlikely that these diseases will be controlled. The U.S. Public Health Service cannot ever hope to gather accurate statistics on this social problem when most people do not want to mention these diseases since they originate in behavior that is taboo (i.e., the old testament makes numerous references to what appears to be both gonorrhea and syphilis - Book of Leviticus, Book of Numbers, Thirty-Eighth Psalm).[48]

It is obvious that both state and federal governments must deal properly with this issue as has been done in the District of Columbia Code (i.e., find, treat, and cure those affected with venereal disease) rather than punish individuals for having a contageous disease. Proper sex education would be a real benefit to all members of the community. The opening of more treatment clinics that are free or charging a nominal fee would also help. Finally hotlines that answer questions concerning venereal diseases and inform individuals where they can seek medical and psychological advice are needed. In our society only the military take a proper approach to the venereal disease problem through both preventative and control methods. The United States should follow the proven methods utilized in Great Britain since World War II concerning venereal disease.

106

Notes

1. R.S. Morton, <u>Venereal Diseases</u>, Baltimore: Penquin Books, 1966, 20; A. Fessler, Advertisements in the Treatment of Venereal Disease and the Social History of Venereal Disease, <u>British Journal of Venereal Diseases</u>, 25 (1949), 84; S.M. Laird, <u>Venereal Disease in Britain</u>, Baltimore: Penquin Books, 1943; Theodore Roseburv, <u>Microbes and Morals: The Strange Story of Venereal Disease</u>, New York: Viking Press, 1971.

2. Morton, <u>op. cit.</u>, 20.

3. <u>Ibid.</u>, 24.

4. <u>Ibid.</u>

5. Fessler, <u>op. cit.</u>, 84; Morton, <u>op. cit.</u>, 30.

6. Morton, <u>op. cit.</u>, 30.

7. <u>Ibid.</u>

8. <u>Ibid.</u>, 31.

9. <u>Ibid.</u>, 140.

10. <u>Ibid.</u>, 32.

11. <u>Ibid.</u>, 136.

12. <u>Ibid.</u>, 141.

13. <u>Ibid.</u>, 163.

14. Robert Bell, <u>Social Deviance</u>, Homewood, Illinois: Dorsey Press, 1976, 93.

15. Ralph Thomlinson, <u>Population Dynamics</u>, New York: Random House, 1976, 298.

16. <u>Ibid.</u>, 298-299.

17. Bell, <u>op. cit.</u>, 94, 115; Norman St. John-Stevas, History and Legal Status of Birth Control, in Edwin Schur (ed.), <u>The Family and the Sexual Revolution</u>, Bloomington, Indiana: Indiana University Press, 1964, 337-338.

18. Bell, op. cit., 261.

19. Ibid., 262.

20. Ibid.

21. Carey v. Population Services International, 1977.

22. Henry Black, Black's Law Dictionary, St. Paul, Minnesota: West Publishing Company, 1968, 1726.

23. Morton, op. cit., 15-16.

24. Ibid., 16-18

25. District of Columbia Code, Annotated, Washington, D.C.: U.S. Government Printing Office, 1973, 1, 6-119, 610.

26. Ibid., 6-119a, 610.

27. Ibid., 6-119b, 610-611.

28. Ibid., 6-119d, 612.

29. Ibid., 6-119e, 612.

30. Ibid., 6-119g, 612.

31. Ibid., 6-119h, 613.

32. Ibid., 6-119j, 613-614.

33. Code of Virginia, 5A, title 32-94, Charlottesville, Virginia: The Michie Company, 1950.

34. United States Code, title 42, Washington, DC: US Government Printing Office, 1971, 247.

35. Morton, op. cit., 112-133; Bell, op. cit., 260-263; William Brown et al., Syphilis and Other Venereal Diseases, Cambridge, Massachusetts: Harvard University Press, 1970; Stewart Brooks, The V.D. Story, New York: A.S. Barnes Company, 1971; Margaret Hyde, V.D.: The Silent Epidemic, New York: McGraw-Hill, 1973; Robert Helmer, The Venus Dilemma, Los Angeles: Nash Publishing Company, 1974; Robert Richards, Venereal Diseases and and Their Avoidance, New York: Holt, Rinehart and Winston, 1974; Celia Deschin, Teenagers and Venereal Disease: A Sociological Study of 600 Teenagers in New York City's Social Hygiene Clinics, American Journal of Nursing, 1963; Richard Stiller, The Love Bugs, New York: Thomas Nelson, 1974; Eric

108

Johnson, <u>V.D.</u>, Philadelphia: J. B. Lippincott, 1973; Louis
Lasagna, <u>The V.D. Epidemic</u>, Philadelphia: Temple University
Press, 1975; A. J. King and C. S. Nichol, <u>Venereal Diseases</u>,
London: Cassell, 1964; M. Schofield, <u>The Sexual Behavior
of Young People</u>, London: Longmans, 1965.

36. Morton, <u>op</u>. <u>cit</u>., 114

37. Deschin, <u>op</u>. <u>cit</u>.

38. Brown, <u>op</u>. <u>cit</u>., 78; Morton, <u>op</u>. <u>cit</u>., 115.

39. Deschin, <u>op</u>. <u>cit</u>.; Morton, <u>op</u>. <u>cit</u>., 116; Schofield, <u>op</u>. <u>cit</u>.

40. Bell, <u>op</u>. <u>cit</u>., 263.

41. <u>Ibid</u>., 259-260; Lawrence Galton, VD: Out of Control?, <u>Medical
Aspects of Human Sexuality</u>, (January, 1972), 18-22.

42. Stiller, <u>op</u>. <u>cit</u>., 56; Morton, <u>op</u>. <u>cit</u>., 119-123.

43. Lasagna, <u>op</u>. <u>cit</u>., 8-9; Morton, <u>op</u>. <u>cit</u>., 128-130; E.R. Trice,
Venereal Disease and Homosexuality, <u>Medical Aspects of Human
Sexuality</u>, (January, 1969), 70-71.

44. Johnson, <u>op</u>. <u>cit</u>., 79; Stiller, <u>op</u>. <u>cit</u>.; Brown, <u>op</u>. <u>cit</u>.;
Brooks, <u>op</u>. <u>cit</u>.; Hyde, <u>op</u>. <u>cit</u>.; Helmer, <u>op</u>. <u>cit</u>.;
Richards, <u>op</u>. <u>cit</u>.

45. Deschin, <u>op</u>. <u>cit</u>.; Morton, <u>op</u>. <u>cit</u>., 115-119; Schofield, <u>op</u>. <u>cit</u>.

46. Interviews with Captain Clayton Clark and officer Selma Partner,
Sex Offender Branch, Metropolitan Police Department of
Washington, D.C., 1977, 1978.

47. Bell, <u>op</u>. <u>cit</u>., 252-254.

48. Stiller, <u>op</u>. <u>cit</u>., 17-18.

VIII

FAMILY CONFLICTS

<u>Legal History</u>

The legal status of members of the family stems from Roman Law as interpreted by ecclesiastical law after the time of the Code of Justinian.[1] The Code of Aethelberht (600 A.D.) in England states that problems of a domestic nature were to be treated as torts and handled as both family and church matters.[2] Thus the English Common Law that deals with family conflicts (i.e., domestic relations) is based primarily on church law and later on equity or chancery law.[3]

According to the Common Law all deviance in connection with the institution of the family, were torts (i.e., husband/wife, parent/child, affinal and consanguinal relations) with the exceptions of adultery and incest. These crimes were handled by ecclesiastical law in England.[4] Bigamy was not a crime until the time of King James I when it was made a felony.[5] Such family problems as child and wife abuse were dealt with by family members, a fact that has legal status going back to Roman Law. The Common Law allowed the husband to deal with wife and children as he wished which included deprivation of liberty and corporal punishment short of death.[6]

Adultery, incest, and bigamy were punished in the ecclesiastical courts in the early period of the Common Law in England. Adultery and incest were considered criminal acts and both parties were considered liable except in cases of incest where the child was under age seven. The reasons for the severity of punishment for adultery and incest were the probable creation of illegitimate offspring that threatened family stability, violated that sanctity of the marriage contract, and created challenges to the legitimate heirs to the family estate. Further at Common Law illegitimate children could not inherit from either mother or father although there were challenges made on behalf of bastards of the upper classes. Finally illegitimate children could not obtain support from their fathers' at Common Law.[7]

In Colonial New England of the seventeenth century, statutes were passed making adultery punishable by death and fornication punishable by public whipping. Usually the offender was fined, sometimes whipped, rarely branded, and never hanged.[8] The Puritans tried to resolve their problems concerning illegitimacy by passing statutes making the father of the child responsible for its upbringing.[9]

At Common Law, domestic relations problems were under the jurisdiction of the ecclesiastical courts who had jurisdiction over all problems of marriage and also dealt with divorce. It was not until the nineteenth century that the traditional authoritarian relationship of the husband legally dominating wife and children was challenged in England by the chancery or equity court. This institution was absent or incorporated into the civil court structure in the early United States.[10] Until 1857 England had no satisfactory solution for individuals who wished to divorce which was a continual source of problems from adultery to desertion.[11] The divorce laws were not any better in colonial America. In 1682 the colony of Pennsylvania allowed divorce if one spouse was convicted of adultery. This statute was later expanded to allow divorce on the grounds of incest, bigamy, and homosexuality. Divorces were granted by the colonial governor and later the colonial legislatures of Pennsylvania, New Jersey, and New Hampshire.[12]

After Independence from Great Britain, the United States government allowed each state to decide the divorce issue for itself. Legislative divorce was only allowed in the South and very rarely granted so the problems of adultery, bigamy, seduction, fornication and prostitution continued. All the states in the North (i.e., Pennsylvania, Massachusetts, New York, New Jersey, all the other New England states and Tennessee) had general divorce laws by 1800.[13] For example New York only allowed divorce for adultery; this law remained basically unchanged from 1787 until the early 1970's, Vermont in 1798 allowed divorce for adultery, desertion, and other grounds while Rhode Island allowed divorce for any type of sexual deviance (i.e., homosexual as well as heterosexual).[14]

Desertion of the family by a husband was dealt with indirectly by the Common Law as the wife and children were to be cared for by other members of the immediate family. According to the Common Law, a wife did not have legal standing outside of the marital context (i.e., her legal existence disappeared in favor of her husband).[15] The states had to make allowances for wives who were deserted so that they could sell the family land and other possessions in order to pay bills and live without going on welfare. This first happened in Massachusetts in 1787 and by 1850 several states allowed married women some legal rights.[16] Thus the gradual move toward legal equality for married women was not motivated by ideological principles but by the pragmatic concern about keeping deserted women and children off of welfare.

The poor house was essentially the same in eighteenth and nineteenth century America as it had been in England since 1601. Parents who neglected or deserted their children could not be held liable for taking care of them so the states allowed dependent youths to be apprenticed or be trained as servants (i.e., the former for boys and the latter for girls). Abuses by master were notorious of their wards but little in the way of legislation took place until well into the nineteenth century. It was not until 1899 that the Illinois legislature passed the first Juvenile Court Act in America that brought together under one jurisdiction all cases of child neglect, dependency, and delinquency.[17]

It was not until 1920 that the Nineteenth Amendment to the U.S. Constitution allowed women the right to vote. This did not alter to a great degree their legal status in the family since husbands still dominated the marital context in terms of divorce settlements.[18] It was not until the Civil Rights Act of 1964 that sex discrimination was outlawed by Congress. This aided in pushing the states to modernize their divorce and dependency statutes but the pending Equal Rights Amendment to the Constitution has speeded up the concern by many states in the problems of spouse and child abuse.[19]

Legal Definitions

Black defines adultery as the voluntary sexual intercourse of a married individual with someone other than the offender's spouse. A distinction is sometimes made whether one or both parties are married (i.e., single and double adultery respectively). Open and notorious adultery constitutes the flagrant and public living together as husband and wife of individuals one of whom is married.[20] Bigamy is the crime of deliberately marrying a second person while knowingly still married to another spouse. By statute the second marriage is not legal and any children of the void marriage are considered by law to be illegitimate.[21]

Black defines abuse of a child as ill treatment which may be injurious, improper, hurtful, or sexually offensive.[22] Another name for the maltreatment of juveniles by parents or guardians is the battered-child syndrome.[23] An abandoned child is one who is deserted by his or her parents or guardian and who is without proper care or the ability to pay for his or her proper care. A neglected child is one who is not receiving proper care, education, and upbringing from his or her parents or guardian according to the statutes for such care established by law in a given jurisdiction.[24]

Desertion is the actual abandonment or cessation of matrimonial cohabitation by either spouse and a refusal to fulfil the duties and obligations of the marital relationship, with an intent to abandon or give up entirely and not to return to or resume the marital relationship, occurring without legal justification either in the consent or the wrongful conduct of the other party. Constructive desertion arises when an existing cohabitation is ended by the misconduct of one spouse providing that the misconduct is itself a legal ground for divorce.[25]

Divorce is the legal separation of husband and wife effected for cause by the judgment of a court, either totally dissolving the marriage (i.e., a vinculo matrimonii) or suspending its effects so far as concerns the cohabitation of both spouses (i.e., a mensa et thoro or from bed and board).[26]

One who is illegitimate is usually a term applied to a child whose parents were not married legally.[27] Black defines a bastard as an illegitimate child or one born of an unlawful intercourse and before the legal marriage of his or her parents. The term also describes a child born after marriage but under circumstances which make it impossible that the husband of his mother can be his father.[28] There are two types of the latter situation (1) adulterine or adulterous bastards (i.e., children produced by an illegal sexual liaison between two people who at the time when the child was born were either of them or both married to some other individual) and (2) incestuous bastards (i.e., children produced by an illegal sexual liaison between two people who are relations within the guidelines prohibited by law).[29]

Incest is the crime of sexual intercourse or cohabitation between a man and a woman who are related to each other within the guidelines set up by the jurisdiction that prohibits marriage between the two by law.[30]

Statutes and Enforcement Policy

Whoever commits adultery shall on conviction be punished by a fine not exceeding five hundred dollars, or by imprisonment not exceeding one year, or both; and when the act is committed between a married woman and an unmarried man, both parties to such act shall be found guilty of adultery; and when such act is committed between a married man and an unmarried woman, the man shall only be guilty of adultery.[31] A person who has a living husband or wife and who marries another shall be guilty of bigamy, and on conviction shall be imprisoned for not less than two nor more than seven years. This statute shall not apply to any person whose spouse has been continually absent for five successive years next before such marriage without being known to such person to be living within that time, or whose marriage to said living spouse shall have been dissolved by a valid decree of a competent court, or shall have been pronounced void by a valid decree of a competent court on the ground of the nullity of the marriage contract.[32]

Cruelty to children is defined as any act of torture, beating, abuse, or otherwise willfully maltreat any child under the age of eighteen years; or any individual having the custody or possession of a child under the age of fourteen years who shall expose, or aid and abet in exposing such child in any highway, street, field, house, or other place, with the intent to abandon said child; or any person having in his custody or control a child under the age of fourteen years who shall in any way dispose of said child with a view to its being employed as an acrobat, or a gymnast, or a contortionist, or a circus rider, or a rope-walker, or in any exhibition or like dangerous character, or as a begger, or merchant, or pauper, or street singer, or street musician; or any person who shall take, receive, hire, employ, use, exhibit, or have in custody any child of the age last named for any of the purposes enumerated shall be deemed guilty of a misdemeanor and upon conviction shall be fined not more than two hundred and fifty dollars or imprisoned for a term not exceeding two years, or both.[33]

Any person of sufficient financial ability who shall refuse or neglect to provide for any child under the age of fourteen years of which he or she shall be the parent or guardian, such food, clothing, and shelter as will prevent the suffering and secure the safety of such child shall be guilty of a misdemeanor and upon conviction shall be fined not more than one hundred dollars or imprisoned not more than three months, or both.[34]

The District of Columbia has no specific statute dealing with spouse abuse since a wife or husband can file charges of assault, battery, and/or false imprisonment. Divorce and desertion are not crimes but behavior that is causal in creating the grounds for divorce may be (i.e., adultery, bigamy, seduction, etc.). It is not a crime to be illegitimate but the behavior that produces the illegitimate issue may be criminal (i.e., adultery or incest). In most states it is a crime for a husband to fail to support his wife and/or children.[35]

If any individual related to another person within and not including the fourth degree of consanguinity computed according to the rules of the Roman or civil law shall marry or cohabit with or have sexual intercourse with such other so-related individual, knowing him or her to be within said degree of relationship, the individual so offending shall be found guilty of incest and upon conviction shall be punished by imprisonment for not more than twelve years.[36]

Most of the offenses against the family and children are quite difficult to enforce by the agencies of law enforcement. This is due to the fact that most members of the community do not care about these offenses since they are so common. Thus the public prosecutor does not press the police for more stringent enforcement of the statutes since he is usually reluctant to prosecute most types of cases (i.e., adultery, spouse abuse, child abuse, and even bigamy and incest). Desertion cases are rarely prosecuted since the husband who has failed to provide support for wife and children would serve no useful purpose to the state if he goes to jail.[37]

Most of the cases of child abuse and sexual assaults on children in the District of Columbia originate through reports of Children's Hospital and other private and public hospitals that investigate suspicious cases. Cases of spouse abuse are usually reported by either the spouse who has been injured or a neighbor who calls the police. In some cases the Department of Social Services will refer a case to the police but more likely the social worker will refer an abused wife to the House of Ruth that provides counselling and treatment for battered wives.[38]

The Corporation Counsel's Office, Juvenile Section of the District of Columbia government reports that there were 548 cases of child abuse and sexual assault on children in 1976. According to the Metropolitan Police Department Sex Offense Branch and Youth Division, this figure is approximately five times lower than the actual incidence of offenses but they are not reported to the police. The police receive 24 percent of the reported cases while Children's and D.C. General report the majority of cases of abuse and neglect. Other reporting agencies are the schools, social workers, neighbors, relatives, the child himself, parent or guardian, and private social agencies.[39]

The Prevention of Child Abuse and Neglect Act of 1977 (D.C.) requires that every physician, psychologist, medical examiner, dentist, chiropractor, registered nurse, licensed practical nurse, person involved in care and treatment of patients, police officer, school administrator, classroom teacher, social worker, day care worker, and mental health professional, who knows or has reasonable cause to suspect that a child known to him or her or her professional or official capacity has been or is in immediate danger of being a mentally or physically abused or neglected child shall immediately report or have a report made to the Metropolitan Police Department or the Child Protective Services Division of the D.C. Department of Human Resources. Also any person, hospital, or institution participating in good faith in the making of a report shall have immunity from liability, civil or criminal. Neither the husband/wife privilege nor the physician/patient privilege shall be grounds for excluding evidence. Any person who willfully fails to make such a report shall be fined not more than one hundred dollars or imprisoned not more than thirty days, or both.[40]

One percent of those arrested in 1976 were for alleged offenses against family and children. Ninety percent of these offenses were perpetrated by males and ten percent by females.[41] Of all those held for prosecution for offenses against family and children (i.e., 5,766) fifty percent plead guilty to the original offense, two percent plead guilty to a lessor charge, twenty-four percent were acquitted or had the case dismissed, and twenty-four percent of the cases were referred to juvenile court.[42]

Description of Specific Deviance

There are no specific profiles on the typical individuals who commit adultery, bigamy, or get divorced. Adultery is quite common today and individuals from all social classes, races, ethnic groups, and religions are guilty of this victimless crime. Comarital sex or swinging is popular with many middle and upper class couples.[43] Bigamy is quite rare in today's society since divorce laws allow a person who has been deserted to remarry after the requisite number of years of desertion have elapsed. Divorce is quite common in American society and cuts across all subcultural lines and age groups, although marriages are also broken by annulment, voluntary separation, as well as desertion. Divorce rates are increasing for those under thirty five and those over fifty five for a variety of reasons, both criminal and noncriminal. Post-marital sex is seen as more normal than deviant for the formerly married individual of either sex.[44]

Spouse abuse (i.e., usually wife abuse) is a serious and growing problem in the United States. Battered wives have usually kept the incidents of violence directed towards them by husbands to themselves for a variety of reasons (i.e., fear of further violence, shame and guilt, need for financial support for themselves and their children, and feelings that the police will be ineffective in resolving the problem). The Office of Abused Persons of the Montgomery County, Maryland Department of Social Services states that 263 women were served in 1977. Counselling services and shelter capabilities are offered to these women. The House of Ruth, Battered Women Program in the District of Columbia also offers similar services.[45]

Child abuse is becoming an increasing serious problem in the United States. It is estimated that more than one million children are victims of physical and/or sexual abuse and neglect by parents, relatives, or guardians in the United States. Of these abused children approximately two thousand die yearly from the effects of abuse and/or neglect. These figures are quite conservative as most cases go unreported or are reported as accidents.[46]

Persons who are child abusers are parents, guardians, close relatives (i.e., uncles, aunts, siblings, cousins), and friends of the family. These people are typically mentally unstable, drug addicts, alcoholics, and/or sexual deviants.[47]

The types of injuries to children are physical, sexual, and psychological in nature. Burns, beatings, whippings, starving, sexual assaults, and various degrees of psychological torment are perpetrated upon children every day leading to permanent injury and death. A number of selected case studies will show the diversity of the problem of child abuse. A nine year old girl was subjected for a period of two weeks to hot baths with liquid clorox poured into the water that was administered to her by her stepmother. Between these baths the child was whipped on a regular basis. Two days before the child died the stepmother beat the child so severely that she was covered with open wounds. The stepmother proceeded to pour clorox and peroxide into these wounds and then scrubbed the wounds with an SOS pad. The child died from shock the next day.[48]

An eleven year old girl was subjected to sexual abuse by the boyfriend of the mother who allowed him to live with her and her children. The mother did not discover the fact that her daughter and boyfriend were having sexual relations until approximately a year's time elapsed. The boyfriend had taken the daughter on shopping trips where he bought her presents and then to motels where he had sexual intercourse with her. She was told not to tell her mother or the boyfriend would take all the gifts away from her. At the time the mother discovered the relationship, her daughter already had experienced her menstrual cycle and could have gotten pregnant. The mother was upset that her boyfriend was sleeping with her daughter, not that the child was regularly exposed to sex and could have gotten pregnant.[49]

A five year old girl living with her drug addict aunt and her alcoholic grandfather was brought to the hospital by a neighbor. The little girl complained of severe pains eminating from her urinogenital tract. Upon examination the girl was found to have a severe case of gonorrhea. Investigation of the case by the police revealed that the girl had been abandoned by her addict mother and given to her sister who said she would take care of her niece. The aunt in turn began to drink and take drugs and left the child in the care of the alcoholic grandfather. He and his drinking buddies would when drunk take liberties with the little girl who subsequently contracted venereal disease. The aunt and grandmother paid no attention to the medical problem of the child until the neighbor brought her to the hospital.[50]

A mother brought her eighteen month old son to the hospital where the child upon examination was shown to be suffering from what appeared to be a rare skin disease. Closer medical examination showed that the child had been severely burned upon his face with a hot iron and that his body was encrusted with layers of dirt (i.e., the mother had never bathed the child). The mother complained that her son was "mean" just like his father and that she punished him by neglecting him and then burning him when he cried too much. The mother was committed to the public mental hospital and her son placed in a foster home. The mother upon release began to drink heavily and subsequently wanted her child back. She was very upset when the case worker would not allow her to ever see her child again.[51]

Incest is another crime that is rarely discussed in public but occurs with a frequency that would surprise the average member of the community. Most often these crimes occur between father and daughter, brother and sister, and sometimes between mother and son. A parent or sibling will endulge in sexual activities with another member of the immediate family because of psychological problems, problems with one's spouse who denies one access to acceptable sexual relations, adolescent experimentation where there is no proper parental authority present to prevent such activity, and perverted interest in sexual intercourse with members of the nuclear family.[52] The Guyon Society of Alhambra, California is a group dedicated to the practice of incest among members of the nuclear family. This society believes that the parent is the logical person from which the child should learn about sexuality. Members of this society take contraceptive precautions so that daughters, sisters, and mothers will not become pregnant.[53]

Decriminalization

Family conflicts are a diverse problem for the legislatures and law enforcement agencies to handle. Some problems are not presently dealt with through the criminal court but by domestic relations, family, and/or juvenile courts in the United States. These are problems such as adultery, desertion, divorce, and battered wives and children. Some jurisdictions like the District of Columbia have criminalized social deviance that deals with child abuse, both physical and sexual but most leave the problems to be handled by the local jurisdictions through actions taken by departments of social welfare. The police are only called in when an emergency situation occurs (i.e., someone's life is being threatened or seriously endangered).

Bigamy and incest are crimes in most jurisdictions of the United States but most victims do not report the offenses because of the negative publicity they would receive in the press and in

118

the community in general. Thus most cases of bigamy and incest go
unknown and unreported to the police or when known to the police
are left unprosecuted since the public prosecutor does not want to
follow through on such negative cases unless other crimes are also
involved. Many times criminal or juvenile court feels it is in
the best interest of the offender to have the individual seek out
voluntary psychiatric treatment as an alternative to incarceration.[54]

Research has pointed out that those who commit family related
crimes are usually immature, frustrated, sociopathic or psychopathic,
or suffering from the pathological effects of alcohol, drugs, or
other physiological problems.[55] Adultery is very rarely seen on
the arrest records of police departments since it is so common and
divorces granted on this ground rarely result in the guilty party
being turned over to the proper authorities for criminal prosecution. Divorce is not a crime but many of the grounds for same
could be easily prosecuted by the public prosecutor who usually
never sees such a source for his caseload. The increasing number
of divorced fathers who fail to pay child support has prompted
some jurisdictions to criminalize this behavior as a potent threat
to force reluctant ex-husbands to pay for the support of their
children so that local social welfare authorities do not have to
pay for these children.[56]

Thus in the case of family conflict problems, one can see that
crimes stemming from deviant behavior of family members has often
been criminalized but lack of public interest and/or the commonality
of such behavior leads the criminal justice authorities to overlook
most of the offenses. Yet in the cases of child and spouse abuse
there is a growing feeling that these forms of deviance should be
criminalized and specialized staff recruited and trained to handle
such victims and rehabilitate their offenders.

Notes

1. Henry Maine, _Ancient Law_, Boston: Beacon Press, 1963, 153–154.

2. _Ibid._, 140.

3. Arthur Diamond, _The Evolution of Law and Order_, Westport, Connecticut: Greenwood Press, 1951, 148.

4. Morton Hunt, _The Natural History of Love_, New York: Alfred A. Knopf, 1959; G.R. Taylor, _Sex in History_, New York: Vanguard Press, 1954; Isabel Drummand, _The Sex Paradox_, New York: G.P. Putnam's Sons, 1953; Morris Ploscowe, _Sex and the Law_, New Jersey: Prentice-Hall, 1951.

5. 1 James I, c. 11.

6. Maine, _op. cit._

7. _Ibid._

8. Edmund Morgan, The Puritans and Sex, in Michael Gordon (ed.), _The American Family in Social-Historical Perspective_, New York: St. Martin's Press, 1973, 284–290.

9. _Ibid._, 289–291.

10. Lawrence Friedman, _A History of American Law_, New York: Simon and Schuster, 1973, 179–184.

11. Gerhard Mueller, Inquiry into the State of a Divorceless Society: Domestic Relations Law and Morals in England from 1660 to 1857, _University of Pittsburgh Law Review_, 18 (1957), 545.

12. Nelson Blake, _The Road to Reno: A History of Divorce in the United States_, 1962, 34–47.

13. _Ibid._, 50.

14. _Ibid._

15. Friedman, _op. cit._, 184–185.

16. _Ibid._, 185–186.

17. _Ibid._, 188–191; Robert Rich, _Juvenile Delinquency: A Paradigmatic Perspective_, Washington, DC: University Press of America. 1978, 221–222.

18. Robert Bell, *Social Deviance*, Homewood, Illinois: The Dorsey Press, 1971, 320.

19. *Ibid.*, 386–387.

20. Henry Black, *Black's Law Dictionary*, St. Paul, Minnesota: West Publishing Company, 1968, 71–72; The Dushkin Publishing Group, *Encyclopedia of Sociology*, Guilford, Connecticut: The Dushkin Publishing Group, 1974, 4.

21. Black, *op. cit.*, 206; Dushkin, *op. cit.*, 21.

22. Black, *op. cit.*, 25.

23. Dushkin, *op. cit.*, 37.

24. Henry Fairchild (ed.), *Dictionary of Sociology*, Paterson, New Jersey: Littlefield, Adams and Company, 1962, 39; Black, *op. cit.*, 533.

25. Black, *op. cit.*, 532–533; Dushkin, *op. cit.*, 77–78.

26. Black, *op. cit.*, 566; Dushkin, *op. cit.*, 83.

27. Fairchild, *op. cit.*, 149.

28. Black, *op. cit.*, 192–193.

29. *Ibid.*, 71, 904.

30. Black, *op. cit.*, 904; Fairchild, *op. cit.*, 150; Dushkin, *op. cit.*, 135.

31. *District of Columbia Code*, Annotated, Washington, DC: US Government Printing Office, 1973, 2, 22–301, 1345.

32. *Ibid.*, 22–601, 1368.

33. *Ibid.*, 22–901, 1374.

34. *Ibid.*, 22–902, 1375.

35. Martin Haskell and Lewis Yablonsky, *Criminology: Crime and Criminality*, Chicago: Rand McNally, 1978, 114.

36. D.C. Code, *op. cit.*, 22–1901, 1437.

37. Haskell and Yablonsky, *op. cit.*, 114–115.

38. Interview with Officer Selma Partner, Sex Offense Branch, Metropolitan Police Department of Washington, DC, 1978; Interview with Captain George Henry, Watch Commander, Youth Division, Metropolitan Police Department of Washington, DC, 1978; Interview with Dr. Veronica Maz, Battered Women Program, House of Ruth, Washington, DC, 1978.

39. Ibid.

40. Prevention of Child Abuse and Neglect Act, Washington, DC: Council of the District of Columbia, 1-22, 1977.

41. Uniform Crime Reports of the FBI, Crime in the United States-1976, Washington, DC: US Government Printing Office, 1977, 184.

42. Ibid.

43. Dushkin, op. cit., 4.

44. Bell, op. cit., 82-86; Dushkin, op. cit., 83; Morton Hunt, The World of the Formerly Married, New York: McGraw-Hill, 1966.

45. Haskell and Yablonsky, op. cit., 115; Interview with Dr. Maz, op. cit.; Interview with Cynthia Anderson, Coordinator, Office of Abused Persons, Department of Social Services, Montgomery County, Maryland, 1978.

46. Haskell and Yablonsky, op. cit., 114.

47. Henri Raffalli, The Battered Child: An Overview of a Medical, Legal, and Social Problem, Crime and Delinquency (April, 1970), 139-150; David Gill, Violence Against Children, Cambridge, Massachusetts: Harvard University Press, 1975; Joseph Goldstein et al., Beyond the Best Interests of the Child, New York: MacMillan, 1973; C.H. Kempe, Helping the Battered Child and His Family, Philadelphia: J.B. Lippincott, 1972; Leontine Young, Wednesday's Children, New York: McGraw-Hill, 1964; Vincent Fontana, Somewhere a Child is Crying, New York: MacMillan, 1973; E.R. Helfer, Child Abuse and Neglect, Washington, DC: Report to the Subcommittee of Children and Youth, Committee of Labor and Public Welfare, United States Senate, 1973; Claire Nissenbaum, A Child is Dead, Reaction (1972), Symposium on Child Abuse, Denver: The American Humane Association-Children's Division, 1972; W.T. Downs, The Meaning and Handling of Child Neglect - A Legal View, Child Welfare (March, 1963), 131-134.

48. Case studies based on officer reports of the Youth Division and Sex Offense Branch, Metropolitan Police Department (D.C.), 1978.

49. _Ibid._

50. _Ibid._

51. _Ibid._

52. Paul Gebhard and John Gagnon, Male Sex Offenders Against Very
    Young Children, American Journal of Psychiatry, 121 (1964),
    576–580; R.E.L. Masters, _Patterns of Incest_, New York: The
    Julian Press, 1963; S.K. Weinberg, _Incest Behavior_, New York:
    Citadel Press, 1955; Irving Kaufman et al., The Family
    Constellation and Overt Incestuous Relations Between Father
    and Daughter, _American Journal of Orthopsychiatry_, 24 (1954),
    266–277; Hector Cavallin, Incestuous Fathers: A Clinical
    Report, _American Journal of Psychiatry_, 122 (1966), 1132–1138;
    C. Bagley, Incest Behavior and Incest Taboo, _Social Problems_,
    16 (1969), 505–519.

53. Haskell and Yablonsky, _op. cit._, 349.

54. _Ibid._, 350.

55. J.H. Fitch, Men Convicted of Sex Offenses Against Children: A
    Follow-Up Study, _British Journal of Sociology_, 13 (1962), 18–37;
    Bagley, _op. cit._; Don Gibbons, _An Introduction to Criminology_,
    New Jersey: Prentice-Hall, 1973, 375–405.

56. Kenneth Eckhardt, Deviance, Visibility, and Legal Action: The
    Duty of Support, _Social Problems_, 15 (1968), 470–477.

IX

ABORTION

Legal History

The English Common Law says nothing about abortions until after the time of fetal "quickening" (i.e., fetal movement which usually occurs between the sixteenth and twentieth week of pregnancy). The ecclesiastical court also ignored the abortion issue. Thus both legal and illegal abortions were fairly commonplace in Great Britain for centuries.[1] In eighteenth century America, the colonial assemblies followed the English example and allowed the pregnant woman to terminate her pregnancy before quickening.[2]

Parliament in 1803 passed Lord Ellenborough's act which declared all abortions criminal except those performed to save the life of the prospective mother. The act specifically dealt with abortions performed by poisoning either before or after quickening. In practice very few persons were convicted of this crime which called for life imprisonment.[3] The United States followed the English example several years later when Connecticut passed an abortion statute in 1821 which was based on the English act of 1803. Most states still allowed abortions before quickening until the time of the Civil War although some states like New York passed abortion statutes that allowed abortion when necessary to save the mother's life (1828).[4]

It was not until 1938 that the 1803 English act was challenged in the famous case of Rex v. Bourne. This case set the tone for future abortions performed by a physician for the sake of saving the life of the prospective mother.[5] The Abortion Law Reform Association since 1952 lobbied parliament to introduce several abortion bills which all failed to be enacted. In the United States The Planned Parenthood Federation in 1955 drafted a model abortion statute.[6] The American Law Institute drafted a model abortion statute in 1962.[7]

The Abortion Act of 1967 passed by Parliament was quite liberal. The act provided for legal termination of pregnancy if two licensed physicians agreed that continuation of pregnancy would involve risk to the life of the prospective mother, or injury to her physical or mental health, or to any children in the family. Abortion was also permitted if there was great risk that the child would be physically or mentally abnormal if born. The act had no provision dealing with rape.[8]

123

124

Colorado and California both reformed their abortion statutes in 1967 which made them quite similar to the British Act of 1967. Colorado allowed abortions in the cases of rape and incest while California did not. The protection of the mental health of the woman was accepted as grounds for abortion in California. New York in 1970 allowed abortions for any reasons at all (i.e., abortion on demand).[9] Hawaii, Alaska, and Washington followed the New York example and approved liberal abortion statutes in 1970. Eleven other states also liberalized their abortion statutes to coincide with either the Colorado or California examples.[10]

In 1973 the United States Supreme Court ruled that abortion is legal in this country and that any woman has the right to have an abortion. In Roe v. Wade the Court held that the right to privacy is broad enough to encompass a woman's decision whether or not to terminate her pregnancy. The right of privacy is not absolute and a state can decide that at some point to regulate a pregnancy. The Court ruled that prior to the end of the first trimester of pregnancy the state may not interfere with or regulate an attending physician's decision reached in conjunction with his patient that a pregnancy should be terminated. After the first trimester and until the point when the fetus becomes viable the state may only regulate an abortion procedure to the extent that such regulation relates to the preservation and protection of maternal health. After the fetus is viable the state may prohibit abortions altogether except when necessary to preserve the life or health of the mother. Last the fetus is not included within the definition of person as used in the Fourteenth Amendment of the Constitution.[11]

In Doe v. Bolton (1973), the Court struck down requirements that abortion must be approved by a hospital committee and that two licensed doctors must confirm the attending physician's recommendation to abort.[12] Thus both 1973 decisions allowed abortion on demand and states did not need to keep an abortion statute.

In 1976, the Supreme Court ruled in Planned Parenthood of Missouri v. Danforth that Missouri's requirement of spousal consent was unconstitutional because it granted the husband the right to prevent unilaterally and for whatever reason, the effectuation of his wife's and her doctor's decision to terminate her pregnancy.[13] The Court also ruled the same year that a minor under the age of eighteen does not need her parents' consent to have an abortion. States may require written informed consent from the woman prior to abortion, but they may not prohibit use of the saline method of abortion after the first trimester of pregnancy.[14]

The Supreme Court in 1977 ruled that the Equal protection Clause of the Constitution does not require a state participating in the medicaid program to pay the expenses incident to nontherapeutic abortions for indigent women simply because it has made a

policy choice to pay expenses incident to childbirth. The
Connecticut regulation does not impinge upon the fundamental right
of privacy recognized in the Roe decision. An indigent woman
desiring an abortion is not disadvantaged by Connecticut's decision
to fund childbirth; she continues as before to be dependent on
private abortion services.[15]

A number of attempts to override the 1973 Supreme Court
decisions have been made in the United States Congress. These
pieces of legislation would be in the form of a constitutional
amendment. As of this date all attempts have failed (i.e., right-
to-life, states rights, fetus-as-persons, Burdick Amendment, Church
Amendment, Helms Amendment, and Hogan-Froelich Amendment).[16]

Legal Definitions

Black defines abortion as the unlawful destruction or bringing
forth of the fetus before the natural time of birth; causing or
procuring an abortion is the actual crime.[17] A criminal abortion
can take place only after the fetus is viable and the life of the
mother is not endangered. It is the illegal destruction of a
fetus by the use of drugs, instruments, or manupulation.[18]

Abortion Statutes and Enforcement Policy

Whoever by means of any instrument, medicine, drug, or other
means whatever, procures or produces, or attempts to procure or
produce an abortion or miscarriage on any woman, unless the same
were done as necessary for the preservation of the mother's life
or health and under the direction of a competent licensed physician,
shall be imprisoned not less than one year or not more than ten
years; or if the death of the mother results therefrom, the person
procuring or producing, or attempting to procure or produce the
abortion or miscarriage shall be guilty of second degree murder.[19]

Since the 1973 and 1976 Supreme Court Decisions the number of
arrests and prosecutions for illegally performed abortions has all
but ended in the District of Columbia.[20] Since the Supreme Court
decision allowing states not to elect to pay for nontherapeutic
abortions in 1977, there might be a return to the illegal abortions
and associated deaths among the lower class poor in society once
again. In New York City alone there were estimated to have been
50,000 illegal abortions annually before 1974 which resulted in the
deaths of twenty-five women annually.[21]

Thus the Supreme Court ruling of 1977 discriminates against
the poor who can least afford a legal, let alone an illegal abortion.
Since the poor cannot pay much they will have to seek out abortionists who are not skilled and utilize unsanitary instruments and

facilities. Thus the poor woman who cannot get funding for a
non-therapeutic abortion will either try to self-induce abortion
or be at the mercy of those offering illicit services under dangerous conditions. This situation might bring back a more disreputable
version of the abortion mill and/or ring as Schur described.[22]

A lengthy literature has been developed concerning the criminal
abortion and the problems of law enforcement.[23] First of all the
woman seeking an abortion must find an abortionist and poor women
have a harder time finding one since they lack the money to seek
out a legal nontherapeutic abortion at a licensed clinic or hospital.
The indigent female must resort to seeking out paramedical and
non-medical hospital staff such as practical nurses, orderlies,
and maintenance staff who have access to medical supplies and have
a little knowledge of medical practices but are not really able to
do any more for a desperate pregnant woman than she can do for
herself.[24]

The police today are not looking for the abortionist but come
across the abortion problem when a woman is found dead or dying
from a self-induced abortion or one performed by the "cheap"
abortionist. Thus the problem is one for the police homicide
squad rather than for a special detail assigned to discover and
break up abortion mills and rings as in the past when abortions
were illegal. There is apparently little police corruption concerning illegal abortion operations since a licensed doctor can
earn more than enough money performing legitimate abortions. Therefore the problem of obtaining evidence through undercover work,
presenting the case at trial, and trying to get a conviction are
relatively rare today. The current problem today is the proper
inspection of abortion clinics by public health authorities to see
that instruments, staff, and operating rooms meet proper health
standards and have proper licenses to perform abortions. This is
a task that the police do not perform. The local medical society
can suspend or revoke a doctor's license to practice medicine if he
or she performs improper abortions but it is almost impossible to
prove that a patient died due to deliberate criminal neglegence of
the physician (i.e., refer to the 1977 case of Dr. Sherman whose
patient died after an incomplete abortion was performed).[25]

Description of Specific Deviance

The majority of women who seek abortions are unmarried women
with teenagers accounting for an estimated forty percent of all
abortions. It is estimated that medicaid financed approximately
thirty percent of all abortions in the United States until 1978.
It is estimated that without medicaid support, poor women would seek
out abortionists who are not licensed or make the attempt themselves
with the result that up to 250 deaths would result and possibly
25,000 complications would occur requiring hospitalization at
public expense.[26]

The assumption can be safely made that most women who seek illegal nontherapeutic abortions today are from the lower classes and are probably urban nonwhites to a great extent (i.e., Blacks, Puerto Rican-Americans, and Mexican-Americans). Since most of these women are poor and not married, they are singled out by the state legislatures, United States Congress, and Supreme Court as socially deviant and penalized for their lack of information about birth control on the one hand and their high rate of illegitimate births with subsequent need for public welfare aid on the other hand. Even with public hospitals offering free nontherapeutic abortions, most poor women would be turned away due to lack of staff and space to perform all the abortions.

Women who have attempted self-induced abortions have used a variety of methods such as oral (i.e., chlorox, turpentine, quinine, tea, gin, and various pills), insertion (i.e., catheter into the uterus or knitting needles, coathangers, wire), and insertion of liquids into the uterus (i.e., chlorox, lye, turpentine, douche). Most of these attempts fail to produce an abortion and the chances for serious medical consequences are one thousand times greater than an abortion performed by a licensed doctor.[27]

Public opinion polls conducted from 1973 through 1976 consistently show that those polled (approximately 54 percent) are in favor of the continuation of legalized abortions in the United States. Three polls in particular broke down their samples by religion (i.e., National Data Program for the Social Sciences, Devries Poll, and National Opinion Research Survey). All three showed that Catholic-Americans were opposed to abortions for single women, poor women, and women not wanting more children. Protestant-Americans were more favorably inclined to grant abortions to these categories of women while Jewish-Americans were the most favorably inclined toward nontherapeutic abortions for all women.[28]

A number of organizations have been active in the abortion issue throughout the years. In 1931 a number of organizations came out in favor of birth control (i.e., Federal Council of the Churches of Christ, American Neurological Association, the Eugenics Society, and the Central Conference of Rabbis).[29] The Roman Catholic Church has opposed abortion since 1930 when Pope Pius XI spoke on Christian Marriage. The 1968 papal encyclical Of Human Life did not ease the controversy.[30] The American Medical Association approved of birth control in 1937.[31] At the present time almost all Protestant and Jewish leaders are in favor of therapeutic abortions and most also favor nontherapeutic abortions.[32]

At present there are a number of organizations organized for and against the continued legalization of abortions in America. The National Abortion Rights Action League, the Religious Coalition for

Abortion Rights, Planned Parenthood Federation of America, and Zero
Population Growth Inc. are in favor of legalized abortions while
the National Conference of Catholic Bishops, Committee for Pro-Life
Activities leads the opposition to abortion. Since 1972 the
Committee for Pro-Life Activities has sponsored a respect life
program (i.e., Respect Life Sunday in October of every year). On
January 22, 1976 approximately fifty thousand people marched in
Washington, DC to persuade Congress to pass a constitutional amendment forbidding abortion. In April and June of 1977 Pro-Life
rallies were also held in Washington to protest Congress' inaction
on the abortion issue. President Carter's opposition to federal
funds being used for nontherapeutic abortions has caused problems
for the abortion supporters for the poor since Congress appears to
be somewhat unsure about federal funding for all types of abortions
for the poor.[33]

Decriminalization

Since abortion is currently not a criminal issue, it does not
belong under the topic of victimless crimes. But the debate
continues in and out of the courts, state legislatures, and Congress
on the topic of abortion. Obviously some people feel very strongly
that abortion and for that matter birth control are forms of social
deviance that should be criminalized. This appears to be a
religious and ethical, not a criminal justice issue at this time in
our national history. The Roman Catholic Church along with some
fundamentalist Protestant and Orthodox Jewish leaders are opposed
to abortion and spearhead the controversy in the United States.[34]

The current debate is not concerned with the decriminalization
of abortion but the decriminalization of nontherapeutic and in some
cases even therapeutic abortions. The abortion issue is further
confused by opposition of these groups to the Equal Rights Amendment
for women, sex education in the public schools, and the availability
of contraceptive devices and information to all age groups at
commercial shopping centers and public health and welfare offices.[35]

The abortion debate should not center around whether abortions
should remain legal or not. The issue should be one of freedom of
access to all forms of family planning which comes through a
thorough understanding of the part sexual behavior plays in the
everyday life of the average person in society. Since it has been
shown that the family does not properly prepare the children of the
next generation in the area of sex education, then the church and
school should take over this public responsibility. If these two
institutions can not assume this responsibility, then only the
state can provide leadership. It is very inconsistent for the

United States government in its foreign policy to push programs of
birth control on other countries while denying a national policy
for our own population. It appears that only the military institution is concerned about sex education, birth control, and family
planning for its membership in our society.[36]

Our Constitution guarantees that every citizen has the right
to freedom of speech. Thus one is not proposing that there should
not be disagreements concerning ethical and religious issues in
society. But there is also the guarantee in this country of
separation of church and state and this means that no religious
group should be able to force any other group or person in society
to follow its particular dictates. The abortion issue is one where
the adherents of the church are attempting to interfere with the
rights of the citizen in a secular state. Let the individual
citizen decide for or against the practice of abortion in the
privacy of his or her home, not in the public courts or legislatures
where it constitutionally has no place in our society.

130
Notes

1. Gilbert Geis, Criminal Abortion, in Simon Dinitz et al., (eds.), Deviance: Studies in Definition, Management, and Treatment, New York: Oxford University Press, 1975, 320; David Granfield, The Abortion Decision, Garden City, New York: Doubleday, 1969, 73-76.

2. Robert Bell, Social Deviance, Homewood, Illinois: The Dorsey Press, 1971, 122; Granfield, op. cit.

3. Geis, op. cit., 320; Granfield, op. cit.

4. Bell, op. cit., 122; Geis, op. cit.; Granfield, op. cit.

5. Mary Calderone (ed.), Abortion in the United States, New York: Paul B. Hoeber, 1958, 193-194.

6. Edwin Schur, Crimes Without Victims: Deviant Behavior and Public Policy, New Jersey: Prentice-Hall, 1965, 57.

7. American Law Institute, Model Penal Code, Philadelphia: American Law Institute, 1962, 189-190.

8. Granfield, op. cit., 107; Geis, op. cit., 321.

9. Geis, op. cit., 316-319; Granfield, op. cit., 76, 112.

10. Geis, op. cit., 319-320.

11. Roe v. Wade, 410 U.S. 113 (1973).

12. Doe v. Bolton, 410 U.S. 179 (1973).

13. Planned Parenthood of Missouri v. Danforth, 428 U.S. 52, 70-71 (1976).

14. Bellotti v. Baird, 428 U.S. 132, 147 (1976).

15. Maher, Commissioner of Social Services of Connecticut v. Roe et al., 75-1440, June 20, 1977, Washington, DC: Supreme Court of the United States, I-II of Syllabus.

16. Susan Lowe, The Right to Choose: Facts On Abortion, Family Planning Perspectives, 7 (1975), 225.

17. Henry Black, Black's Law Dictionary, St. Paul, Minnesota: West Publishing Company, 1968, 20.

18. Henry Fairchild (ed.), Dictionary of Sociology, Paterson, New Jersey: Littlefield, Adams and Company, 1962, 1.

19. District of Columbia Code, Annotated, Washington, DC: US Government Printing Office, 1973, 2, 22-201, 1085.

20. Interview with Captain Joseph O'Brien, Homicide Squad, Metropolitan Police Department of Washington, DC, 1977.

21. J. Pakter et al., Impact of the Liberalized Abortion Law in New York City on Deaths Associated with Pregnancy: A Two-Year Experience, Bulletin of the New York Academy of Medicine, 49 (1973), 804.

22. Schur, op. cit., 31-34; Jerome Bates, The Abortion Mill: An Institutional Analysis, Journal of Criminal Law and Criminology, 45 (1954), 157-163; Jerome Bates and E. S. Zawadzski, Criminal Abortion: A Study in Medical Sociology, Springfield, Illinois: Charles C. Thomas, 1964.

23. Bell, op. cit., 139-143; Schur, op. cit., 31-38; Abraham Rongy, Abortion: Legal or Illegal, New York: Vanguard Press, 1933; Lucy Freeman, The Abortionist, New York: Doubleday and Company, 1962; National Committee on Mental Health, The Abortion Problem, Baltimore: Williams and Wilkins Company, 1944; Glanville Williams, The Sanctity of Life and the Criminal Law, New York: Alfred A. Knopf, 1957; Calderone, op. cit.; Zad Leavy and Jerome Kummer, Criminal Abortion: Human Hardships and Unyielding Law, Southern California Law Review, 35 (1962), 139-140; Russell Fisher, Criminal Abortion, Journal of Criminal Law and Criminology, 42 (1951), 246-250; Paul Gebhard et al., Pregnancy, Birth, and Abortion, New York: Paul B. Hoeber, 1958; Nancy Howell, The Search for an Abortionist, Chicago: University of Chicago Press, 1969; Roy Lucas, Federal Constitutional Limitations on the Enforcement and Administration of State Abortion Statutes, The North Carolina Law Review, (July, 1969), 730-778; Alice Rossi, Abortion Laws and Their Victims, Trans-Action, (September, 1966), 7-12.

24. Freeman, op. cit.; Howell, op. cit.

25. Ex-Abortionist is Probed By U.S. Attorney, Washington Post, October 26, 1977.

26. Lowe, op. cit.; Zero Population Growth, 15 Facts You Should Know About Abortion, Washington, DC: Zero Population Growth, Inc., 1976; Bell, op. cit., 132-139; Schur, op. cit., 45-51.

27. Polgar and Fried, op. cit., 126-127.

28. National Abortion Rights Action League, <u>Public Opinion Polls Since the Supreme Court Decisions of 1973</u>, Washington, DC: NARAL, 1976.

29. Norman St. John-Stevas, History and Legal Status of Birth Control, in Edwin Schur (ed.), <u>The Family and the Sexual Revolution</u>, Bloomington, Indiana: Indiana University Press, 1964, 377-378.

30. Bell, <u>op</u>. <u>cit</u>., 131.

31. St. John-Stevas, <u>op</u>. <u>cit</u>.

32. Bell, <u>op</u>. <u>cit</u>., 131.

33. <u>Washington Post</u>, September 29, 1977; <u>Washington Star</u>, October 18, 1977; <u>Washington Post</u>, September 28, 1977.

34. Schur, <u>op</u>. <u>cit</u>., 51-55; Bell, <u>op</u>. <u>cit</u>., 130-132; Harold Rosen (ed.), <u>Therapeutic Abortion</u>, New York: Julian Press, 1954, 153-165, 155-174; Williams, <u>op</u>. <u>cit</u>., 192-206; Joseph Fletcher, <u>Morals and Medicine</u>, Boston: Beacon Press, 1960; Norman St. John-Stevas, <u>Life, Death and the Law</u>, Bloomington, Indiana: Indiana University Press, 1962.

35. Daniel Callahan, <u>Abortion: Law, Choice and Morality</u>, New York: MacMillan, 1970; Thomas Diennes, <u>Law, Politics and Birth Control</u>, Urbana, Illinois: University of Illinois Press, 1972; Henry Rudel et al., <u>Birth Control, Contraception and Abortion</u>, New York: MacMillan, 1973; Betty Sarvis and Hyman Rodman, <u>The Abortion Controversy</u>, New York: Columbia University Press, 1973; St. John-Stevas, <u>Life, Death, and the Law</u>, <u>op</u>. <u>cit</u>.

36. <u>Ibid</u>.; Edwin Schur and Hugo Bedau, <u>Crimes Without Victims</u>, New Jersey: Prentice-Hall, 1975.

X

EUTHANASIA

Legal History

The first mention of mercy killing or euthanasia is an
article published in 1870 in England. The first appeal for legalizing the practice of euthanasia also occurred in England in 1901
when a bill was rejected by Parliament. Ohio in 1906 was the first
state where an attempt was made to legalize euthanasia but the
legislation never passed the state legislature. A second attempt
to get Parliament to enact euthanasia legislation failed in England
in 1931. In 1938 the Euthanasia Society of America was founded and
began the difficult task of lobbying legislatures and educating the
general public on this issue.[1]

The first court case involving a doctor took place in 1950
when he was tried for killing a terminally ill cancer patient. The
judge declared that the euthanasia issue had no place in the trial
but the jury acquitted the physician. Most cases of mercy killing
that go to court end with the jury either acquitting the defendant
or refusing to indict the offender.[2]

The New Jersey State Supreme Court in 1976 rendered a decision
that recognized the legality of passive, involuntary euthanasia for
a patient whose mental and physical health has irrevocably declined
to a level of vegetative existence. The Court noted that the state
has an interest to preserve life and allows the physician the
decision on how best to accomplish this end but there is a point in
time when the interest of the state must give way to the individual's
right to privacy. The Court based its ruling on Roe v. Wade (410
U.S. 113, 1973) which guarantees the right of privacy and in
certain instances protects a person's decision to terminate medical
care. The New Jersey Supreme Court refused to order the state to
terminate medical care for the terminally ill in this decision.[3]

The Court had to decide the issue whether passive euthanasia
constitutes criminal homicide. The Court rejected this view and
felt that death resulting from discontinuation of life support
systems constitutes expiration from natural causes, not homicide.
The Court set up guidelines by which a life support system of a
terminally ill patient could be withdrawn in order to protect the
rights of the patient and relieve the doctor of legal responsibili-
ties. First the doctor must state that there is no possibility that
the patient will recover. Second the doctor with concurrence of the
family or guardian must determine that the life support system be
stopped. Last a hospital board must agree that the attending
physician's decision to terminate life support is correct.[4]

As of this date there is still no legal basis for distinguishing euthanasia from homicide since the Quinlan case dealt specifically with the technical aspects of death.

Legal Definitions

Black defines euthanasia as the act or practice of painlessly
killing people suffering from incurable and distressing disease
(i.e., an easy or agreeable death).[5] The concept of euthanasia can
be divided into two categories: voluntary or non-voluntary (i.e.,
the former involving the consent of the person while the latter term
applies where the person is not capable of making a rational decision)
and active or passive (i.e., the former involves some positive act
of commission while the latter term involves an act of omission).[6]

An issue closely related to euthanasia is the legal definition
of death. Black defines death as the cessation of life or the total
stoppage of the circulation of the blood (i.e., natural death).[7]
Medical technology has advanced our definition of death beyond that
expressed by a legal authority like Black (i.e., an absence of
spontaneous respiration and cardiac function). There is currently
disagreement among medical, psychological, and sociological experts
as to what constitutes death (i.e., cellular, physiologic, intellectual, spiritual, and social).[8] This disagreement concerns certain
categories of people such as the terminally ill, the deformed, and
those suffering from permanent brain damage.

A new definition of death has been proposed by Harvard Medical
School and a number of states including Virginia and Maryland have
adopted this definition (i.e., six additional states have adopted
the Harvard definition and fifteen other states have legislation
pending). Brain death is defined as unreceptivity and unresponsive-
ness to external stimuli; no movement or breathing for one hour, or
three minutes on a respiratory machine; no reflexes; and a flat
electroencephalogram for a time period varying from ten minutes
to twenty-four hours.[9]

Statutes and Enforcement Policy

There are no criminal statutes dealing specifically with
euthanasia. There are only statutes dealing with homicide and
aiding or abetting a suicide.[10] A person who practices euthanasia
will most likely be charged with homicide or manslaughter if the
matter is brought to the attention of the police department.[11]
This is because the beneficial intention of the person practicing
euthanasia on another must be disregarded in a court of law since
the offender knows that his act can cause death of another and
malice aforethought is assumed since his intention is to cause the
death of another.[12]

The practice of euthanasia rarely comes to the attention of the police as performed by physicians although relatives or close friends may be exposed as practitioners if an autopsy is requested by the coroner's office as to cause of death. Only a small percentage of doctors are ever charged for practicing euthanasia by the public prosecutor although most friends or relatives are charged with murder or manslaughter. Very few juries will convict a physician or relative for a mercy killing. Those who are convicted are usually given suspended sentences by presiding judges.[13]

Description of Specific Deviance

Three groups of people have been identified with the euthanasia issue. People who are terminally ill with only a short time to live would obviously benefit from euthanasia. This category is the easiest to deal with since there is no hope that they will survive. Most are in great physical pain and a great number would like to end their suffering rather than be kept alive in such a horrible state. The second group of people who could benefit from euthanasia are persons considered defective or degenerate. This group includes those who are in a permanent unconscious vegetative state (i.e., through disease or accident), those who are severely retarded and unable to care for themselves, those who are hopelessly mentally ill, the senile, and those suffering from gross physical defects. There are difficulties in dealing with some members of this category on ethical and religious grounds. The third category of people who could benefit from euthanasia are infants and young children with gross physical or mental defects.[14]

Recent polls show that a sizeable minority of people are in favor of some form of legalized euthanasia.[15] This is in part due to the activities of numerous organizations, both secular and religious. The Roman Catholic Church issued a statement in 1957 concerning euthanasia. Both protestant and jewish groups have also taken a stand on the euthanasia issue, some positive and others opposed.[16] The Euthanasia Education Council was established in 1972 as part of the Euthanasia Society of America to educate citizens and lobby for legislation. As to date, eight states have enacted right-to-die laws (i.e., California, New Mexico, Idaho, Nevada, Oregon, Texas, Arkansas, and North Carolina). The statutes are basically the same with the person determining his or her future and no doctor or nurse having to take any action contrary to their personal beliefs. These statutes deal only with passive euthanasia. Currently Idaho, Montana, and Oregon are considering legislation making active euthanasia legal.[17]

The American Hospital Association in 1973 prepared a patient's bill of rights which allows the patient to receive that information

necessary to give informed consent and to refuse treatment to the
extent permitted by law. The concept of utilizing the hospice was
also brought over from England. Hospice care involves making a
dying patient comfortable, both physically and mentally with family
and friends away from hospital life support systems and the
impersonality of hospital rules and regulations.[18]

Decriminalization

Proponents of the euthanasia movement are asking for legislation, not seeking decriminalization. The right-to-die laws and the
use of the "living will" have enabled people to control their
destiny without creating problems for physicians and the hospitals
in which they are treated.[19] Many opponents to euthanasia are
misinformed about the topic and react emotionally without examining
the actual facts and looking at the state laws where euthanasia
is allowed (i.e., California Natural Death Act of 1977). Some of
the most valid arguments against euthanasia involve the fear of its
abuse concerning individuals other than the terminally ill. There
is also the basic religious arguments that taking another person's
life is immoral as well as illegal. Finally, physicians and other
medical personnel are not quite sure what their legal and moral
status and obligations are concerning euthanasia.[20]

The controversy over euthanasia will continue for as long as
medical technology keeps prolonging life. The basic question should
be whether life should be preserved at all costs if the patient is
technically dead or incapable of functioning normally or be allowed
to painlessly die with dignity. In a society that is concerned
with overpopulation, disappearing natural resources, and a deterio-
rating quality of life, the euthanasia issue should be carefully
examined before being rejected by any state legislature.

Notes

1. Glanville Williams, The Sanctity of Life and the Criminal Law,
    New York: Alfred A. Knopf, 1957; O.R. Russell, Freedom to
    Die: Moral and Legal Aspects of Euthanasia, New York: Human
    Sciences Press, 1975; Charles and Diane Triche, The Euthanasia
    Controversy: 1812-1974, Troy, New York: Whetson Publishing
    Company, 1975; Jerry Wilson, Death By Decision: The Medical,
    Moral and Legal Dilemmas of Euthanasia, Philadelphia:
    Westminister Press, 1975.

2. Russell, op. cit., 258-260.

3. Marvin Kohl, On Death, Dying, and the Karen Ann Quinlan Case,
    The Humanist, 16 (1976), 18-19; In Re Quinlan: Defining the
    Basis for Terminating Life Support under the Right of Privacy,
    Tulsa Law Journal, 12 (1976), 150-167; Congressional Research
    Service, Library of Congress, The Right to Die, HU-6251-c3
    (June 2, 1976), 16-20.

4. Ibid.

5. Henry Black, Black's Law Dictionary, St. Paul, Minnesota:
    West Publishing Company, 1968, 654; Henry Fairchild (ed.),
    Dictionary of Sociology, Paterson, New Jersey: Littlefield,
    Adams and Company, 1962, 109.

6. Russell, op. cit., 20-22.

7. Black, op. cit., 488.

8. Henry Beecher, Ethical Problems Created by the Hopelessly
    Unconscious Patient, The New England Journal of Medicine,
    284 (1971), 260; Orville Brim et al., (eds.), The Dying
    Patient, New York: Russell Sage Foundation, 1970.

9. Harvard Medical School Ad Hoc Committee to Examine the
    Definition of Death, A Definition of Irreversible Coma,
    Journal of the American Medical Association, 205 (1968),
    85-88; Wilson, op. cit.; Donald Culter (ed.), Updating Life
    and Death: Essays on Ethics and Medicine, Boston: Beacon
    Press, 1969; John Behnke and Sissela Bok, The Dilemma of
    Euthanasia, New York: Doubleday, 1975.

10. District of Columbia Code, Annotated, Washington, DC: US
    Government Printing Office, 1973, 2, 22-2401, 2402, 2403,
    2404, 2405, 1463-1488.

138

11. Interview with Captain Joseph O'Brien, Homicide Squad, Metropolitan Police Department of Washington, DC, 1977.

12. Eike-Henner Kluge, The Practice of Death, New Haven: Yale University Press, 1975; Marvin Kohl, The Morality of Killing, New York: Humanities Press, 1974.

13. Williams, op. cit.; Legal Aspects of Euthanasia, Albany Law Review, 36 (1972), 679-686; Right to Die, Houston Law Review, 7 (1970), 667-670; E.J. Gurney, Is There a Right to Die? - a Study of the Law of Euthanasia, Cumber-Sam Law Review, 3 (1972), 245-248; Right to Die, California Western Law Review, 10 (1974), 613-627; Morris Forkosch, Privacy, Human Dignity, Euthanasia - Are These Independent Constitutional Rights?, University of San Fernando Valley Law Review, 3 (1974), 1-20; Richard Delgado, Euthanasia Reconsidered - the Choice of Death as an Aspect of the Right of Privacy, Arizona Law Review, 17 (1975), 474-494; Daniel Maguire, Death: Legal and Illegal, Atlantic, 833 (1974), 72-77; David Meyers, the Legal Aspects of Medical Euthanasia, Bioscience, 23 (1973), 467-470; Joseph Sanders, Euthanasia: None Dare Call it Murder, The Journal of Criminal Law and Criminology, 60 (1969), 351-359.

14. Group for the Advancement of Psychiatry, The Right to Die: Decision and Decision Makers, Philadelphia: Group for the Advancement of Psychiatry, 1973; A.B. Downing (ed.) Euthanasia and the Right to Death, Los Angeles: Nash Publishing Company, 1969; Richard Trubo, An Act of Mercy: Euthanasia Today, Los Angeles: Nash Publishing Company, 1973; Robert Williams (ed.), To Live and to Die: When, Why and How, New York: Springer-Verlag, 1973; Melvin Grant, Dying and Dignity: The Meaning and Control of a Personal Death, Springfield, Illinois: Charles C. Thomas, 1974; Mary Mannes, Last Rights, New York: William Morrow and Company, 1974; Milton Heifetz, The Right to Die: A Neurosurgeon Speaks of Death with Candor, New York: G.P. Putnam's Sons, 1975; Marvin Kohl (ed.), Beneficient Euthanasia, Buffalo, New York: Promethus, 1975; Eric Cassell, Permission to Die, Bioscience, 23 (1973), 475-478; R.S. Duff and A.G. Campbell, Moral and Ethical Dilemmas in the Special Care Nursery, New England Journal of Medicine, 289 (1973), 890-894.

15. U.S. Senate Special Committee on Aging, Death With Dignity: an Inquiry into Related Public Issues, Hearings, 92nd Congress, 2nd Session, Washington, DC: US Government Printing Office, 1972.

16. Russell, op. cit., 200-214; Immanuel Jacobovits, Jewish
    Medical Ethics, New York: Bloch Publishing Company, 1959;
    Charles McFadden, Medical Ethics, Philadelphia: F.A. Davis,
    1967; American Friends Service Committee, Who Shall Live?
    Man's Control Over Birth and Death, New York: Hill and Wang,
    1970; Paul Ramsey, The Patient as Person: Explorations in
    Medical Ethics, New Haven: Yale University Press, 1970;
    Daniel Maguire, Death By Choice, New York: Doubleday, 1974.

17. Euthanasia News, 3 (1977), New York: Euthanasia Education
    Council, 1-5.

18. L.K.Altman, Doctor and Patient: Bill of Rights, a Break with
    old Paternalism, New York Times, January 1, 1973, 1; Sheila
    Kast, Hospice: A New Way to Combat Loneliness of a Loved
    One's Final Days of Life, Washington Star, November 28, 1977,
    B1-2.

19. Euthanasia News, op. cit., 2-4.

20. Russell, op. cit.; Jacobovits, op. cit.; McFadden, op. cit.;
    Ramsey, op. cit., Maguire, Williams, op. cit.

XI

GAMBLING

Legal History

The first recorded lottery in England was in 1569 during the time of Elizabeth I. A good part of the monies raised by the lottery was to go toward the construction and maintenance of public works. In 1612 James I gave his permission for the establishment of a lottery in the colony of Virginia. Lotteries were held in London in 1627, 1631, and 1689 in order to raise money for public works projects. Under William and Mary, the crown took charge of all lotteries.[1]

In colonial America in addition to the lottery established in Virginia, there were lotteries in Boston but some Quakers in Philadelphia were opposed to a lottery for Pennsylvania in 1699. In the eighteenth century, lotteries were used as a way to finance public works projects (i.e., road building, construction of bridges and canals, and the establishment of schools and colleges). Philadelphia in 1748 held a lottery in order to purchase cannon for the defense of the city. Connecticut held a lottery to make additions at Yale in 1750 Several other colleges like Harvard, Dartmouth, Brown, William and Mary, and Union benefitted from public lotteries during the eighteenth century in several colonies. The construction of Washington, DC was partially financed by lottery.[2]

By 1832 approximately 420 lotteries were drawn in eight states. The popularity of these lotteries lead to the organization of a lottery business run by the forerunners of organized crime. Some deviant operators of lotteries sold large blocks of tickets with no intention of holding a raffle and thus obscounded with the proceeds. Others would arrange for confederates to be the winners or would award inferior prizes than those advertised. Thus in response to the growing criminal influence in the lottery business, Pennsylvania and Massachusetts passed statutes prohibiting the sale of lottery tickets and the operation of lotteries in 1833. New York state followed with its prohibition against lotteries in 1834 and by 1840 most states had prohibitions against lotteries.[3]

While the majority of states enacted legislation banning lotteries by the time of the Civil War, Louisiana built its lottery into a large interstate project that brought in millions of dollars annually. The United States Congress in 1890 passed legislation that forbade the distribution of lottery machines and tickets through the mail. Finally in 1895 congressional statutes forbade interstate transportation of lottery tickets. This put an end to the Louisiana lottery.[4]

By the beginning of World War I, gambling had become a crime in the United States although more people than ever had an active interest in this form of social deviance. Gambling became the greatest source of revenue for organized crime. It controlled and expanded its interests from lotteries (i.e., numbers and bolita), off-track betting, bets on sports events, large dice games, to illegal casinos.[5]

The federal government began dealing with illegal gambling on a national basis in 1948 when Congress passed a statute prohibiting the operation of gambling ships off the coasts of the United States.[6] The Special Senate Committee to Investigate Organized Crime in Interstate Commerce headed by Senator Kefauver began hearings in 1950. It produced a number of statutes aimed at organized crime and in particular prohibited the interstate transportation of gambling devices. The series of statutes enacted were known as the Johnson Act.[7] During the 1950's the federal government tried to control the spread of gambling by creating statutes that allowed the Internal Revenue Service to monitor and tax betting through the use of excise and occupational stamp taxes.[8]

The United States Department of Justice in the early 1960's began seriously looking into the organized crime aspect of gambling. The federal government believed that illegal gambling provided much of the revenue for most organized crime operations. Congress passed three statutes which attacked interstate gambling facilities and prohibited the use of public communications facilities to transmit wagering information on an interstate basis.[9] In 1960 Parliament enacted the first of a series of laws legalizing gambling in Great Britain. The Omnibus Crime Control and Safe Streets Act passed by Congress in 1968 allowed the F.B.I. to use wiretapping in order to catch bookmakers.

The Organized Crime Control Act of 1970 expanded federal control over interstate gambling.[10] The Act defined a gambling business as one that involves five or more persons in the conducting, financing, directing, managing, or ownership doing a gross volume of two thousand dollars per day or which operates continuously over a thirty day period and which is in violation of the law of the state where it occurs. The Act also prohibits conspiracy to obstruct justice on the part of those involved in these operations.[11]

The federal lottery statutes were strengthened to restrict those operating lotteries from using postal, mass media, and interstate commerce facilities. The intent of these statutes was to protect the public from corrupt and fraudulent practices on an interstate level.[12]   In 1975 these statutes of the United States Code were not applied to the various states that had legislated legal lotteries into operation (i.e., New Hampshire established its lottery in 1964 followed by Delaware, Illinois, Maine, Connecticut, Maryland, Massachusetts, Michigan, New Jersey, New York, Ohio, Pennsylvania, and Rhode Island).[13]

Legal Definitions

Black defines gambling as the playing or gaming for money or other stakes (i.e., to stake money or other valuables on an uncertain event). Gambling not only involves chance but the hope of gaining more money than one originally wagered. A gambler is a person who practices games of chance with the expectation of earning a living from this activity. A gambling device is an apparatus that is used and employed in gambling so that one may win or lose money or other valuables in the process of utilizing the device.[14]   A gaming (i.e., gambling) house is any building, place, or room kept for the purpose of gambling. A gaming table is any table that could be used for playing any game of chance for money or valuables.[15]   A lottery is a chance for a prize for a price. A scheme whereby one person pays another money and becomes entitled to receive more money or nothing in return as some formula of chance may determine. A game of chance in which small sums of money are bet for the chance of obtaining a larger sum of money.[16] A Numbers game is a game of chance in which one person selects any number and makes a bet on that number and gives amount of bet and number to the runner who enters it on a pad, the player receiving a copy, and whereby winning number is determined each day by computation based upon prices paid on the horse races, stock market, etc. that are published in a newspaper, the holder of the winning number receiving approximately 500 times the amount of the bet.[17]

Statutes and Enforcement Policy

Any person keeping, setting up, or promoting, or being concerned as owner, agent, or clerk, or in any other manner, in managing, carrying on, promoting, or advertising, directly or indirectly, any policy lottery, policy shop, or any lottery, or shall sell or transfer any chance, right, or interest, tangible or intangible, in any policy lottery, or any lottery or shall sell or transfer any ticket, certificate, bill, token, or other device, purporting or intended to guarantee or assure to any person or entitle one to a chance of drawing or obtaining a prize to be drawn in any lottery, or in a game or device commonly known as policy lottery or policy or shall for himself or another person sell or transfer, or have in his possession for the purpose of sale or transfer, a chance or

ticket in or share of a ticket in any lottery or any such bill,
certificate, token, or other device, shall be fined for each said
offense not more than one thousand dollars or be imprisoned not
more than three years or both.[18]

Any person knowingly having in his possession or under his
control, any record, notation, receipt, ticket, certificate, bill,
slip, token, paper, or writing, current or not current used or to
be used in violating the other provisions dealing with gambling
will for each offense be fined not more than one thousand dollars
or be imprisoned not more than one year, or both.[19]

Any individual knowingly permitting on any premises under his
control, the sale of any chance or ticket in or share of a ticket
in any lottery or policy lottery, or shall knowingly permit any
lottery or policy lottery, or policy shop on such premises, shall
be fined not less than fifty dollars nor more than five hundred
dollars, or be imprisoned not more than one year, or both.[20]

Whoever shall set up or keep any gaming table, or any house,
vessel, or place, on land or water, for the purpose of gaming, or
gambling device commonly called A,B, C, faro bank, E), roulette,
equality, keno, thimbles, or little joker, or any kind of gaming
table or gambling device adapted, devised, and designed for the
purpose of playing any game of chance for money or property, or
shall induce, entice, and permit any individual to bet or play at
or upon any such gaming table or gambling device, or on the side of
or against the keeper thereof, shall be imprisoned for a term of
not more than five years.[21]

It shall be unlawful for any individual knowingly, as owner,
lessee, agent, employee, operator, occupant, or otherwise, to
maintain or aid or permit the maintaining of any gambling premises.
All moneys, vehicles, furnishings, fixtures, equipment, stock
(including without limitation, furnishings and fixtures adaptable
to nongambling uses, and equipment and stock for printing, recording,
computing, transporting, safekeeping, or communication) or other
things of value used or to be used in carrying on or conducting any
lottery, or the game or device commonly known as a policy lottery
or policy, contrary to the provisions of the statute; in setting
up or keeping any gaming table, bank, device contrary to the
provisions of this statute; in maintaining any gambling premises,
shall be subject to seizure by any member of the Metropolitan
Police Department for the jurisdiction, and any property seized
regardless of its value shall be proceeded against in the Courts
by libel action brought in the name of the jurisdiction by the
public attorney, and shall, unless good cause be shown to the
contrary, be forfeited to the jurisdiction, and shall be made
available for the use of any agency of the government or otherwise

disposed of as may, by order or by regulation. Whoever violates this statute shall be imprisoned not more than one year or fined not more than one thousand dollars, or both, unless the violation occurs after one has already been convicted of a previous violation of this statute, in which case he may be imprisoned for not more than five years, or fined not more than two thousand dollars, or both.[22]

Whoever shall deal, play, or practice, or be in any manner accessory to the dealing or practicing of the confidence game or swindle known as three-card monte, or of any such game, play, or practice, or any other confidence game, play, or practice, shall be punished by a fine not exceeding one thousand dollars and by imprisonment for not more than five years.[23]

It shall be unlawful for any individual, or association of people, to purchase, possess, own, or acquire any chance, right, or interest, tangible or intangible, in any policy lottery, or any lottery, or to make or place a bet or wager, accept a bet or wager, gamble or make books or pools on the result of any athletic contest (i.e., football, baseball, softball, basketball, hockey, polo, tennis, golf, wrestling, boxing, trotting, running of horses, running of dogs, or any other sporting or athletic event or contest). Any person or association found guilty shall be fined not more than one thousand dollars or imprisoned not more than one year, or both.[24]

Bucketing or bucket-shopping is the making of or offering to make any contract respecting the purchase or sale, either upon credit or upon margin, of any securities or commodities wherein both parties thereto intend, or such keeper intends, that such contract shall be, or may be, terminated, closed, or settled according to or upon the basis of the public market quotations of prices made on any board of trade or exchange upon which said securities or commodities are dealt in and without a bona fide purchase or sale of the same. Bucketing is also the making of or offering to make any contract respecting the purchase or sale, either upon credit or upon margin, of any securities or commodities, wherein both parties intend, or such keeper intends, that such contract shall be, or may be, deemed terminated, closed, or settled when such public market quotations of prices for the securities or commodities named in such contract shall reach a certain figure without a bona fide purchase or sale of the same. Finally bucketing is the making of or offering to make any contract respecting the purchase or sale, either upon credit or upon margin, of any securities or commodities wherein both parties do not intend, or such keeper does not intend, the actual or bona fide receipt or delivery of such securities or commodities, but do intend, or

such keeper does intend, a settlement of such contract based upon
the differences of such public market quotations of prices at
which said securities or commodities are or are asserted to be
bought and sold.[25]

The individual who makes or offers to make any contract or
who is the keeper of any bucket-shop shall upon conviction be
fined a sum not exceeding one thousand dollars or by imprisonment
for not more than one year. Any person convicted of a second
offense shall be imprisoned for not more than five years. The
continuing of the keeping of a bucket-shop by any person after the
first conviction shall be deemed a second offense. If a domestic
corporation shall be convicted of a second offense, it shall be
dissolved. If a foreign corporation shall be convicted of a
second offense, it shall be restrained from doing business in the
jurisdiction.[26]

Any individual who shall communicate, receive, exhibit, or
display in any manner any statement of quotations of prices of any
securities or commodities with the intent to make, or offer to
make, or to aid in making, or offering to make any contract
prohibited shall be fined not more than one thousand dollars or
imprisoned for not more than one year for the first offense.[27]

It is unlawful for one to pay or give, or agree to pay or
give, or to promise or offer, any valuable thing to any individual
with intent to influence such individual to lose or cause to be
lost, or to attempt to lose or cause to be lost, or to limit or
attempt to limit his or his team's margin of victory or score in
any professional or amateur athletic contest in which said individual is or may be a contestant or participant; or with intent to
influence such individual, in the case of any professional or
amateur athletic contest in connection with which such individual
(i.e., manager, coach, owner, second, jockey, trainer, handler,
groom, etc.) has or will have any duty or responsibility with
respect to a contestant, participant, or team who or which is
engaging or may engage therein, to cause or attempt to cause the
loss of such athletic contest by such contestant, participant, or
team; or the margin of victory or score of such contestant,
participant, or team to be limited; or with intent to influence
such individual, in the case of any professional or amateur
athletic contest in connection with which such individual is to be
or may be a referee, judge, umpire, linesman, starter, timekeeper,
or other similar official, to cause or attempt to cause the loss
of such athletic contest by any contestant, participant, or team
who or which is engaging or may engage therein; or the margin of
victory or score of any such contest, participant, or team to be
limited. Whoever violates this statute shall be punished by
imprisonment for not less than one year nor more than five years
and fined not more than ten thousand dollars.[28]

It shall be unlawful for any person to solicit or accept, or agree to accept, any valuable thing or a promise or offer of any valuable thing to influence such individual to lose or cause to be lost, or to attempt to lose or cause to be lost, or to limit or attempt to limit his or his team's margin of victory or score in, any professional or amateur athletic contest in which such individual is or may be a contestant or participant; or to influence such individual, in the case of any professional or amateur athletic contest in connection with which such individual (i.e., manager, coach, owner, second, jockey, trainer, handler, groom, etc.) has or will have any duty or responsibility with respect to a contestant, participant, or team who or which is engaging or may engage therein, to cause or attempt to cause the loss of such athletic contest by such contestant, participant, or team; or the margin of victory or score of such contestant, participant, or team to be limited; or to influence such individual, in the case of any professional or amateur athletic contest in connection with which such individual is to be or may be a referee, judge, umpire, linesman, starter, timekeeper, or other similar official, to cause or attempt to cause the loss of such athletic contest by any contestant, participant, or team who or which is engaging or may engage therein; or the margin of victory or score of any such contestant, participant, or team to be limited. Whoever violates any provision of this section of the statute will be imprisoned for not more than one year and by a fine of not more than five thousand dollars.[29]

Whoever is found in a gambling establishment or an establishment where intoxicating liquor is sold without a license or any narcotic drug is sold, administered, or dispensed without a license, if he knew that it was such an establishment and if he is unable to give a good account of his presence in said establishment shall be imprisoned for not more than one year or fined not more than five hundred dollars, or both.[30]

Most of the responsibility for enforcement of anti-gambling laws rests with the Metropolitan Police Department although the Federal Bureau of Investigation does enter the picture if a huge gambling operation is uncovered. Gambling enforcement has been a traditional source of serious problems to the police. Enforcement efforts have never had more than a minimal impact on illegal gambling because of public enthusiasm for the activity. Investigations of police corruption usually show that gambling is the prime source of this problem in police departments.[31]

The Gambling Branch of the Morals Division of the Metropolitan Police Department (District of Columbia) deals with all gambling law violations. Gambling squad officers serve a two year tour of duty. A large percentage of the investigations by the gambling squad is initiated as a result of unhappy bettors who have not been paid off when they have won the lottery. Many other gambling investigations are initiated based on information supplied by informants. There is a selective enforcement policy towards gambling activities by the gambling section as they would like to obtain evidence against those who organize gambling operations rather than arrest those who gamble so that gambling activities can be completely shut down.[32]

The broadness of the gambling statutes and the difficulty in obtaining evidence that stands up in court (i.e., paid informers and wire taps) have caused members of the criminal justice system to approach gambling in a predictable pattern. The members of the gambling section of the Metropolitan Police Department work with the Major Violators Branch of the United States Attorney's Office and the F.B.I. The common problem of gambling in an urban area with the generality of the statutes allows both the prosecutor and the defendant much lattitude in resolving the case. Most prosecutors allow the offender to plead guilty to lessor offenses in order to get a quick conviction. The gambler knows this and readily accepts the plea to a lessor charge since many of those arrested are repeat offenders (i.e., compulsive gamblers) and sometimes cooperate with the police in gaining information on especially corrupt gambling operations. The fact that the gambling statutes carry more severe punishment for repeat offenders does not stop gamblers since they know they will only be fined the minimum or have the original charge reduced by the prosecutor.[33]

Thus the criminal justice system really would like to arrest those in organized crime who setup and provide the money to initially operate the various types of gambling operations in a metropolitan area. But for the most part those constantly arrested are the average person who gambles. Therefore the public prosecutor allows the typical defendant to plead guilty to a lessor charge, judges usually impose fines or dismiss the charges rather than heavily fine or imprison offenders, and gambling continues to be a common problem in the jurisdiction.[34]

The District of Columbia has a conviction rate of approximately fifty-two percent for gambling violations although less than three percent of those convicted received jail sentences. Forty-eight percent of the cases were dismissed by the prosecutor or the judge. Thus police administrators feel that their use of manpower and financial resources are best used in attempting to make strong cases against organized crime figures involved in gambling operations or use their resources for other work than that of enforcement of gambling laws.[35]

Only one percent of those arrested for all crimes in 1976 were for gambling according to the F.B.I.[36] A sample of jurisdictions

148

in 1976 that showed the disposition of all cases indicates that
out of 6,259 arrests for gambling, seventy-five percent of those
arrested plead guilty to the offense charged, three percent plead
guilty to a lessor offense, nineteen percent were acquitted of the
charge or had their cases dismissed, and three percent were
referred to juvenile court.[37]

Description of Specific Deviance

According to the National Gambling Commission, more than
sixty percent of all adult Americans gamble, both legally and
illegally. It is estimated that at least thirty billion dollars
has been wagered in any given year during the 1970's with approximately one-third going to organized crime. At present thirty-three
states have some form of legalized gambling (i.e., Nevada and New
Jersey have legalized almost every form of gambling; paramutual
betting is legal in thirty-three states; bingo is legal in eleven
states; five states allow slot machines; poker is legal in Gardena,
California; and gambling type pinball machines is legal in
Illinois).[38]

It appears that most individuals gamble with friends. Approximately one in twenty individuals who gamble are of the compulsive
type. This type of person ultimately has problems with his or her
family or marriage, commits the crime of embezzlement, or gets
involved with loan sharks who represent organized crime. Despite
these forms of deviance attributed to gambling, most people
surveyed are in favor of some form of legalized gambling in their
state.[39]

Most gambling operations in metropolitan areas of the United
States have been established and are controlled by organized crime.
An elaborate hierarchy has been created where the customer places
his bet with the small operator who in turn turns over the money
collected and policy slips to runners who in turn deliver the
money and slips to district offices. Those at the district level
turn the money over to persons at the main office. The profits
that eventually go into other organized crime operations such as
loan sharking are passed from so many levels of the organization
that it is virtually impossible to trace those at the top who make
decisions as to where the illicit funds ultimately should be best
put to use. The telephone has been used widely for lottery and
sports betting. The gambling syndicate is structured in such a way
so as to prevent heavy losses (i.e., more money may be bet on a
number or sports event than an operator can pay off if the number
should win). To counteract this problem operators bet some of their
own money on that number or game. This "layoff" betting is performed through a network of local, regional, and national layoff
personnel who take bets from the street level of gambling
operations.[40]

Decriminalization

Those who favor the legalization of all forms of gambling state that most people are going to gamble anyway so one might as well decriminalize this form of supposed social deviance. Economically decriminalization of gambling is the only politically feasible way to raise new public revenue for municipal, county, state, and the federal governments. Currently only Nevada and New Jersey benefit from almost all forms of legalized gambling in terms of gained revenues. A gambling tax is not regressive and is voluntary since only those who gamble are taxed. Gambling does not compete with the business community as it actually attracts more potential business for an area that may be economically depressed.[41]

Decriminalization of gambling would aid in the destruction of secondary crimes associated with gambling. Loan sharking (i.e., lending money at usurious interest rates) which is operated by organized crime lends money to compulsive gamblers in order to pay their debts (i.e., interest rates may vary from one to one hundred-fifty percent per week depending on the circumstances of the loan and the characteristics of the person in debt). The loan shark makes an average of twenty percent per client and makes more money on the interest so usually encourages continued gambling as long as the gambler keeps up his payments on the debt. Associated with loan sharking is another type of secondary crime, extortion. This is the threat of force or use of brutal force if the gambling debt is not quickly paid. Thus the gambler is intimidated into promptly paying any interest rate charged, is afraid of going to the police, and does not protest very much about his treatment since the loan shark's customer may be severely beaten, members of his family threatened, or even be killed if he does not pay promptly and quietly.[42]

Thus legalization of gambling would deny organized crime its largest single source of revenue (i.e., gambling and loan sharking that goes with indebtedness due to gambling). Organized crime would then be denied the use of ready funds that are utilized for paying graft to police, politicians, and members of the business community. Further the criminal justice system has not been able to effectively prosecute members of organized crime involved in either gambling or loan sharking, let alone the average person who gambles since most individuals desire to gamble. The criminal justice system can best utilize its personnel and monitary resources elsewhere.[43]

There is no conclusive evidence that freedom to gamble legally will cause a great increase of compulsive gamblers. Gambling may be a positive social force that will allow people to escape the

tensions and frustrations of everyday life and is a legitimate
form of recreation. Thus it is highly improbable that the legalization of gambling will cause a breakdown of the family, work
ethic, and one's responsibility toward local government and the
community in general. Research has pointed out that gambling allows
the poor and minorities the opportunity to achieve success through
winning at gambling. The numbers game supposedly allows Blacks
the hope that if they win the "big one" they will be able to escape
the ghetto. Some research even points to the fact that gambling
provides members of the ghetto community with jobs that they would
not otherwise have.[44]

The National Gambling Commission concludes that the states
should have the primary responsibility for determining what forms
of gambling may be allowed. The federal government should prevent
interference by one state with the gambling policies of another.
Specifically the Commission states that winnings derived from legal
gambling should not be part of one's gross income but be part of
the taxpayer's responsibility to report all sources; that states
refrain from legalizing single-event sports wagering under the
present structure of federal taxation; that on-track takeout in
paramutual racing be reduced in order to increase revenues; that
racing commissioners be prohibited from holding financial interests
in racetracks within their jurisdictions and public disclosure of
all financial interests be made of all racing operations; that
states fully inform the public of the odds of winning in all types
of lotteries; that states legalize all forms of public gambling;
and that statutes dealing with gamblers who are associated with
organized crime and gambling establishments that are fronts for
organized crime be stringently enforced.[45]

Those who are opposed to the decriminalization of gambling
feel that the existing statutes should be thoroughly enforced and
corrupt police and public officials be severely punished. Legalization of gambling would lead to more crime since more people would
gamble. Easy access to gambling would produce more compulsive
gamblers and the family and community would suffer a breakdown of
moral ties and become anomic. The poor and minorities would be
hurt since they would not try to improve themselves socio-
economically but rely on winning it big through gambling. The
taxation of gambling would be regressive since the poor who can
least afford more taxes are the most frequent bettors. Legalized
gambling would increase law enforcement costs and also cause more
people to be forced on welfare since the breadwinner would gamble
away money that is for food and rent. Legalized gambling will not
create new jobs and will hurt the legitimate businesses in any
community in which it is located. Gambling revenues are unreliable
and each state would compete for the gambling population that would
ultimately force more federal regulation of state and local
community tax sources. Taxation of gambling is not a cure for
public fiscal problems.[46]

Notes

1. John Ashton, <u>A History of English Lotteries</u>, London: Leadenhall Press, 1893; John Ezell, <u>Fortune's Merry Wheel</u>, Cambridge, Massachusetts: Harvard University Press, 1960; Robert Herman (ed.), <u>Gambling</u>, New York: Harper and Row, 1967; Commission on the Review of the National Policy Toward Gambling, <u>Gambling in America</u>, Washington, D.C.: Government Printing Office, 1976.

2. <u>Ibid.</u>

3. <u>Ibid.</u>

4. Ezell, <u>op. cit.</u>, 13-14.

5. Herbert Marx, Gambling in America, <u>The Reference Shelf</u>, 23 (1952); Fred Cook, Gambling, Inc., <u>The Nation</u>, 191 (1960); Henry Chafitz, <u>Play the Devil</u>, New York: C.N. Potter Publishing Company, 1960; Gambling, <u>The Annals</u>, 269 (1950); The President's Commission on Law Enforcement and Administration of Justice, <u>Task Force Report: Organized Crime</u>, Washington, DC: US Government Printing Office, 1967, 2.

6. <u>United States Code</u>, title 18, section 1083.

7. <u>United States Code</u>, title 15, sections 1171-1177.

8. <u>United States Code</u>, title 26, sections 4401-4411.

9. <u>United States Code</u>, title 18, sections 1084, 1952, 1953.

10. Public Law 91-452, 84 Stat. 922, October 15, 1970.

11. <u>United States Code</u>, title 18, sections 1955, 1511.

12. <u>United States Code</u>, title 18, sections 1301-1304; 1307, 1953; title 39, section 3005.

13. <u>Gambling in America</u>, op. cit.; Congressional Research Service, Library of Congress, <u>Legalized Gambling in the United States: A Survey</u>, August 11, 1971, 1-3.

14. Henry Black, <u>Black's Law Dictionary</u>, St. Paul, Minnesota: West Publishing Company, 1968, 808.

15. <u>Ibid.</u>, 809.

16. <u>Ibid.</u>, 1097.

17. Ibid., 1218.

18. District of Columbia Code, Annotated, Washington, DC: US Government Printing Office, 1973, 2, 22-1501, 1407.

19. Ibid., 22-1502, 1411.

20. Ibid., 22-1503, 1415.

21. Ibid., 22-1504, 1415.

22. Ibid., 22-1505, 1416-1417.

23. Ibid., 22-1506, 1419

24. Ibid., 22-1508, 1419-1420.

25. Ibid., 22-1509, 1420-1421.

26. Ibid., 22-1510, 1421.

27. Ibid., 22-1511, 1421.

28. Ibid., 22-1513, 1422.

29. Ibid.

30. Ibid., 22-1515, 1423.

31. Lawrence Sherman (ed.), Police Corruption: A Sociological Perspective, Garden City, New York: Anchor Books, 1974; Gambling In America, op. cit.; Task Force Report, Organized Crime, op. cit., 2.

32. Interview with Inspector Charles Light, commander, morals division of Metropolitan Police Department of Washington, DC, 1977; interview with Lt. Richard Simmonds, commander, gambling section, M.P.D. (D.C.), 1977; interview with sergeant William Martin, gambling squad, M.P.D. (D.C.), 1977.

33. Ibid.

34. Ibid.; Donald Cressey, Theft of the Nation: The Structure and Operations of Organized Crime in America, New York: Harper and Row, 1969, 74-77, 267-268.

35. Ibid.; Cressey, op. cit., 283-287.

36. Uniform Crime Reports of the F.B.I., Crime in the United States-1976, Washington, DC: US Government Printing Office, 184.

37. Ibid., 217.

38. Gambling in America, op. cit.; Rufus King, Gambling and Organized Crime, Washington, DC: Public Affairs Press, 1969; Herbert Bloch, The Gambling Business: An American Paradox, Crime and Delinquency, 8 (1962), 355-364; Robert Pursley, Introduction to Criminal Justice, Encino, California: Glencoe Press, 1977, 99.

39. Bloch, op. cit.; Gambling in America, op. cit.; Ned Polsky, Hustlers, Beats, and Others, Garden City, New York: Anchor Books, 1969; Louis Lawrence, Bookmaking, The Annals, 269, (1950), 46-54; Herman, op. cit.; Cook, op. cit.; Irving Zola, Observations on Gambling in a Lower Class Setting, in Howard Becker (ed.), The Other Side, New York: Free Press, 1964, 247-260; George McCall, Symbiosis: The Case of Hoodoo and the Numbers Racket, in Becker, The Other Side, 51-66.

40. King, op. cit.; Cressey, op. cit.; Task Force Report: Organized Crime, op. cit.; Pursley, op. cit.; Marshall Clinard and Richard Quinney, Criminal Behavior Systems: A Typology, New York: Holt, Rinehart and Winston, 1973; 224-226, 239-241, 247; Herbert Bloch and Gilbert Geis, Man, Crime and Society, New York: Random House, 1970, 190-216; Combating Organized Crime, The Annals, 347 (1963); Estes Kefauver, Crime in America, Garden City, New York: Doubleday, 1951; Organized Crime, Crime and Delinquency, 8 (1962), 325-407; Gus Tylor (ed.), Organized Crime in America: A Book of Readings, Ann Arbor, Michigan: University of Michigan Press, 1962; Permanent Subcommittee on Investigations, Senate Committee on Government Operations, Gambling and Organized Crime, Senate Report number 1310, 87th Congress, 2nd Session, Washington, DC: US Government Printing Office, 1962.

41. Gambling in America, op. cit.

42. Task Force Report: Organized Crime, op. cit., 3; New York Commission of Investigation, The Loan Shark Report, 17 (1965); Pursley, op. cit., 100.

43. Ibid.

44. Task Force Report: Organized Crime, op. cit.; Zola, op. cit., 360; Thomas Johnson, Numbers Called Harlem's Balm, The New York Times, March 1, 1971; St. Clair Drake and Horace Clayton,

Black Metropolis: A Study of Negro Life in a Northern City,
New York: Harcourt Brace, 1945, 470-494; McCall, op. cit.;
William Furlong, Out of the Bleachers, Where the Action Is,
Harpers, 233 (1966), 49-53; Julian Roebuck, The Negro Numbers
Man as a Criminal Type: The Construction and Application of a
Typology, Journal of Criminal Law and Criminology, 54 (1963),
48-60.

45. Gambling in America, op. cit.

46. Pursley, op. cit., 100; Edwin Schur and Hugo Bedau, Victimless
Crimes: Two Sides of a Controversy, New Jersey: Prentice-Hall,
1974.

XII

ALCOHOLISM

Legal History

The English Common Law did not define an alcoholic as a criminal and his drunken behavior was tolerated in public or private as long as he did not breach the peace or become disorderly. The church had jurisdiction over the chronic alcoholic since his behavior showed a lack of moral character. In 1606, Parliament passed the Intoxication Act (I James) which made public intoxication a crime. Colonial America accepted drunkenness as criminal although most alcoholics were not really treated the same as other criminals.[1]

The first Congress of the United States was lobbied to impose prohibitive tariffs on the importation of alcoholic beverages into the country by members of the temperance movement which based their beliefs on puritan doctrines. By the 1830's there was an ideological war between the prohibitionists who wanted to stop the manufacture and sale of alcohol and the manufacturers and consumers of spirits. By the 1850's approximately forty percent of the states prohibited the manufacture and sale of alcohol but most of these laws were rescinded or modified by the 1860's. The Habitual Drunkards Act was passed by Parliament in 1879. It authorizes confinement in a retreat, upon the person's own application and admission that one is an habitual drunkard who cannot manage one's own affairs and is a danger to oneself and others in the community.[2] Another attempt at prohibiting the manufacture and sale of alcoholic beverages through legislation came during the 1880's when eight states enacted statutes that were prohibitionist in nature.[3]

After 1890, the prohibitionists (i.e., Women's party, the Woman's Christian Temperance Union, The National Temperance League of America, Prohibition Party, Anti-Saloon League and the International Order of Good Templars) attempted to get the state legislatures to pass statutes that curtailed the manufacture and sale of alcohol. These state laws failed to stop the sale of alcoholic beverages between states so the prohibitionists lobbied for congressional action. In 1913 Congress passed the Webb-Kenyon law that prevented the shipping of alcohol from "wet" states to "dry" jurisdictions. The Jones-Randall law was enacted in 1917 that made it a crime to use the United States mail to send liquor advertisements to people who lived in states that prohibited the manufacture and sale of alcohol. In 1917 Congress passed the Eighteenth Amendment to the Constitution which prohibited the manufacture, sale, and public consumption of alcohol. The Volstead Act passed by Congress in 1919 enforced the Amendment by defining what an intoxicating beverage was and forbade the wholesale manufacture, transportation, and sale of liquor but not the buying, using, or making of it for private use.[4]

155

By 1929 the problem of dealing with the Volstead Act made the federal government appoint a commission to study the problems of enforcement of the Act and the growing disrespect for the Eighteenth Amendment by both respectful members of the community and organized crime that provided the illicit alcohol. The Wickersham Commission reported in 1931 that there was a breakdown of federal enforcement of the liquor laws and an increase of crime and corruption on the state level concerning control of alcohol. In 1933 Congress repealed the Eighteenth Amendment and passed the Twenty-First Amendment which was adopted by the states in the same year. Thus control of liquor reverted to the states which could remain dry or become wet as each legislature decided.[5]

The campaign to change the legal status of alcoholics began in a series of test cases in the District of Columbia in 1964. Four test cases were dropped by the public prosecutor before the Easter case was heard in court.[6] The District of Columbia Court of Appeals in 1966 stated that a chronic alcoholic cannot be convicted of the crime of public drunkenness which should be handled as a public health problem. The Court stated that chronic alcoholism is a sickness and a good defense to a drunkenness charge since the defendant lacks the necessary criminal intent to be guilty of a crime and cannot be punished under the criminal law.[7] The District Court of Appeals ruled in the Driver case that the Eighth Amendment (i.e., rules against cruel and unusual punishment) applies to chronic alcoholics as they cannot be convicted of public drunkenness.[8]

Congress passed the Hagan Act (i.e., District of Columbia Alcoholic Rehabilitation Act) in 1967 which repealed the public intoxication statute and established a comprehensive detoxification system under the civil law. Hawaii became the first state in 1968 to abolish public drunkenness as a crime and replace it with civil statutes dealing with rehabilitation of the alcoholic.[9] The President's Commission on Law Enforcement and Administration of Justice Task Force Report on Drunkenness recommended alternatives to incarceration for alcoholics in 1967.[10]

The United States Supreme Court in 1968 upheld the Texas trial court conviction of Powell for the crime of public drunkenness but agreed with the decisions reached by the lower courts in the Easter and Driver cases. The Court concluded that they could not decide that alcoholism is a disease or not, that the defendant was not found guilty because he was an alcoholic but because he was drunk in public, that defendant's conviction did not violate his Eighth Amendment rights, that until rehabilitation centers are created - a jail sentence can be of some use in sobering the alcoholic, and indefinite civil commitment for treatment purposes

157

would be worse than a criminal sentencing, and that the Court does
not have the expertise to decide whether an alcoholic lacks the
necessary criminal intent to be guilty of a crime.[11]   The Supreme
Court's decision in Powell is somewhat confusing when compared to
the lower courts' findings in Easter and Driver.

     In 1966 the National Center for Prevention and Control of
Alcoholism was established in the National Institute of Mental
Health of H.E.W. to develop and deal with programs concerning the
use of alcohol in society. In 1968 Congress passed the Alcoholic
and Narcotic Addict Rehabilitation Act. Congress passed the
Comprehensive Alcohol Abuse and Alcoholism Prevention, Treatment,
and Rehabilitation Act and established the National Institute on
Alcohol Abuse and Alcoholism within NIMH in 1970.[12]

     The American Medical Association defined alcoholism as a form
of drug dependence and an illness in 1970.[13]   The American Bar
Association and the American Medical Association Joint Committee on
Alcoholism published a model act in 1971 that stated that the laws
against public drunkenness should be rescinded except where the
individual is disorderly. All alcoholics who were not disorderly
should be handled at civil detoxification centers.[14]   This was one
of the recommendations of the Task Force on Drunkenness of the
President's Commission of 1967. Also in 1971, the National Conference of Commissioners, representing the fifty state governments
adopted the Uniform Alcoholism and Intoxication Treatment Act that
recommended the decriminalization of public intoxication and the
civil treatment of alcoholics as ill people. The Department of
Health, Education, and Welfare of the federal government has been
working with the states to have them accept the noncriminal definition of the alcoholic and develop treatment programs.[15]   As of 1976
twenty-five states have adopted the Uniform Act and another twelve
states have adopted some of the basic provisions of the act while
three states had legislation pending.[16]

                        Legal Definitions

     Black defines a drunk as one who is so far under the influence
of alcohol that his judgment is impaired and his self-control is
lost. A drunkard is one who is always getting drunk.[17]   An
habitual drunkard is an individual who has a fixed habit of frequently getting drunk but has periods of being sober that may last
weeks at a time.[18]

     Alcoholism is the pathological effect of excessive indulgence
in alcoholic beverages.[19]   Drunkenness is the condition of an
individual whose mind is affected by the immediate use of alcoholic
beverages (i.e., the normal mental and physical condition of the
person is altered due to intoxication).[20]   Habitual drunkenness,
intoxication, or intemperance is the custom or habit of getting

drunk. These terms do not imply continuous drinking but
constitutes the normal routine for a person that interferes with
one's daily routine at home and work and is a source of problems
for both the individual and others dealing with him on a continuous
basis.[21]

Statutes and Enforcement Policy

At the present time half the states of the United States have
decriminalized public intoxication. Several other states have
adopted some form of comprehensive treatment legislation but have
not decriminalized all forms of public drunkenness.[22] The Uniform
Alcoholism and Intoxication Treatment Act states that it is the
policy of the state that alcoholics and intoxicated persons may not
be subjected to criminal prosecution of their consumption of alcoholic beverages, but should be given a series of treatments in order
that they may be able to lead as normal a life as possible so as to
be a productive member of the community.[23]

The Uniform Act requires that the states establish programs
for the treatment of alcoholics and those who are drunk. Intoxicated
individuals and drunkards should be assisted to their residences
or to treatment facilities by the police or emergency service
personnel (i.e., fire department or ambulance services) in protective
custody under civil law. Political subdivisions of each state (i.e.,
counties and municipalities) are prohibited from adopting any
statute making public drunkenness or any related behavior or condition with the exception of drunk driving a criminal offense or the
subject of any sanction of any kind.[24]

Last the Uniform Act suggests a treatment program that should
be part of the administrative procedure for the state to follow.
There should be emergency treatment provided in dealing with the
alcoholic or drunkard who is incapacitated and in need of immediate
care. There should also be inpatient treatment or institutionalized
care for those who need it. Treatment should be a combination of
out-patient as well as in-patient services. Last there should be
community follow-up services to attempt to reintegrate the former
alcoholic back into a normal life style.[25]

The statute dealing with the alcoholic in the District of
Columbia states that all public officials shall take cognizance of
the fact that public intoxication shall be handled as a public
health problem rather than as a criminal offense; that a chronic
alcoholic is a sick person who needs, is entitled to, and shall be
provided adequate medical, psychiatric, institutional, advisory,
and rehabilitative treatment services of the highest caliber for
his illness. The statute specifically provides that the intoxicated

person will be taken into protective custody by the police and either taken to his home or if in need of medical care or a danger to himself taken to the detoxification center in the District and be held for forty-eight hours for treatment.[26]

The D.C. Code states that a chronic alcoholic who is alleged to be unfit to manage or control his estate properly can be summoned before a court and jury and if found to be unfit to manage or control his estate, a fit person shall be appointed by the court to be committee of the person so declared unfit to manage or control his estate.[27] The committee shall control the estate of the alcoholic, both real and personal, and collect all debts owed and pay all debts in the name of said alcoholic. The committee shall apply part of the income of the estate to the maintenance of the alcoholic and his family.[28]

If an individual is found to be driving while under the influence of alcohol, he is liable for a fine of five hundred dollars, a sentence of up to six months in jail, or both, for the first offense. A second arrest for drunk driving can result in a fine up to one thousand dollars, a jail term of up to one year, or both.[29]

The National Institute on Alcohol Abuse and Alcoholism stated that for the year 1971, thirty-five thousand people were arrested for crimes against the person. Arrest reports show that sixty-four percent of all those arrested for homicide had been drinking, forty-one percent of those arrested for assault, thirty-four percent of all those arrested for forcible rape, and twenty-nine percent of those arrested for other sex crimes.[30] It is estimated that offenders processed through the criminal justice system who committed alcohol related violent crimes cost our society over five hundred million dollars annually (i.e., 308 million cost to the police, 43 million cost to the courts, 71 million to the jails, 76 million to the prisons, and 25 million to alcoholic rehabilitation programs).[31]

In states that have not accepted the Uniform Act in all its provisions or rejected the Act entirely, individuals are arrested for drunkenness, public intoxication, habitual or common drunkard, drinking in public, or drunk and disorderly. In states that have adopted the Uniform Act, police still arrest alcoholics but charge them with such offenses as vagrancy, loitering, driving while intoxicated (DWI), or disorderly conduct.[32]

In 1976, fourteen percent of those arrested by the police were for public drunkenness, eleven percent for driving under the influence, four percent for liquor law violations, seven percent for disorderly conduct, and one-half of one percent for vagrancy. It is impossible to deduce what percentage of those arrested for disorderly conduct and vagrancy were alcoholics.[33] A higher percentage of inner city residents were arrested for drunkenness (i.e., 14% to 10%), disorderly conduct (i.e., 8% to 7%), and vagrancy (i.e., .5% to .2%) than suburban residents. On the other hand a higher percentage of suburbanites were arrested for driving under the influence (i.e., 12% to 9%) and liquor law violations (5% to 4%).[34]

The disposition of those processed through the criminal justice systems of selected jurisdictions in 1976 was as follows: 85% of those arrested for drunkenness plead guilty to the original charge, .5% plead guilty to a lessor charge, 12% were acquitted or had their cases dismissed, and 2% were referred to juvenile court. Seventy-six percent of those arrested for driving under the influence plead guilty to the original charge, 13% plead guilty to a lessor offense, 10% were acquitted or had their cases dismissed, and 1% were referred to juvenile court. Sixty-eight percent of those arrested for liquor law violations plead guilty to the offense charged, 1% plead guilty to a lessor charge, 9% were acquitted or had their case dismissed, and 22% were referred to juvenile court. Seventy percent of those arrested for disorderly conduct accepted the original charge, 1% accepted a lessor charge, 20% were acquitted or had their cases dismissed, and 9% were referred to juvenile court. Sixty-one percent of those arrested for vagrancy plead guilty to the offense charged, 1% accepted a lessor charge, 30% were acquitted or had their cases dismissed, and 9% were referred to juvenile court.[35]

The police have a great deal of discretionary power when dealing with a person who is drunk. They can take the individual home, take him to a public detoxification center or hospital that has a unit dealing with alcoholics, or arrest the individual and take him to the municipal or county jail. Arrests for public intoxication vary from jurisdiction to jurisdiction depending on both the type of statutes and the policy of the police departments toward alcoholics. Police officers often arrest an individual on the basis of age, race, and social class as much as the circumstances under which the person is found to be drunk (i.e., skid row bum, college students at a bar or apartment party, minority group members drinking on the street in public, or an apparently affluent citizen who is making a fool of himself at a hotel function or family celebration like a wedding).[36]

An alcoholic who is placed in a municipal or county jail subsequent to arrest is usually placed in what is euphemistically called a drunk tank (i.e., a large holding cell that can accomodate many individuals). The typical drunk tank has no place to sit or lie down and is usually without proper sanitary facilities and ventilation. Thus a drunk who is not sick when he enters the cell usually becomes sick from the stench of others already ill. Since medical care is minimal or not available at all, many alcoholics are not properly screened for any complications resulting from their intoxication. Sometimes a drunk will die in the cell before anyone realizes he was critically ill. The drunk who can make bail is usually released after he sobers up and the forfeiture of the bail bond is accepted in lieu of a court appearance. This usually applies in cases where the alcoholic is middle class or has a steady job.[37]

Skid row types and other indigent alcoholics usually stay in the drunk tank until enough individuals are together to be taken before a magistrate for their hearing. Most often this is the next morning or at night court, especially on Friday and Saturday nights in major metropolitan areas. Criminal law procedure and Constitutional guarantees rarely apply in cases of drunkenness. Most offenders are rapidly processed and either fined and released or sentenced to short term stays in the jail. At any rate most alcoholics find themselves back on the street and if they are chronic sufferers with no job or money will usually be rearrested in a matter of hours or days (i.e., some chronic alcoholics spend much of their time being arrested and released, rearrested and re-released on an average of two or more times in a given week which adds up to possibly fifty arrests per year).[38]

Driving while intoxicated is a crime in all jurisdictions in the United States yet relatively few drivers are arrested and charged with this serious offense. Approximately 838,000 individuals were arrested for drunken driving in 1976.[39] This figure is only the tip of the iceberg since most individuals manage to avoid arrest or are allowed to plead guilty to lessor offenses in court. Approximately one half of the 50,000 highway deaths and 750,000 of those seriously injured in traffic accidents yearly are attributable to drunk driving and drunk drivers.[40] The costs of such motor vehicle accidents with resulting loss of life and property damage is estimated to be approximately five billion dollars in 1976.[41]

Most Americans feel that drunk drivers should be severely punished yet most offenders are usually not treated as criminals by members of the community. More suburbanites are arrested for drunk driving than inner city residents, more males than females, and more individuals over twenty-five years of age than under that age. It appears that those who are initially arrested for drunk driving usually repeat the offense within a relatively short period of time although they may not be apprehended the second time. A fatality caused by a drunk driver could result in a criminal charge of negligent manslaughter and a serious injury to another driver or a pedestrian could bring a five year sentence in prison as a felony conviction but most alcoholics that drive do not consider the consequences of their actions behind the wheel.[42]

Description of Specific Deviance

There are approximately ten million problem drinkers in the
United States today and the problem appears to be on the increase.
Thus alcoholism is the most serious drug problem in the country
with an estimated twenty-five billion dollars wasted in economic
loss due to this problem.[43] In 1976, over one million individuals
were arrested for drunkenness (93% male and 7% female). An
additional one and three quarters million people were also arrested
on alcohol related charges.[44] Thus close to three million individuals were dealt with by the criminal justice system.

Several studies and surveys show that individuals who have
trouble with the police and employers most frequently are those
living in metropolitan areas of the East, Midwest, and West; those
with either high school or higher education past the bachelor's
level; those with either low incomes or high incomes; and those
having unskilled jobs or professional/managerial positions. Those
least likely to have problems with the police and employers are
individuals with grade school educations, residents of rural areas,
those residing in the South, those with low incomes, and those
employed as unskilled workers.[45]

Most of the studies point to the fact that just about any
individual from a given subculture in our society (i.e., race,
ethnic, religious, regional, urban-rural, and social class) or
ascribed status group (i.e., age, sex, and marital status) can be
an alcoholic and have problems with the criminal justice system at
any given time.[46]

It appears that those who most frequently encounter trouble
with the police due to their drinking habits are those in the age
cohorts 18-21 and 40-49 while those having the least problem with
the law and drinking are over sixty-five years of age (i.e., the
latter typically drink in private).[47] More men than women are
problem alcoholics in general but more white males than Black
have difficulties with the police although more Black women than
white are problem drinkers.[48] Married individuals are less often
problem drinkers than unmarried, divorced, or widows/widowers.[49]
Protestants of unspecified denominations, Catholics, and those with
no religious affiliations are more prone to be problem drinkers
than Jews, Methodists, and Mormans.[50] The Irish-Americans appear
to have more problems concerning intoxication than other ethnic
groups while Italian-Americans have the least problems with
alcoholism.[51] Chinese-Americans appear to have the lowest rates
of public intoxication while Blacks and American Indians have the
highest rates of problems with alcohol.[52]

A special class of alcoholics has drawn the wrath of the
community and immediate attention and action by the police. This

class of drunkards is the skid row or skid road bum (male and female). They usually congregate in slum/transitional areas of the largest cities like the bowery area of New York, south State street area of Chicago, and other similar areas of Philadelphia, Los Angeles, San Francisco, etc. These "colorful" vagrants constitute less than ten percent of the chronic alcoholics of our population yet they account for more than sixty percent of the arrests (i.e., some arrested for public drunkenness that are skid row bums have been to court as many as twenty or more times in a given year in some jurisdictions).[53]

The typical skid row alcoholic is more a public nuisance than a criminal. He or she is typically an unemployed individual who has serious personal problems and uses drink as an escape from reality. Many of these individuals and the slum areas with the typical bars and flophouses are tourist attractions and part of our American heritage. Often the police leave the skid row individuals alone unless they cannot take care of themselves or are annoying the general public.[54]

Decriminalization

The criminal justice system has been a failure in its efforts to prevent and control alcoholics and public drunkenness. The President's Commission noted this fact in 1967 and it is even more true in 1978.[55] Public drunkenness and related crimes place an undue burden on the law enforcement system since the individual police officers make arbitrary decisions on the basis of the appearance of the drunk whether to arrest the individual, refer him to a social services organization, and take him home. Those who are most often arrested and booked are usually the skid row type whose Constitutional safeguards are often violated as they are the most familiar inhabitants of the municipal or county jail (i.e., officers have dealt with these recidivists so often that they take for granted that the drunk knows his rights and waives his phone call to a lawyer since he does not want one anyway).

The criminal courts are not any better concerning the processing of public drunkards. Since a defense attorney is rarely present, judges and magistrates take the opinion of the arresting officer that the defendant is intoxicated without applying the various medical tests to determine if in fact that the person is drunk (i.e., coordination, breath, or blood tests). Most court caseloads are overwhelmed with intoxication in public and related cases. Thus most judges are forced to dispose of these cases in bulk with as many as 25-50 alcoholics being dealt with at the same time. These cases represent a drain on the time and money of the court since most often the judge must deal with serious felony and misdemeanor situations. The arresting officer usually is the expert and complaining witness and must be off the street at a time when his services could be put to better utilization.[56]

The alcoholic who is sent to the municipal or county jail cannot be properly provided for and takes up space that should be utilized for those who are in need of incarceration. Often as many as half or more of the jail population is composed of those convicted of public drunkenness and related charges. The jail provides the public with the service of removing temporarily the skid row bum from the streets but all the personnel can do is dry him out, provide food, clothing, shelter, and the most limited sort of medical treatment.[57]

The President's Commission stated that public drunkenness should be decriminalized. They did not advocate decriminalization for alcohol related crimes like driving under the influence, liquor law violations, and crimes such as disorderly conduct and vagrancy.[58] Since the Commission's report, the American Medical Association has defined alcoholism as a sickness and other prestigious national organizations have lobbied for the decriminalization of public drunkenness (i.e., as noted elsewhere in this chapter). The Commission report did request the expansion of detoxification centers around the country as well as aftercare programs for patients who have successfully been "dried out".

The detoxification center in Washington, D.C. is federally funded and the police as well as social service personnel bring alcoholics to the center. The inhabitants of the center are dealt with physically and medically in order to dry them out (i.e., proper diet with vitamin supplements and medication are administered). Alcoholics Anonymous members are allowed to counsel inhabitants in addition to social work staff. Unfortunately once an alcoholic is deemed healthy, he cannot be held any further in the center and if he has committed a crime has to be returned to the custody of the police and processed through the criminal justice system.

A number of programs have been initiated to deal with aftercare services for the chronic alcoholic. The Salvation Army, Alcoholics Anonymous, public hospitals and their outpatient clinics, mental health associations, and psychologists and psychiatrists all deal with the problem drinker. Halfway houses have been utilized to deal with former alcoholics and are operated by a combination of professional staff and former alcoholics. The new resident is expected to get a job in order to pay for his room and board and take part in all facets of the rehabilitation process.[60]

A tremendous amount of work has been done by Alcoholics Anonymous to deal with former drunkards both within and outside of prisons, mental hospitals, and other total institutions. Alcoholics Anonymous has been utilized as an alternative and as a supplement to traditional approaches to treatment of alcoholics. This organization

deals with those convicted of public drunkenness, related crimes
such as driving under the influence, and felons and misdemeants
who admit that their crimes were related to their abuse of
alcohol.[61]

It appears that there is no active organized movement to retain
the public drunkenness statutes in the United States today. Many
who support the decriminalization of this minor offense also support
the continued enforcement of statutes related to alcoholism. A
major criticism of those convicted of these alcohol-related crimes
is the lack of consistency of the criminal justice system in dealing with offenders and the lack of success in rehabilitating them.
This is especially true in the cases of driving while intoxicated
where injuries and deaths result.[62]

166
Notes

1. Marshall Clinard, _Sociology of Deviant Behavior_, New York:
Holt, Rinehart and Winston, 1974, 428; President's Commission
on Law Enforcement and Administration of Justice, _Task Force
Report: Drunkenness_, Washington, DC: US Government Printing
Office, 1967; US Department of Health, Education, and Welfare,
First Special Report to the US Congress on Alcohol and Health,
Washington, DC: US Government Printing Office, 1972; Robert
Bell, _Social Deviance_, Homewood, Illinois: The Dorsey Press,
1971, 171; Alcoholism, Public Intoxication, and the Law,
Columbia Journal of Law and Social Problems, 2 (1966), 109–132;
Robert Merton and Robert Nisbet (eds.), _Contemporary Social
Problems_, New York: Harcourt, Brace and World, 1966; Paul
Horton and Gerald Leslie, _The Sociology of Social Problems_,
New Jersey: Prentice-Hall, 1974, 539.

2. 42, 43 Victoria, c. 19.

3. _Ibid._

4. James Timberlake, _Prohibition and the Progressive Movement_,
1900–1920, Cambridge, Massachusetts: Harvard University Press,
1970; _First Special Report to the US Congress on Alcohol and
Health_, _op. cit._; Merton and Nisbet, _op. cit._; Horton and
Leslie, _op. cit._; John Krout, _United States Since 1865_, New
York: Barnes and Noble, 1955, 182.

5. Krout, _op. cit._, 182–183.

6. _First Special Report to the US Congress on Alcohol and Health_,
op. cit., 85–86.

7. Easter v. District of Columbia, 361 F. 2d (D.C. Cir. 1966);
Clinard, _op. cit._, 485; Herbert Bloch and Gilbert Geis, _Man,
Crime, and Society_, New York: Random House, 1970; Robert
Pursley, _Introduction to Criminal Justice_, Encino, California:
Glencoe Press, 1977.

8. Driver v. Hinnant, 356 F. 2nd 761 (4th Cir. 1966); Bloch and
Geis, _op. cit._, 327–328; Pursley, _op. cit._, 105.

9. District of Columbia Register, _D.C. Rules and Regulations_,
Washington, DC: US Government Printing Office, 1971, title 3,
section 5.1, 16–17; Clinard, _op. cit._, 485.

10. _Task Force Report: Drunkenness_, _op. cit._

11. Powell v. Texas, 392 U.S. 514-516 (1968); Bloch and Geis, op. cit., 328; Pursley, op. cit., 105.

12. National Institute of Mental Health, National Institute on Alcohol Abuse and Alcoholism, Washington, DC: US Government Printing Office, 1971.

13. Horton and Leslie, op. cit., 541.

14. First Special Report to the US Congress on Alcohol and Health, op. cit., 92.

15. National Institute of Mental Health, Alcoholism and the Law, Washington, DC: US Government Printing Office, 1973, 14; Horton and Leslie, op. cit., 541.

16. Alcoholic Topics in Brief, Decriminalization of Public Intoxication- Is It Working? January 31, 1977.

17. Henry Black, Black's Law Dictionary, St. Paul, Minnesota: West Publishing Company, 1968, 587.

18. Ibid., 839.

19. Ibid., 93; Henry Fairchild (ed.), Dictionary of Sociology, Paterson, New Jersey: Littlefield, Adams and Company, 1962, 8.

20. Black, op. cit., 587.

21. Ibid., 839.

22. Alcoholic Topics in Brief, op. cit.

23. Alcoholism and the Law, op. cit., 14; First Special Report to the US Congress on Alcohol and Health, op. cit., 92-93; Department of Health, Education, and Welfare, The Legal Status of Intoxication and Alcoholism, Washington, DC: US Government Printing Office, 1976.

24. Ibid.

25. Ibid.

26. District of Columbia Register, op. cit.

27. District of Columbia Code, Annotated, Washington, DC: US Government Printing Office, 1973, 2, 21-1301, 1326.

28. Ibid., 21-1302, 1326.

29. Ibid., 11-501, 11-921.

30. National Institute on Alcohol Abuse and Alcoholism, Alcohol and Health, Washington, DC: US Government Printing Office, 1974, 42; R.E. Berry et al., Further Analysis of the Economic Costs of Alcohol Abuse and Alcoholism, National Institute on Alcohol Abuse and Alcoholism, Washington, DC: US Government Printing Office, 1977; Julian Roebuck and Ronald Johnson, The Negro Drinker and Assaulter as a Criminal Type, Crime and Delinquency, 3 (1962), 21-33; Marvin Wolfgang, Patterns in Criminal Homicide, Philadelphia: University of Pennsylvania Press, 1958, 166; Austin MacCormick, Correctional Views on Alcohol, Alcoholism, and Crime, Crime and Delinquency, 9 (1963), 24-25; Division of Alcoholic Rehabilitation, Criminal Offenders and Drinking Involvement, Sacramento, California: California State Department of Public Health, 1964; Lloyd Shupe, Alcohol and Crime, Journal of Criminal Law and Criminology, 44 (1954), 661-664; Paul Haberman and Michael Baden, Alcoholism and Violent Death, Quarterly Journal of Studies on Alcohol, 35 (1974), 221-231.

31. Ibid., 42.

32. First Special Report to the US Congress on Alcohol and Health, op. cit.; Department of Health, Education, and Welfare, Second Special Report to the US Congress on Alcohol and Health, Washington, DC: US Government Printing Office, 1975.

33. Uniform Crime Reports of the F.B.I., Crime In the United States-1976, Washington, DC: US Government Printing Office, 1977, 184.

34. Ibid., 192, 201.

35. Ibid., 217.

36. Task Force Report: Drunkenness, op. cit.; Frank Grad, Legal Aspects of Alcoholism, New York: Academic Press, 1973; Raymond Nimmer, The Public Drunk: Formalizing the Police Role as a Social Help Agency, The Georgetown Law Journal, 58 (1970); Nimmer, Two Million Unnecessary Arrests: Removing a Social Service Concern From the Criminal Justice System, Chicago: American Bar Foundation, 1971; Wayne LaFave, Arrest: The Decision to Take a Suspect into Custody, Boston: Little, Brown and Company, 1965, 108-110; John Murtagh, Arrests for Public Intoxication, Fordham Law Review, 35 (1967), 1-14; Melvin Selzer, Alcoholism and the Law, Michigan Law Review, 56 (1957), 237-248; Martin Haskell and Lewis Yablonsky, Criminology: Crime and Criminality, Chicago: Rand McNally, 1978, 337-338; Lloyd Shupe, op. cit.

37. Ibid.

38. David Pittman (ed.), Alcoholism, New York: Harper and Row, 1967; Pittman and Wayne Gordon, Revolving Door: A Story of the Chronic Police Case Inebriate, New York: Free Press, 1958; Earl Rubington, The Chronic Drunkenness Offender, The Annals, 315 (1958), 65-72; Task Force Report: Drunkenness, op. cit., 2, 9; James Spradley, You Owe Yourself a Drunk: An Ethnography of Urban Nomads, Boston: Little, Brown and Company, 1970; Spradley, The Moral Career of a Bum, Transaction, 7 (1970), 17-29; Nimmer, op. cit., 1-2; Keith Lovald and Holger Stub, The Revolving Door: Reactions of Chronic Drunkenness Offenders to Court Sanctions, Journal of Criminal Law and Criminology, 59 (1968), 525-530.

39. Uniform Crime Reports, op. cit., 184.

40. Seldon Bacon, Traffic Accidents Involving Alcohol in the USA: Second Stage Aspects of a Social Problem, Quarterly Journal of Studies on Alcohol, Supplement number 4 (1968); Wolf Middendorff, The Effectiveness of Punishment: Especially in Relation to Traffic Offenses, South Hackensack, New Jersey: Fred Rothman and Company, 1968; A. Dale (ed.), The Drinking Driver in Traffic Accidents, Bloomington, Indiana: Indiana University Press, 1964; Wolfgang Schmidt and Reginald Smart, Alcoholics, Drinking, and Traffic Accidents, Quarterly Journal of Studies on Alcohol, 20 (1959), 631-644; George Beitel, Probability of Arrest While Driving Under the Influence of Alcohol, Quarterly Journal of Studies on Alcohol, 36 (1975), 109-116; R.D. Yoder, Prearrest Behavior of Persons Convicted of Driving While Intoxicated, Quarterly Journal of Studies on Alcohol, 36 (1975), 117-125.

41. Berry et al., op. cit.

42. Bloch and Geis, op. cit., 332-335; Middendorff, op. cit., 20; Clinard, op. cit., 442-444; Merton Hyman, The Social Character-istics of Persons Arrested for Driving While Intoxicated, Quarterly Journal of Studies on Alcohol, 29 (1968), 138-177; Harvey Marshall and Ross Purdy, Hidden Deviance and the Labelling Approach: The Case for Drinking and Driving, Social Problems, 19 (1972), 541-553.

43. Second Report to the National Commission on Marihuana and Drug Abuse, Drug Use In America: Problem in Perspective, Washington, DC: US Government Printing Office, 1973, 143; Second Special Report to the US Congress on Alcohol and Health, op. cit., 49-59; Vera Efron et al., Statistics on Consumption of Alcohol and on Alcoholism, New Brunswick, New Jersey: Rutgers Center of Alcohol Studies, 1974.

44. Uniform Crime Reports, op. cit., 184.

45. Harold Mulford, Drinking and Deviant Behavior, USA, **Quarterly Journal of Studies on Alcohol**, 25 (1964), 634-650; Don Cahalan et al., **American Drinking Practices: A National Study of Drinking Behavior and Attitudes**, New Brunswick, New Jersey: Rutgers Center of Alcohol Studies, 1969; Margaret Bailey et al., The Epidemiology of Alcoholism in an Urban Residential Area, **Quarterly Journal of Studies on Alcohol**, 26 (1965), 19-40; Harrison Trice and Paul Roman, **Spirits and Demons at Work: Alcohol and Other Drugs on the Job**, Ithaca, New York: Industrial and Labor Relations Paperback, Cornell University Press, 1972; Thomas Plaut, **Alcohol Problems: A Report to the Nation by the Cooperative Commission on the Studies of Alcoholism**, New York: Oxford University Press, 1967; **Task Force Report: Drunkenness**, op. cit., Erich Goode, **Deviant Behavior: An Interactionist Approach**, New Jersey: Prentice-Hall, 1978; 284-286; Merton and Nisbet, op. cit., 189.

46. David Pittman and Charles Snyder (eds.), **Alcohol, Culture, and Drinking Patterns**, New York: John Wiley, 1962; Pittman, op. cit.; Harrison Trice, **Alcoholism in America**, New York: McGraw-Hill, 1966; Genevieve Knupfer and Robin Room, Age, Sex, and Social Class as Factors in Amount of Drinking in a Metropolitan Community, **Social Problems**, (Fall, 1964), 224-240.

47. Mulford, op. cit.; Nisbet and Merton, op. cit., 203-206; George Maddox (ed.), **The Domesticated Drug: Drinking Among Collegians**, New Haven: College and University Press, 1970; Peter Park, Dimensions of Drinking Among Male College Students, **Social Problems**, 14 (1967), 473-482; Kaye Fillmore, Drinking and Problem Drinking in Early Adulthood and Middle Age, **Quarterly Journal of Studies on Alcohol**, 35 (1974), 819-840; Muriel Sterne et al., Teen Agers, Drinking, and the Law: A Study of Arrest Trends for Alcohol Related Offenses, in Pittman (ed.), op. cit., 57.

48. Don Cahalan and Robin Room, **Problem Drinking Among American Men**, New Brunswick, New Jersey: Rutgers Center of Alcohol Studies, 1974; Mulford, op. cit.; Cahalan et al., op. cit.; Margaret Bailey et al., op. cit.

49. Ibid.

50. Charles Snyder, **Alcohol and the Jews**, New York: Free Press, 1958; Jerome Skolnick, Religious Affiliation and Drinking Behavior, **Quarterly Journal of Studies on Alcohol**, 19 (1958), 452-470; John Riley and Charles Marden, The Social Pattern of Alcoholic Drinking, **Quarterly Journal of Studies on Alcohol**, 8 (1947), 265-273; Robert Bales, Cultural Differences in Rates

of Alcoholism, Quarterly Journal of Studies on Alcohol, 6
(1946), 480-500; Genevieve Knupfer and Robin Room, Drinking
Patterns and Attitudes of Irish, Jewish, and White Protestant
American Men, Quarterly Journal of Studies on Alcohol, 28
(1967), 676-699; Charles Snyder, Culture and Jewish Sobriety:
the Ingroup-Outgroup Factor, in Pittman and Snyder (eds.),
op. cit., 188-225; D.D. Glad, Attitudes and Experiences
of American-Jewish and American-Irish Male Youth as Related
to Differences in Adult Rates of Inebriety, Quarterly Journal
of Studies on Alcohol, 8 (1947), 452.

51. Bales, op. cit.; Giorgio Lolli et al., Alcohol in Italian
Culture, New York: Free Press, 1958; William and Joan McCord,
Some Current Theories of Alcoholism: A Longitudinal Evaluation, Quarterly Journal of Studies on Alcohol, 20 (1959),
746; Knupfer and Room, op. cit.

52. George Chu, Drinking Patterns and Attitudes of Rooming-House
Chinese in San Francisco, Quarterly Journal of Studies on
Alcohol, (May, 1972), 58-68; Milton Barnett, Alcoholism in
the Cantonese of New York City: An Anthropological Study, in
Diethelm (ed.), Etiology of Chronic Alcoholism, Springfield,
Illinois: Charles C. Thomas, Publisher, 1955, 179-227;
Omer Stewart, Questions Regarding American Indian Criminality,
Human Organization, 23 (1964), 61-66; Edward Dozier, Problem
Drinking Among American Indians: The Role of Socio-Cultural
Deprivation, Quarterly Journal of Studies on Alcohol, 27
(1966), 72-87; Donald Weast, Patterns of Drinking Among
Indian Youth: The Significance of Anomia and Differential
Association, The Wisconsin Sociologist, 9 (1972), 12-28;
Muriel Sterne, Drinking Patterns and Alcoholism Among American
Negroes, in Pittman (ed.), op. cit., 74-98; Roebuck and
Johnson, op. cit., 21-23; Robert Strayer, A Study of the Negro
Alcoholic, Quarterly Journal of Studies on Alcohol, 22 (1961),
111-123.

53. The President's Commission on Law Enforcement and Administration of Justice, The Challenge of Crime in a Free Society,
Washington, DC: US Government Printing Office, 1967, 233-235.

54. Don Gibbons, Society, Crime, and Criminal Careers, New Jersey:
Prentice-Hall, 1973, 437-441; Spradley, op. cit.; Joan Jackson
and Ralph Conner, The Skid Row Alcoholic, Quarterly Journal
of Studies on Alcohol, 14 (1953), 468-486; Donald Bogue, Skid
Rows in American Cities, Chicago: Community and Family Study
Center of University of Chicago, 1963, 272-304; Earl Rubington,
The Bottle Gang, Quarterly Journal of Studies on Alcohol, 29
(1968), 943-955; Jacqueline Wiseman, Stations of the Lost:
The Treatment of Skid Row Alcoholics, New Jersey: Prentice-
Hall, 1970; Pittman and Gordon, op. cit., 16-93, 109-124;

Samuel Wallace, Skid Row as a Way of Life, Totowa, New
Jersey: Bedminster Press, 1965; Francis Feeney et al., The
Challenge of the Skid Row Alcoholic, Quarterly Journal of
Studies on Alcohol, 16 (1955), 647-667; Jack Peterson and
Milton Maxwell, The Skid Row Wino, Social Problems, 5 (1958),
308-316; Sara Harris, Skid Row, New York: Doubleday, 1956.

55. The Challenge of Crime in a Free Society, op. cit., 235.

56. Ibid.; Pursley, op. cit., 103.

57. Ibid.; Pursley, op. cit., 103.

58. Ibid., 235.

59. Pursley, op. cit., 105-106; Peter Kratcoski, Some Alternatives
    to Criminal Prosecution for the Victimless Crimes of
    Drunkenness Offenders, Journal of Alcohol and Drug Addiction,
    18 (Spring, 1973); Rupert Wilkinson, The Prevention of
    Drinking Problems: Alcohol Control and Cultural Influences,
    New York: Oxford University Press, 1970; Trice and Roman,
    op. cit.; Nimmer, Two Million Unnecessary Arrests, op. cit.

60. Ibid.; Clinard, op. cit., 485-486.

61. Harrison Trice, Alcoholics Anonymous, in Gold and Scarpitti
    (eds.), Combatting Social Problems: Techniques of Interven-
    tion, New York: Holt, Rinehart and Winston, 1967, 503-511;
    Joseph Cook and Gilbert Geis, Forum Anonymous: the Techniques
    of Alcoholics Anonymous Applied to Prison Therapy, Journal of
    Social Therapy, 3 (1957), 9-13; Harrison Trice and Paul Roman,
    Sociopsychological Predictions of Successful Affiliation with
    Alcoholics Anonymous, Social Psychiatry, 5 (1970), 51-59;
    Trice and Roman, Delabeling, Relabeling, and Alcoholics
    Anonymous, Social Problems, 17 (1970), 538; Clinard, op. cit.,
    486-492.

62. Pursley, op. cit.; The Challenge of Crime in a Free Society,
    op. cit.; Middendorff, op. cit.

XIII

DRUG ADDICTION

Legal History

The nonmedical use of opium was legal in England as well as the United States in the late eighteenth century and throughout the nineteenth century in both countries. Opium was legally imported as well as grown within the United States during this period. In fact opium was legally grown in America until almost mid-twentieth century.[1]

State Laws

San Francisco was the first municipality to pass an ordinance in 1875 prohibiting the smoking of opium in so-called opium dens. The penalty for violation of this statute was a fine, imprisonment, or both.[2] Virginia City, Nevada passed an ordinance in 1876 prohibiting the smoking of opium in smoking houses. This was followed by a tougher state law in Nevada in 1878.[3] Oklahoma was the first state to ban peyote in an 1899 statute but rescinded the law in 1908.[4] The period 1883-1914 in the United States shows a gradual increase in the number of statutes passed by state and municipal governments against opium smoking and other drugs (i.e., twenty-seven laws were passed). Several of these statutes also made it a crime to possess an opium pipe.[5]

Most states since 1914 adopted statutes in line with those of the federal government dealing with the possession, sale, and giving away of such drugs as morphine, heroin, and cocaine.[6] After the enforcement of the Volstead Act (i.e., prohibition) in 1920, marijuana slowly became a partial substitute for alcohol among many Americans.[7] In 1921 fourteen states had enacted legislation prohibiting cigarettes and bills to the same effect were under consideration in twenty-eight other state legislatures. But by 1927, all states had rescinded their anti-cigarette statutes except for the sale to minors.[8] In 1922, several states passed statutes providing the prosecution did not have to prove that the offender was in illegal possession of drugs since the burden of legality of possession of narcotics rested with the defendent. Some states made it a criminal offense to make an attempt to provide narcotics to a minor (i.e., the intent was an offense). Finally a number of jurisdictions made the buying, possessing, or selling of a hypodermic syringe or needle or other equipment without a prescription an offense.[9]

Louisiana in 1927 passed a statute providing a maximum penalty of five hundred dollars fine or six months jail term for possession or sale of marijuana. The penalties were later increased to thirty years at hard labor or even the death penalty for sale to youth

under twenty-one for the first offense.[10] Colorado passed a similar
statute against marijuana in 1929.[11] New Mexico outlawed peyote in
1929 but never enforced the statute and amended it in 1959 to permit
ritual use of the substance by the Native American Church of North
America.[12] By 1937 forty-six states and the District of Columbia
had laws against marijuana. The substance was often designated as
a narcotic and penalties were as severe as those applying to the
opiates and cocaine.[13] Since 1937 restrictive legislation on
marijuana increased in both quantity and severity (i.e., most state
statutes stated that penalties should be the same as for heroin).
Thus as penalties rose for law violations concerning the opiates,
they rose for law violations concerning marijuana. Nineteen states
made no distinction as to the quantity of marijuana or opiates sold
or in one's possession and giving away the substances was also a
crime.[14] Thus the various states between 1914 and the early 1950's
passed hundreds of statutes dealing with marijuana, opiates, and
cocaine. Maximum penalties were increased from five years in 1914
to ten years in 1922 to twenty, forty, or ninety-nine years by 1953.
Minimum sentences were increased over the decades and in most states
neither probation nor a suspended sentence were allowed.[15]

By the late 1940's states began passing laws against non-prescription barbiturates.[16] By 1962 some states followed the federal
example and passed statutes on the use of amphetamines for non-
medical purposes.[17] The same year legislation was initiated in some
states against glue-sniffing.[18] New York, California and several
other jurisdictions had provisions in the 1960's that made it
manditory for the incarceration not only of drug addicts but also
those who were in supposed danger of becoming addicts. This involuntary commitment of pre-addicts became known as civil committment as
initiated in California legislation in 1961 and followed by New York
statute in 1963.[19] During the period 1965-1969, several states
banned by statute LSD (i.e., New York, California, and Maryland).[20]
By 1977, eight states (California, Colorado, Alaska, Maine, Minnesota,
Ohio, Oregon, and South Dakota) passed laws reducing penalties for
marijuana possession. The California statute makes possession by an
individual of an ounce or less of marijuana a misdemeanor subject to
a traffic type citation and a fine of up to one hundred dollars.
Possession of more than an ounce or possession for sale are felony
offenses. Individuals under age eighteen can be arrested for
possession of any amount of marijuana.[21]

Federal Laws

The first federal legislation concerning narcotics was a
statute passed in 1887 by Congress that prohibited the importation
of a type of opium that was used for smoking. This statute also
prohibited the importation of opium by ethnic Chinese living in the
United States. Congress in 1890 limited the manufacture of opium

for smoking to American citizens.[22] The Pure Food and Drug Act of
1906 required that medicines containing opiates and certain other
drugs state the contents on their labels. The Act also stated that
the quantity of each drug must be truly noted on the label and
every drug must meet official standards of identity and purity.[23]
In 1909 Congress enacted a law prohibiting the importation of opium
except for medicinal purposes. Violation of the statute could bring
as long as a two year jail sentence.[24] The 1909 statute was amended
in 1914.[25] Congress passed another statute dealing with opium in
1914 which imposed a prohibitive tax on opium prepared for smoking
within the United States.[26]

The Harrison Narcotic Act of 1914 was the first major drug
legislation of the twentieth century in America. The Act provided
for the registration of, with collectors of internal revenue, and
to impose a special tax upon all persons who produce, import,
manufacture, compound, deal in, dispense, sell, distribute, or give
away opium or coca leaves, their salts, derivatives, or preparations
and for other purposes. The Act specifically applied to manufacturers, importers, pharmacists, and doctors who were licensed.
The license could be obtained at a moderate cost. Patent-medicine
manufacturers were exempted from both licensing and tax provisions
provided that their products did not contain more than a specified
amount of opium, morphine, cocaine, or heroin. The Act was quite
clear that doctors, dentists, and veterinarians could prescribe
these drugs if registered in the course of their professional
practice only. Punishment for violation of this Act was up to five
years imprisonment.[27]

The Jones-Miller Act of 1922 made importation of opiates and
other narcotics illegal. The Act also provided that the prosecution
need not prove that the defendant is in illegal possession of
narcotics as the burden of proof is on the defendant to prove that
his possession is legal. Whenever on trial for a violation of this
Act, if the offender is shown to have or to have had possession
of a narcotic drug, such possession shall be deemed sufficient
evidence to authorize conviction unless the defendant explains the
possession to the satisfaction of the jury. The punishment for
violation of this Act was up to a five thousand dollar fine and a
ten year prison term.[28]

Congress passed a statute in 1924 prohibiting the importation
of heroin even for medicinal use.[29] The Federal Bureau of Narcotics
established the Uniform Narcotic Drug Act of 1932 that was designed
to aid the states in creating uniform statutes and law enforcement
procedures and practices when dealing with narcotics.[30] The Federal
Bureau of Narcotics also lobbied the various states to enact legislation against marijuana. By 1937 forty-six states and the District

of Columbia had laws as severe as those enacted against morphine,
heroin, and cocaine although like the latter drug, marijuana was
not a narcotic.[31]

The Marijuana Tax Act of 1937 fully recognized the medicinal
use of the drug and specified that physicians, dentists, veterinarians, and other licensed persons could continue to prescribe
cannabis if they paid a license fee of one dollar per year, that
druggists who sold it should pay a license fee of fifteen dollars
per year, that growers should pay twenty-five dollars per year, and
that importers, manufacturers, and compounders should pay fifty
dollars per year. Only the nonmedicinal untaxed possession or sale
of marijuana was outlawed on the federal level.[32] The Federal
Bureau of Narcotics pressured the United States Pharmacopeia to
remove marijuana as an accepted drug in 1942 although it had been
listed since 1850.[33] The Opium Poppy Control Act of 1942 prohibited the growth of this poppy in the United States and its terri-
tories except under license.[34] By the late 1940's the Food and
Drug Administration and Federal Bureau of Narcotics began seizing
illicit supplies of nonprescription barbiturates and arresting
individuals selling and possessing them.[35]

The Boggs Amendment of 1951 was a response to the Kefauver
Committee on Crime of the United States Senate that examined the
link of organized crime to narcotics and marijuana. This congressional amendment attached mandatory minimum sentences to narcotic
violations with no suspended sentence or probation for repeaters.[36]
The Narcotics Control Act of 1956 made penalties for possession and
sale of narcotics and marijuana more severe and inflexible than the
Boggs Amendment, especially sales to juveniles.[37]

In 1962 the Food and Drug Administration began a crackdown on
legal sources of amphetamines.[38] By 1965 the Food and Drug Administration passed regulations concerning LSD and Congress passed a
law restricting the use of the drug for scientific purposes. The
National Institute of Mental Health controlled the distribution of
LSD for research.[39] The Community Mental Health Centers Act of
1963 provided federal aid for state and local treatment of mental
illness which included drug dependence cases.[40]

The Federal Drug Abuse Control Amendments of 1965 were made to
strengthen further the drug laws relating to amphetamines, barbiturates, and other drugs. It allowed the Food and Drug Administration to keep tabs on the manufacturers and wholesalers of these substances. The Amendment made it a crime to possess these substances
without a prescription and added severe penalties for sale of
these drugs to youth under age of 21.[41] The Narcotic Addict
Rehabilitation Act of 1966 allowed civil commitment of drug addict
in lieu of incarceration. The Act implied that a ninety day

manditory treatment could be imposed if the individual did not
volunteer for treatment.[42]   The Alcoholic and Narcotic Addict
Rehabilitation Amendment of 1968 provided special grants for treatment of addicts. The Federal Bureau of Prisons would provide
institutional and community aftercare for certain types of narcotic
offenders.[43]

The Comprehensive Drug Abuse Prevention and Control Act of
1970 removed the tax base of control and eliminated the Harrison
Act, the Opium Smoking Act, the Marijuana Tax Act, the Narcotics
Control Act, and other congressional acts dealing with drugs. The
Act defined categories (i.e., schedules) of drugs on the basis of
potential abuse and harm. Federal law took jurisdiction over all
scheduled drugs and enforcement authority resided in the Department
of Justice. Criminal penalties were generally reduced for all
opiates, cocaine, marijuana, and other "dangerous" substances.[44]
This Act simplified all the fifty-five previous federal drug laws
that were passed since 1914 to supplement the Harrison Act. The
year 1970 also was noted for an act of Congress allowing federal
agents under certain circumstances to enter the homes or apartments
of private citizens without knocking in order to secure evidence
against drug dealers, manufacturers, or addicts. Thus the Act of
1970 made conviction of drug abusers easier and "No-Knock" laws
made arrests easier.[45]

Federal Court Decisions

The Supreme Court ruled in the Webb case (1919) that a
prescription of drugs for an addict not in the course of professional
treatment in the attempted cure of the habit, but issued for the
purpose of providing the user of morphine sufficient to keep him
comfortable by maintaining his customary use was not a prescription
within the meaning of the law and was not included within the
exemption for the doctor-patient situation.[46]   In the Moy case
(1920), the Supreme Court ruled that possession of smuggled drugs
by an addict was a violation of the law. Thus physicians were
the only legal source of drugs but the Court ruled that a doctor
could not legitimately prescribe drugs to cater to the appetite
or satisfy the craving of one addicted to the use of the drug.[47]

In the Behrman decision (1922), the Supreme Court ruled that
narcotic drug prescriptions were illegal regardless of the purpose
the doctor may have had.[48]   The Supreme Court ruled in the Lindner
case (1925), that addiction is a disease and that a physician
acting in good faith and according to fair medical standards may
give an addict moderate amounts of drugs to relieve withdrawal
symptoms without necessarily violating the law.[49]

In the decisions reached by the federal courts in the 1930's
a number of conclusions can be reached (i.e., Strader, Anthony, and
Carey cases). First the courts have decided when a doctor acts in
good faith and have never defined what good faith is. Second a
doctor's determination that an addict needs treatment has not been
a good defense. Third reputable doctors have been constantly
convicted of violations of federal and state drug laws. Further
medical experts have also been silenced via convictions for their
treatment of addicts. Last the courts have rejected their own
statement that addiction is an illness, not social deviance.[50]

The Supreme Court ruled in Rochin (1952) that the police
cannot forcibly pump the contents of a drug peddler's stomach
because they suspect that he had swallowed drugs that have not been
taxed.[51] The federal courts ruled in the Blackford case (1957) that
a forcible search of a drug dealer's rectum is legal on the grounds
that probable cause existed for believing that drugs were concealed
there.[52] In the Sherman case (1958) the courts dealt with the problem of police entrapment in drug cases.[53] In the Robinson case (1962),
the Supreme Court ruled that imprisonment merely for being an addict
was prohibited by the Eighth Amendment to the Constitution. This
decision did not remove the stigma of criminality from drug addiction
since both purchase and possession of narcotics were still punishable
offenses. But the case set precedent for the concept of civil
commitment as an alternative to incarceration for drug addicts.[54]

Federal Agencies and Commissions

From the early 1900's until 1920, the Narcotics Division of the
Treasury Department dealt with enforcement of federal drug laws.
The Narcotics Division became part of the Bureau of Prohibition from
1920 until 1930. In 1931 the Bureau of Narcotics was set up in the
Treasury Department.[55] Although the Narcotics Division closed
down all privately run narcotic dispensing clinics by 1924, the
United States Public Health Service set up the first Public Health
Service Hospital in 1935 followed by a second in 1938.[56]

The various federal agencies of the Departments of Treasury and
Health, Education, and Welfare responsible for control of narcotics
were merged and transferred in 1968 to the Department of Justice as
the Bureau of Narcotics and Dangerous Drugs.[57] In 1971 the United
States Bureau of Prisons established a Drug Abuse Program in sixteen
federal prisons.[58] The same year a Special Action Office of Drug
Abuse Prevention was set up in the Executive Office of the President
to coordinate the fourteen federal agencies that were engaged in
research, prevention, training, treatment, education, and rehabilitation of drug addicts (SAODAP). In 1972 the Treatment and Alternatives
to Street Crime (TASC) became the primary federal mechanism for refer-
ral of pretrial and posttrial criminal offenders into community based
treatment programs financed by the federal government.[59]

The National Institute of Drug Abuse of the Alcohol, Drug
Abuse, and Mental Health Administration of the Public Health
Service of the U.S. Department of Health, Education, and Welfare
was established in 1972. This institute deals with non law enforcement aspects of drug addiction and abuse, prevention, control,
and treatment programs. The institute conducts research on drug
addiction and abuse, trains professional and paraprofessional
personnel at state and federal levels, and advises states, counties,
and municipalities on training and planning for drug addiction and
abuse prevention programs.[60]

The Drug Enforcement Administration of the Department of
Justice was established in 1973. The DEA is charged with national
and international control of narcotic and dangerous drugs. This
Administration has law enforcement as well as non law enforcement
programs to achieve its purpose. It regulates the legal trade in
narcotic and dangerous drugs; provides training for state, federal,
and foreign law enforcement personnel; and performs law enforcement
functions in coordination with state, other federal, and foreign
police department personnel dealing with criminals involved in all
aspects of the narcotic drug and dangerous substances trade.[61]

The Kefauver Committee (i.e., Senate Special Committee to
Investigate Organized Crime in Interstate Commerce) in 1951 turned
its attention to the topic of narcotics and marijuana. The
McClellan Subcommittee (i.e., Permanent Subcommittee on Investigations of the Senate Committee on Government Operations) during the
period 1963-1965 also dealt with investigating narcotics.[62] In 1962,
the White House Conference on Narcotic and Drug Abuse was held.[63]
The President's Advisory Commission on Narcotic and Drug Abuse was
established as an outcome of the White House Conference in 1963.[64]
The President's Commission on Law Enforcement and Administration of
Justice set up a task force on narcotic and drug abuse which issued
a report and series of recommendations in 1967.[65] The National
Commission on Marihuana and Drug Abuse was set up in 1971 and
ussued reports in 1972 and 1973 that were critical of both traditional law enforcement and correctional facilities.[66]

Non Governmental National Committees

The Joint Committee on Narcotic Drugs, American Bar Association
and American Medical Association (ABA-AMA) issued an interim report
in 1958 and a final report in 1959 which was critical of the
criminal justice system's way of handling drug addicts and abusers.[67]
The American Medical Association and the National Research Council
of the National Academy of Sciences (AMA-NRC) issued a report in
1963 dealing with the use of narcotics in medical practice.[68] The
first National Conference on Methadone Treatment was held in New
York City in 1968.[69]

British Laws and Commissions

The English Parliament in 1920 enacted the Dangerous Drugs Act.[70] The Rolleston Committee in 1924 recommended that physicians freely prescribe morphine and heroin for addicted patients The Committee after visiting the United States rejected the American model that was based on the crime control model (i.e., Harrison Narcotics Act of 1914).[71] The British Interdepartmental Committee of 1961 did not approve changes in the official policy toward drug addicts (i.e., no compulsory committal of addicts, no compulsory registration of addicts, no specialized treatment facilities for addicts). Thus the treatment of addicts remained on a voluntary basis utilizing a non criminal justice medical approach to the problem.[72] The Brain Committee of 1966 recommended the establishment of heroin dispensing clinics in place of physician prescriptions. This change of policy applied only in the case of heroin addicts as doctors could still prescribe morphine or methadone.[73] The clinics could prescribe all three drugs to addicts. The Dangerous Drugs Act of 1967 put the Brain Committee recommendations into operation.[74]

International Laws and Commissions

The Hague International Opium Convention of 1912 was held in an attempt to get all nations to pass statutes preventing and controlling the growth, processing, and sale of opiates to drug addicts.[75] The United Nations Commission on Narcotic and Drug Abuse was established in 1950 to gather statistics and provide advice on the international drug problem to member countries. In 1961 the United Nations Single Convention on Narcotic Drugs established international treaty obligations for all participating countries.[76]

Legal Definitions

A drug is defined by Black as any substance (i.e., animal, vegetable, or mineral) used as a medicine.[77] An addict is an individual who has acquired the habit of using alcohol or narcotics[78] to such an extent as to deprive oneself of reasonable self-control. Drug addiction is the voluntary regular use of a drug (i.e., morphine, opium, cocaine, and marijuana) which causes the person to become psychologically dependent on the substance.[79] Addiction is the psychological or physiological dependence of an individual on a drug which is manifested when the person becomes dysfunctional when the supply of the drug is abruptly terminated.[80]

The Expert Committee on Addiction-Producing Drugs of the World Health Organization differentiates between drug addiction and drug habituation. Drug addiction is a state of periodic or chronic intoxication produced by the repeated consumption of a drug. It includes an overpowering desire or need to continue taking the drug and to obtain it by any means; a tendency to increase the dose; both a psychological and physical dependence on the effects of the drug; and a detrimental effect on the person and on society. Drug habituation on the other hand is a condition resulting from the repeated consumption of a drug. It includes a desire but not a need to continue taking the drug for the sense of improved well-being which it produces; little or no tendency to increase the dose; some degree of psychological dependence on the effect of the drug, but absence of physical dependence and lack of withdrawal symptoms; and detrimental effects are primarily on the individual.[81]

The National Commission on Marihuana and Drug Abuse (1973) believe that the definitions proposed by the World Health Organization are confusing. The Commission proposes to use the term, drug dependence (i.e., actually a dependence continuum). Drug dependence involves most of our American population. The concept should be seen as a continuum starting from a low degree of dependence as measured by minimal individual preoccupation with drug-using behavior and minimal disruptive effects upon interruption of the behavior, and escalating to compulsive dependence as measured by total preoccupation with drug-using behavior and serious behavioral disruption attending deprivation of the drug. Drug dependence exists in many patterns and in all degrees of intensity depending upon the nature of the drug, the route of administration, the dose and frequency of administration, other pharmacological variables, the personality of the user, and the nature of the environment. There is no static model of drug dependence within which finite values are assigned to these various factors (i.e., drug dependence is a dynamic phenomenon).

The primary basis of dependence for all drug use is psychological reinforcement based on reward. Reward is composed of two elements (i.e., conscious and subconscious experiences of the individual and the psycho-social environment which shape the needs that produce drug-seeking behavior and result in drug experiences). When physical dependence is a part of chronic drug administration, the threat of adverse withdrawal symptoms serves as a powerful secondary reinforcement for continued drug-using behavior. Drug dependence is not necessarily harmful either to the person or to the community. The social cost of drug dependence is related directly to the intensity of user-preoccupation. The compulsive extreme of drug dependence could lead to disorders or defects of behavior with serious implications for the criminal justice system as well as medical and social service administrations. On the other hand, there are many forms of drug dependence that do not cause negative social consequences for the individual and the community (i.e., widespread chronic use of tobacco and coffee).[82]

The Commission attempts to clarify the confusion concerning the definitions of drug abuse by examining the history of the definitions. The Commission states that a drug can be defined in either a scientific or a social manner. The former definition leads to the concept of drug use while the latter definition leads to the concepts of drug abuse, narcotics (i.e., habit forming, opiates and cocaine), dangerous drugs (i.e., amphetamines, barbiturates, etc.), soft drugs (i.e., marijuana, LSD, etc.), and hard drugs (i.e., opiates, etc.).

The scientific definition of a drug is any substance other than food which by its chemical nature affects the structure or function of a human being.[83] Drug use must be understood in the cultural context of the society in which it occurs. Drugs have effects other than those which are sought (i.e., drug effects vary with amount and frequency of use, the characteristics of the user, and the environment in which they are used). Therefore different cultures have applied different value-attitudes to the presumed consequences of drug use (i.e., beneficial or harmful). Each society has determined which needs are legitimate concerning drug use (i.e., legitimate and valuable with tolerable risks involved). These judgments are based on the normative system concerning specific drugs, their effects, the reasons for using a particular drug, and the type of people who use the drug. Members of society do not continue to use drugs that do not fulfill some imagined or real need. People use drugs because they feel it is useful socially or psychologically despite the fact that the drug may have no real positive effect physically on the individual. Use of specific drugs may determine group membership or status within an institution or the total community. Drugs may function as symbolic representations of rebellion, alienation, independence, or sophistication within society. Drug use cannot be explained pharmacologically (i.e., classifying substances, listing effects, and counting users and non-users) but must be explained in terms of meaning and function to people in society.[84]

Thus drug use has been a common feature of all societies throughout the history of civilization. No society has successfully eliminated drug use altogether, although most have attempted to set limits, and modern societies have tried to contain specific groups that opposed all drug use among their own members (i.e., the Mormons and other fundamentalist religious sects). Drug use can be socially controlled when it is routinized, ritualized, and structured in ways which reduce to a minimum the occurrence of drug-induced behavior which society considers harmful to its members. This is easier to accomplish in traditional (i.e., gemeinschaft) rather than urban-industrial (i.e., gesellschaft) societies. In American society responsibility for control of drug use has passed from the family and church to the school, the mass media, and the

state. Thus formal, impersonal institutions have made the task of
social control of drug-taking behavior very difficult, especially
since the economy produces such a variety of drugs each and every
year. Therefore the criminal justice system in cooperation with
public legislative bodies has taken an increased role in trying to
contain undesirable drug use within supposedly tolerable cultural
limits.[85]

The social definition of a drug is anything but a socially
neutral concept. Thus one usually thinks of a drug as a social
problem or a substance that has been abused. Drug abuse is therefore synonymous with drug use. Drug abuse refers to any type of
drug without regard to its pharmacologic actions. The concept
creates the impression that all drug-using behavior is either good,
safe, beneficial, and without negative social consequences or is
bad, harmful, without benefit, and having negative social consequences.[86]

The term narcotic means a habit-forming substance such as the
opiates and cocaine. Many identify narcotics with deviant subcultures and conclude that any drug used by these types of individuals is a narcotic. The term has become a symbol of socially
disapproved use of drugs whether addicting or not.[87] The term
dangerous drugs evolved to define those substances (i.e., hallucinogens, barbiturates, and amphetamines) that were non-narcotic.[88]
Finally the terms hard and soft drugs were evolved to differentiate
between the opiates and cocaine (i.e., hard) and marijuana, hallucinogens, barbiturates, and the amphetamines.[89]

Statutes and Enforcement Policy

The District of Columbia Code consists of two sections dealing
with drug offenses, narcotic drugs (chapter 4) and drugs other than
narcotics (chapter 7). Narcotic drugs are defined as coca leaves,
opium, cannabis, isonipecaine, and opiate, and every substance not
chemically distinguishable from them, and any compound, manufacture,
salt, derivative, or preparation of coca leaves, opium, cannabis,
isonipecaine, or opiate, whether produced directly or indirectly
by extraction from substances of vegetable origin, or independently
by means of chemical synthesis, or by a combination of extraction
and chemical synthesis. Coca leaves includes cocaine and any
compound, manufacture, salt, derivative, mixture, or preparation
of coca leaves except derivatives of coca leaves that do not contain
cocaine, ecgonine, or substances from which cocaine or ecgonine may
be synthesized or made. Opium includes morphine, codeine, and
heroin and any compound, manufacture, salt, derivative, mixture, or
preparation of opium. Cannabis includes all parts of the plant
Cannabis sativa L., whether growing or not; the seeds thereof; the
resin extracted from any part of such plant; and every compound,

manufacture, salt, derivative, mixture, or preparation of such
plant, its seeds, or resin, including specifically the drugs
known as American hemp, marijuana, Indian hemp or hasheesh, as
used in cigarettes, or in any other articles, compounds, mixtures,
preparations, or products whatsoever, but shall not include the
mature stalks of such plants; fiber produced from such stalks; oil
or cake made from the seeds of such plant; any compound, manufacture, salt, derivative, mixture, or preparation of such mature
stalks (except the resin extracted therefrom); fiber, oil, or cake;
or the sterilized seed of such plant which is incapable of germina-
tion.[90]

It shall be unlawful for any person to manufacture, possess,
have under his control, sell, prescribe, administer, dispense, or
compound any narcotic drug except as authorized. Arrests without
warrant and searches of the person and seizures pursuant thereto
may be made for a violation by police officers upon probable cause
that the person arrested is violating such statute at the time of
arrest.[91]

A narcotic drug user is any person who takes or otherwise uses
narcotic drugs, except a person using such narcotic drug as a result
of sickness or accident or injury, and to whom such narcotic drugs
are being furnished, prescribed, or administered in good faith by
a duly licensed physician in the course of his professional practice.
A vagrant shall mean any person who is a narcotic drug user or who
has been convicted of a narcotic offense and who has no lawful
employment or visible means of support; is found in any place, abode,
house, shed, dwelling, building, structure, vehicle, boat in which
any illicit narcotic drugs are kept, found, used, or dispensed; or
wanders about in public places either alone or in the company with
a narcotic drug user or convicted narcotic law violator.[92]

Any police officer with probable cause can arrest such vagrant
and submit him to be examined by a physician to determine whether
there is evidence of narcotic drug usage. Upon affirmative determination that the person is a narcotic drug user, or if the person
has been convicted of a narcotic offense in D.C. or elsewhere, and
if such person is also a vagrant, he shall be arraigned and prosecuted under this statute. Any person found guilty shall be fined
not more than five hundred dollars or jailed for more than a year,
or both. The court in sentencing may in its own discretion impose
conditions upon the offender which can include medical and mental
examinations and treatment by proper public health and welfare
authorities and confinement in a suitable institution.[93]

All narcotic drugs which are not in lawful possession and come
into possession of a police officer shall be either disposed of
according to regulation or turned over as evidence in any criminal

proceeding.[94] No person shall obtain or attempt to obtain a
narcotic drug, or procure or attempt to procure the administration
of a narcotic drug by fraud, deceit, misrepresentation, or subter-
fuge; by the forgery or alteration of a prescription or of any
written order; or by the concealment of a material fact; or by the
use of a false name or the giving of a false address. Information
communicated to a physician in an effort unlawfully to procure a
narcotic drug, or unlawfully to procure the administration of any
such drug shall not be deemed a privileged communication. No
person shall wilfully make a false statement in any prescription,
order, report, or record required by law. No person shall for the
purpose of obtaining a narcotic drug falsely assume title of, or
represent himself to be a manufacturer, wholesaler, pharmacist,
physician, dentist, veterinarian, or other authorized person. No
person shall make or utter any false or forged prescription or
false or forged written order. No person shall affix any false or
forged label to a package or receptacle containing narcotic drugs.[95]

A person violating any statute or regulation for which no
specific penalty is otherwise provided shall be fined not less than
one hundred dollars nor more than one thousand dollars or imprisoned
for not more than one year, or both. A person convicted of an
offense who shall have previously been convicted of such offense or
who shall have previously been convicted either in D.C. or elsewhere of a violation of the laws of the United States or of a state
or subdivision thereof which would have been a violation of this
statute shall be fined not less than five hundred dollars nor more
than five thousand dollars, or imprisoned for not more than ten
years, or both.[96]

The term dangerous drug means amphetamine, desoxyephedrine, or
compounds or mixtures thereof, including all derivatives of
phenolethylamine or any of the salts thereof which have a stimulating
effect on the central nervous system, except preparations intended
for use in the nose and unfit for internal use; barbituric acid,
also known as malonylurea, and its salts and derivatives, and
compounds, preparations, and mixtures thereof; other drugs or
compounds, preparations, or mixtures thereof which are habit-
forming, excessively stimulating, or to have a dangerously toxic,
or hypnotic or somnifacient effect on the body of a human or animal.
The term dangerous drug shall not include any drug the manufacture
or delivery of which is regulated by federal narcotic drug laws or
by the narcotic drug laws of D.C.[97]

The following acts, the failure to act as hereinafter set forth,
and the causing of any such act or failure are unlawful: The delivery of any dangerous drug unless such dangerous drug is delivered
by a pharmacist upon a prescription and there is affixed to the
immediate container of such or in which such drug is delivered a

label bearing the name and address of the owner of the establishment
from which such drug was delivered; the date on which the prescription for such drug was filled; the number of such prescription as
filed in the prescription files of the pharmacist who filled such
prescription; the name of the practitioner who prescribed such drug;
the name and address of the patient; and directions for the use of
the drug as contained in the prescription; or such dangerous drug is
delivered to a practitioner by a pharmacist for this professional
to use in his practice; in which case the pharmacist may deliver the
drug without affixing any additional label to the original package
of such drug and must immediately record such sale and delivery by
filing a suitable record of such sale and delivery in the prescription file as maintained for prescriptions for such drugs; or[98]

Such dangerous drug is delivered by a manufacturer's represen-
tative or drug salesman to a practitioner in the course of calling
upon the practitioner; in which case the manufacturer's representa-
tive or drug salesman shall immediately record in a suitable record
book the name and quantity of the drug delivered, the date such
drug was delivered, and the name and address of the practitioner
to whom the drug was delivered; or such dangerous drug is delivered
by a practitioner in the course of his practice and the immediate
container in which such drug is delivered bears a label on which
appears the directions for use of such drug, the name and address
of such practitioner, and the name and address of the patient.[99]

The refilling of any prescription for a dangerous drug except
as designated on the prescription or by the consent of the practitioner. The delivery of a dangerous drug upon prescription unless
the pharmacist who filled such prescription files and retains it as
required. The possession of a dangerous drug by any person, unless
such person obtained such drug on the prescription of a practitioner, or in accordance with this statute. The making or uttering
by any person of any false or forged prescription or false or forged
written order for the purpose of obtaining any dangerous drug. The
delivery of any dangerous drug to any person not lawfully entitled
to receive such drug. The willful making of or concealment of any
material false statement or representation of any prescription,
order, report, or record required by law. The refusal to make
available and to accord full opportunity to check any record or
file as required by law. The failure to keep records as required
by law.[100]

Drugs exempted from the statute are such compound, mixture, or
preparation of barbituric acid, its salts and derivatives that have
or contain no habit-forming properties and do not have a dangerously
toxic or hypnotic or somnifacient effect on the human body or of an

animal; or such compound, mixture, or preparation of amphetamine,
desoxyephedrine, phenolethylamine, or their salts or derivatives
that do not have an excessively stimulating effect upon the central
nervous system and do not have any habit-forming properties or
dangerously toxic effect upon the body of a human or animal.[101]

The statute shall not be applicable to the delivery of dangerous
drugs to persons included in any of the classes hereinafter or to
agents or employees of such persons, for use in the normal or usual
course of their business or practice or in the performance of their
official duties, as the case may be; or to the possession of
dangerous drugs by such persons or their agents or employees for
such use: pharmacists, practitioners, persons who procure dangerous
drugs for handling by or under the supervision of pharmacists or
practitioners, or for the purpose of lawful research, teaching, or
testing and not for resale; Hospitals which procure dangerous drugs
for lawful administration or use by practitioners; Laboratories
which procure dangerous drugs for lawful medical and scientific
purposes; Officers or employees of appropriate enforcement agencies
of federal, state, D.C., or local governments, pursuant to their
official duties; manufacturers and wholesalers; manufacturers'
representatives and drug salesmen; and carriers and warehousemen.[102]

Any person who violates this statute or any regulation shall be
punished for the first offense by a fine of not less than one
hundred dollars nor more than one thousand dollars or by imprisonment
of not more than one year, or both; and for any subsequent offense
by a fine of not less than five hundred dollars nor more than five
thousand dollars, or by imprisonment for not exceeding ten years, or
both. The conviction of any person for a violation of this statute
involving any dangerous drug shall constitute ground for suspension
or revocation or denial of renewal of the professional license of
such person.[103] Any dangerous drug seized pursuant to any lawful
search or which may have come into the custody of a police officer,
the lawful possession of which cannot be established or the title
to which cannot be ascertained, shall be forfeited and destroyed in
the manner provided for narcotic drugs.[104]

There were approximately 500,000 arrests in the United States
in 1976 for narcotic drug law violations.[105] A sample of over
seven thousand persons processed through the criminal justice systems
of selected jurisdictions shows that 45 percent plead guilty to the
offense charged, 4 percent plead guilty to a lessor charge, 24
percent were acquitted or had their cases dismissed, and 27 percent
were referred to juvenile court.[106] As Haskell and Yablonsky state
the possession of a narcotic or dangerous drug or the equipment

associated with such drugs provides the police with a prima facie
case against anyone apprehended but there is a great amount of
official disagreement on the amount and types of crimes attributable
to drug addicts and abusers.[107]

The National Commission on Marihuama and Drug Abuse stated
clearly that the relationship between drugs and criminal behavior
is difficult to comprehend despite public opinion showing that most
drug addicts supposedly resort to crime to support their habits.[108]
The perpetuation of this dope fiend myth goes back to the nineteenth
century and in its present form attributes all forms of violent
crime to not only those addicted to the opiates but also users of
marijuana and abusers of amphetamines, barbiturates, and the
hallucinogens.[109]

The Commission states that marijuana use is neither a cause
nor directly associated with crime (i.e., violent or non-violent).
The only crimes which can be directly attributed to marijuana-using
behavior are those resulting from the use, possession, or transfer
of an illegal substance.[110] Barbiturates have a similar effect on
people to alcohol and various studies on the relationship between
the use of alcohol and the commission of violent crimes (i.e.,
murder, assault, etc.) show that alcohol was used by at least half
of the offenders just before the crime took place. Thus a high
level of barbiturate use may also be linked to violent crime.[111]
Studies of amphetamine users shows that they were disproportionately
involved in criminal activities (i.e., assaults, robberies).[112]

The various studies show that most opiate addicts (i.e.,
usually heroin) are individuals who have had long histories of
delinquent or criminal behavior prior to their being identified as
drug addicts. It has also been shown that opiate use becomes a
further expression of deviant tendencies and most heroin addicts
continue to be arrested subsequent to release from prison, hospital,
or rehabilitation programs. It appears that opiate addicts tend to
escalate the seriousness of their offenses and to experience more
arrests after identification as addicts than before becoming addicted.
Most of the crimes committed by addicts are crimes against property
and/or non-violent crimes against the person in order to obtain
money or goods easily converted to cash. The research shows that
opiate addicts are less likely to commit homicide, rape, and assault
than users of amphetamines and barbiturates.[113] Users of cocaine
suffer from the same reactions as amphetamine abusers (i.e.,
paranoia, hostility, impulsiveness) but data indicates they commit
more crimes against property than against the person.[114]

Users of hallucinogens, non-barbiturate sedative-hypnotics, glue
and similar volatile inhalants are not inclined toward violent

criminal behavior except in cases where there is drug-induced panic
or toxic reactions. Some of the non-barbiturate sedatives (i.e.,
methaqualone) and the hydrocarbon solvents have a potential for
inducing violent behavior although crime statistics are lacking.[115]

A thorough review of the literature by the Commission and others
shows that it is difficult to establish a direct relationship between
crime and the use of various drugs. But it is possible to show that
drug use in combination with a number of physiological, psychological,
and sociological factors may assume an important role in the causation of deviant behavior of a delinquent or criminal nature.[116]

The costs to society from criminal activity associated with all
types of drugs from opiates to hallucinogens is in the billions
of dollars. Most of the research has concentrated on heroin addicts
and findings indicate that suppliers and users spend and earn close
to one billion dollars per year.[117] If one adds to this cost, the
money spent in selling and buying marijuana, cocaine, amphetamines,
barbiturates, and the hallucinogens, the costs could go as high as
fifteen billion dollars a year. This estimate is based on a
comparison with costs of alcoholic consumption.[118] Costs to the
criminal justice system can only be roughly estimated. If we assume
that all 500,000 persons arrested went to jail for one twenty-four
hour period at twenty dollars per person per day, the cost would be
ten million dollars. If one attempts to estimate the cost of police
investigation and arrest, trial, sentencing, treatment and
rehabilitation in addition to incarceration, the costs must easily
be somewhere in the area of one billion dollars or more (i.e.,
making the comparison to alcohol related criminal justice costs).[119]

The legal policy of American society towards the use of all
types of drugs, whether opiates, marijuana, or the prescription
drugs that are abused has been quite punitive-oriented since 1914.
Thus as with alcoholic beverages during prohibition the official
policy of federal, state, and local jurisdictions has been preventing
people from abusing drugs and controlling individuals who are
currently misusing drugs. This has left the hard and soft drug
market wide open to organized crime which has found ways of always
supplying and catering to the needs of Americans, poor and affluent,
white and nonwhite, who want to use drugs.[120]

The Bureau of Customs, Drug Enforcement Administration, F.B.I.,
and the U.S. Border Patrol all work at the federal level to deal
with both international and interstate problems concerning the drug
market. All federal agencies are supposed to cooperate with state,
county, and municipal police department divisions dealing with
narcotics and dangerous drugs. The smuggling of narcotics into

190

the United States has proven to be an impossible phenomenon to
prevent since there are as many ways to smuggle as there are smug-
glers. Organized crime as well as amateurs have been successful
at smuggling the opiates. Such drugs as marijuana are grown almost
everywhere so enforcement is quite difficult. Hallucinogens can
be made quite easily and transported in a variety of ways that defy
detection. The drug industry cannot keep control over all the legal
amphetamines and barbiturates manufactured, stored, shipped, and
delivered to pharmacies and hospitals - let alone deal with those
clandestine laboratories that manufacture the same substances.[121]

Local and state police are not equipped to deal with the
millions of people who may be violating the criminal code statutes
on drugs of any given jurisdiction. Thus most police departments
have traditionally concentrated crime prevention and control efforts
on the opiates and cocaine. Since the early 1960's more effort has
been directed in dealing with marijuana and the other soft drugs
(i.e., hallucinogens, amphetamines, and barbiturates). The drug
problem is no longer one that takes the time of only metropolitan
police officers since much of the soft drug and cocaine problems
tend to be increasingly prevelant in the suburbs.[122]

Law enforcement practices dealing with importers and wholesalers
are usually left to federal officials. Street traffic deals with
the pusher and the addict or drug abuser depending on whether one
is dealing with hard or soft drugs. Effective enforcement of narcotic
and dangerous drug statutes is rather difficult since all aspects of
a drug transaction are illegal and carried out as covertly and
rapidly as possible. Police must utilize covert operations and
resort to utilizing addict-informers, prostitutes, and other social
deviants who are paid to give information on the drug trade in a
given jurisdiction. Informers are either paid for their information,
supplied with drugs, or let off from arrest for an offense for their
cooperation with the police. The officers assigned to narcotics
operations must use informant information to learn what is happening
on the street and then spend time and money on the street as part of
the drug subculture in order to gather evidence. This may take from
several months to a year at considerable time and cost. Police may
use entrapment to obtain evidence and naturally officers, prosecutors,
and judges do not like these procedures since they are either
unconstitutional or border on it. Further undercover officers may
be exposed and either become part of the drug operation as bribed
onlookers or be targets of organized crime or pushers to be shot or
beaten up. Usually a discovered detective is left alone and the
drug traffic moves to a different location.[123]

Description of Specific Deviance

In 1970 over 200 million legal prescriptions for drugs (i.e., stimulants, sedatives, tranquilizers, and depressants) were filled for Americans who had consulted their doctors. Barbiturates and barbiturate substitutes accounted for twenty-nine percent of these prescriptions, minor tranquilizers accounted for thirty-nine percent, stimulants made up thirteen percent, anti-psychotics accounted for ten percent, and anti-depressants made up the rest of the total. Americans also obtained large quantities of non-prescription drugs such as sleeping agents, tranquilizing agents, and caffeine stimulants. Thus a substantial percentage of the American population of all ages, both sexes, and all types of socio-economic backgrounds use drugs legally. This does not count the millions of Americans who smoke cigarettes and use alcoholic beverages.[124]

Concerning illicit drug use in American society, all we have are estimates of the problem. It has been estimated that over one million people abuse barbiturates, almost the same number abuse amphetamines, and over one million regularly smoke marijuana. It is estimated that there are sixty thousand drug addicts in society, most of whom are dependent on heroin. This estimate is based on arrest records. Estimates of heroin users who have not been arrested are approximately 500,000 individuals. The National Commission on Marihuana and Drug Abuse survey of almost 2500 individuals concludes that six percent of the sample abused over the counter sedatives, tranquilizers, and stimulants; three percent abused prescription sedatives, four percent abused prescription tranquilizers and stimulants, fifteen percent smoked marijuana, five percent used hallucenogens, four percent abused inhalants, two percent used cocaine, and only one percent used heroin.[125]

Most of the data gathered by researchers has been on drug addicts (mainly heroin) since these people come in contact with the criminal justice system and rehabilitation programs sooner or later. Most heroin addicts are young (i.e., under age thirty). Most state they started abusing drugs by age sixteen and became addicted to heroin by age nineteen or twenty. Once addicted these individuals soon turned to crimes against property and eventually crimes against the person to secure money for their habit. Most had been arrested within five years of initiating their dependence on heroin. Few heroin addicts completed high school and while in school most were labeled as delinquent despite normal intelligence and achievement potential. Without educational and occupational skills most addicts were employed at unskilled or at best semi-skilled jobs. Many state that their heroin habit keeps them from working since they either are out looking for new supplies or more money. Thus many addicts

192

are on welfare, being supported by friends, pimping, or prostituting
themselves to take care of their habit. Consequently most addicts
are poor job and vocational training risks even after being in such
programs in prison or community treatment centers since their
recidivism rate is high.[126]

Heroin addicts are generally inner city or older suburban area
residents. Their environment is typically characterized by economic
instability and family problems. Drinking and other forms of social
deviance are common among immediate family members and close friends.
Marital instability with high desertion and divorce rates character-
izes both the addict's parents and his or her own marital situation.
The addict's preoccupation with drug use is a major contributing
factor in his or her social isolation and prevents him from attempting to make proper adjustments to adult roles in both the family
and the community. The heroin addict has been characterized as
immature, resentful of authority, passive-aggressive, sexually
inadequate, anxiety-ridden, rebellious, withdrawn, socially isolated,
depressed, and suicidal. The typical addict tends to repress
aggressive and hostile feelings, to require immediate gratification,
to be easily frustrated, and to lack self-respect.[127]

There is one special type of drug addict that does not fit this
description. This is the junkie physician, nurse, dentist, and
pharmacist. These individuals have access to prescription narcotics
and most are able to carefully control their habit and are able to
afford to maintain it. Thus these respectable members of the
community rarely come in contact with the criminal justice system
yet are responsible for the health and welfare of others. It is
estimated that approximately ten percent of those in the medical
and paramedical professions are drug addicts although few are
addicted to heroin.[128]

Decriminalization

The treatment of drug addicts (i.e., opiates) by physicians
actually preceded the criminalization of drug addiction in the
United States. From 1870 to 1900 most drug addicts did not receive
any special treatment since clinics were mostly private. Thus the
addict either was treated by a doctor or utilized patent remedies,
most of which were opium-based. During the years 1900-1915 many
private clinics for alcoholics and drug addicts were opened. The
first narcotic dispensing clinics were established in Florida and
Tennessee in 1912 and 1913. A medical model was developed to deal
with drug addicts.[129]

After the passage of the Harrison Act, the Treasury Department
began to discourage doctors from prescribing opiates to addicts and

a number of court cases resulted in most physicians losing interest
in a medical cure for addiction. The Treasury Department did
encourage the establishment of temporary clinics for the maintenance
of drug addicts after doctors stopped prescribing opiates in 1919.
By 1921 there were forty-four such clinics in the United States.
These clinics were to treat addicts and cure them but in reality
were opiate maintenance centers. Some clinics were careless about
the distribution of narcotics and by 1925 the Treasury Department
closed all clinics. Thus the therapeutic model was a failure and
gave way to the punitive model of dealing with drug addicts.[130]

Congress authorized the establishment of two drug treatment
hospitals in 1929 but the facility at Lexington, Kentucky was not
established until 1935 and the second at Fort Worth, Texas in 1938.
These facilities were designed to deal with federal drug law
offenders but accepted voluntary patients as well. Studies showed
that ninety percent of the patients relapsed into drug addiction
after release.[131] These two federal facilities remained the only
drug addict treatment programs in America until 1952 when Riverside
Hospital in New York City was opened to deal with juvenile addicts.
Under state law the patients were kept in custody for three years
and then released. The program was closed in 1963 since ninety-five
percent of the patients returned to drug addiction after release.[132]
In 1956 New York state set up a special narcotic parole project
that lasted until 1959.[133] Between 1930 and 1960 the laws of thirty-
four states allowed drug addicts to receive treatment in state mental
hospitals although only California and New York for the most part
did send addicts to such facilities.[134]

The failure of the criminal justice system to deal with prevention and control of drug addicts became increasingly apparent by
the early 1960's. In 1961 California set up statewide treatment
programs for addicts followed by New York in 1962. These programs
were to place addicts in mandatory programs that were indeterminate
in nature so that the individual could be truly physically and
mentally rehabilitated. Many addicts chose to go to prison rather
than enter treatment since the period of incarceration was shorter.[135]
In 1966 the federal Narcotic Addict Rehabilitation Act was passed by
Congress and was modeled after the California and New York state
programs that were based on the civil commitment procedure. Forty-
eight community based treatment facilities were in operation financed
by the federal government by 1971 under this Act.[136]

A number of private organizations also became active in the
1960's concerning rehabilitation of addicts. Synanon was founded
in 1959 to deal with addicts based on the Alcoholics Anonymous
model.[137] A methadone maintenance program was set up in New York

City in 1964 which was successful and led to the annual conferences on methadone treatment (first national conference held in 1968).[138] Liberty Park Village was established in 1969 in New Jersey and Daytóp Lodge in New York City.[139]

Those who are opposed to decriminalization of drug addiction and abuse (i.e., opiates, marijuana, and cocain) state that any legal provision of addicting or harmful drugs to people would constitute the condoning of such social deviance in society. Secondly legalization would cause more harm than benefits to society since more people would become addicted and abuse drugs. The critics of decriminalization have mixed into one class of social deviants all drug addicts, drug abusers, and drug users (both over the counter and prescription purchasers). The critics of the de-criminalization concept have made their argument difficult to defend since they are dealing with all types of drugs (i.e., barbiturates, amphetamines, hallucinogens, cocaine, opiates, and marijuana) not just the opiates.

It is obvious that there must be different solutions to the personal and social problems created by using and abusing different kinds of drugs. It would appear from the continuous attempts to deal with the medical management of drugs that a medical solution (both physiological and psychological) would be more appropriate than a simple criminal justice approach. Federal as well as local officials have for too long feld that both the drug addict and abuser are criminals, not people in need of medical and psychiatric attention.[140]

Those who favor decriminalization are quite selective in how best to deal with what types of drugs. Obviously drug addicts have different problems than drug abusers. The latter group is composed of individuals who use cocaine, marijuana, hallucinogens, amphetamines, and barbiturates. Each one of these substances have its own particular properties and potential for abuse. Thus one must approach each substance from the point of view that there will be different types of people utilizing these substances for a variety of reasons. Some people will abuse several substances, others will be quite selective in their use or abuse of these drugs. It is well known that many individuals combine one or more of these drugs with alcohol, tobacco, or coffee. These latter drugs can be dangerous in and of themselves in large quantities so the problem is more difficult to deal with when combinations of legal drugs are utilized along with illicit drugs.[141]

Those who favor decriminalization believe that the legal sup-pression of all types of drugs has made it impossible for law enforce-ment personnel to control the traffic in drugs. This is due to the

fact that organized crime has a willing and interested class of
people wanting to experiment, defy the law, and just plain enjoy
the effects of certain types of drugs. The drug addict (i.e.,
heroin user) is the least of our problems today since that population appears to have been approximately 58,000 known addicts since
the 1920's.[142] All drug abusers become criminals under our current
drug laws and are stigmatized by society by their arrest records
which makes rehabilitation difficult and makes a career as a drug
deviant more easy.[143]

Many individuals and prestigious groups have advocated that
drug addiction and abuse be considered primarily as a medical
problem. Thus the Joint Committee of the American Bar Association
and the American Medical Association on Narcotic Drugs, The National
Commission on Marihuana and Drug Abuse, The President's Commission
on Law Enforcement and Administration of Justice, as well as
Lindesmith, Schur, Geis, Reasons, and others have been pushing for
alternatives to incarceration for drug addicts and abusers and the
decriminalization of certain types of criminal statutes.[144]

Brecher succinctly sums up the most probable solution to
America's drug proglem with six caveats: (1) stop emphasizing
measures designed to keep drugs away from people; (2) stop publici-
zing the horrors of the so-called drug menace; (3) stop increasing
the damage done by drugs; (4) stop misclassifying drugs; (5) stop
viewing the drug problem as primarily a national problem that can
only be solved on a national basis; and (6) stop trying to wipe out
illicit drug use.[145] One more point should be added to Brecher's
caveats, start paying attention to all the national commissions
dealing with analysis and potential solutions to our drug problems
rather than the misdirected and sometimes damaging statements of
some of our politicians.[146]

196
Notes

1. A Gordon, The Relation of Legislative Acts to the Problem of
   Drug Addiction, Journal of Criminal Law and Criminology, 8
   (1971), 211-215; Gilman Udell, Opium and Narcotic Laws,
   Washington, DC: US Government Printing Office, 1968, ii-iv;
   Edward Brecher et al., Licit and Illicit Drugs, Boston: Little,
   Brown and Company, 1972; Charles Terry and Mildred Pellens,
   The Opium Problem, New York: Committee on Drug Addictions,
   Bureau of Social Hygiene Inc., 1928; Alfred Lindesmith, Opiate
   Addiction, Evanston, Illinois: Principia Press, 1947;
   Lindesmith, The Addict and the Law, Bloomington, Indiana:
   Indiana University Press, 1965; Lawrence Kolb and A.G. DuMez,
   The Prevalence and Trend of Drug Addiction in the United States
   and Factors Influencing It, Treasury Department, Washington,
   DC: US Government Printing Office, 1924; The President's
   Commission on Law Enforcement and Administration of Justice,
   Task Force Report: Narcotic and Drug Abuse, Washington, DC:
   US Government Printing Office, 1967; William Eldridge,
   Narcotics and the Law, Chicago: University of Chicago Press,
   1967; John O'Donnell and John Ball (eds.), Narcotic Addiction,
   New York: Harper and Row, 1966; Ball Two Patterns of Narcotic
   Drug Addiction in the United States, Journal of Criminal Law,
   56 (1965), 203-211; David Maurer and Victor Vogel, Narcotics
   and Narcotic Addiction, Springfield, Illinois: Charles C.
   Thomas, 1967; Troy Duster, The Legislation of Morality: Laws,
   Drugs, and Moral Judgement, New York: Free Press, 1970; David
   Musto, The American Disease: Origins of Narcotic Control, New
   Haven: Yale University Press, 1973; Gilbert Geis, Not the
   Law's Business, Washington, DC: US Government Printing Office,
   NIMH, 1972; David Cantor, The Criminal Law and the Narcotics
   Problem, Journal of Criminal Law and Criminology, 51 (1961),
   512-527.

2. Brecher, op. cit., 42-43.

3. Ibid., 43-44.

4. Ibid., 339.

5. Ibid., 44.

6. Ibid., 276.

7. Ibid., 410.

8. Ibid., 231.

9. Ibid., 59.

10. Robert Walton, Marijuana: America's New Drug Problem, Philadelphia: JB Lippincott, 1938, 29-33.

11. Ibid., 37.

12. Brecher, op. cit., 329.

13. Bureau of Narcotics, U.S. Treasury Department, Traffic in Opium and Other Dangerous Drugs for the Year Ending December 31, 1935, Washington, DC: US Government Printing Office, 1936, 30; David Solomon (ed.), The Marijuana Papers, New York: Bobbs-Merrill, 1966, xv.

14. Brecher, op. cit., 419-420.

15. Udell, op. cit., ii-iv; Brecher, op. cit., 56.

16. Brecher, op. cit., 254-255.

17. Ibid., 282-283.

18. Ibid., 328-329.

19. Ibid., 73.

20. Ibid., 370-372.

21. Martin Haskell and Lewis Yablonsky, Criminology: Crime and Criminality, Chicago: Rand McNally, 1978, 313.

22. Terry and Pellens, op. cit., 747.

23. Brecher, op. cit., 47.

24. Public Law Number 221, 60th Congress.

25. Public Law Number 46, 63rd Congress.

26. Public Law Number 47, 63rd Congress.

27. Public Law Number 233, 63rd Congress; Brecher, op. cit., 48-55.

28. Brecher, op. cit., 59.

29. Ibid., 51.

30. Ibid., 413.

31. Solomon, op. cit., xv.

198

32. Public Law Number 238, 75th Congress; Brecher, op. cit.,
    415-416.

33. Brecher, op. cit., 405.

34. Public Law Number 400, 78th Congress.

35. Brecher, op. cit., 254-255.

36. 21 U.S.C., Sec. 174 (65 Stat., 767); Charles Reasons, The Addict
    as a Criminal: Perpetuation of a Legend, Crime and Delinquency,
    21 (1975), 22-23.

37. Public Law Number 78-728, 84th Congress; Brecher, op. cit.,
    420; Eldridge, op. cit., 177-231; Reasons, op. cit., 23.

38. Brecher, op. cit., 282-283.

39. Ibid., 366-372.

40. The President's Commission on Law Enforcement and Administration
    of Justice, The Challenge of Crime in a Free Society, Washington,
    DC: US Government Printing Office, 228-229.

41. Brecher, op. cit., 283.

42. Narcotic Addict Rehabilitation Act of 1966, Public Law Number
    793, Title II, The Narcotic Addict Rehabilitation Act of 1966,
    Public Health Service, U.S. Department of Health, Education,
    and Welfare, Washington, DC: US Government Printing Office,
    1969.

43. Ibid., 2-3.

44. Brecher, op. cit., 420; Reasons, op. cit., 25.

45. Ibid., 60.

46. Webb v. United States, 249 U.S. 96 (1919); Alfred Lindesmith,
    Federal Law and Drug Addiction, in Chambliss (ed.), Crime and
    the Legal Process, New York: McGraw-Hill, 1969, 64.

47. Jin Fuey Moy v. United States, 254 U.S. 189 (1920); Lindesmith,
    op. cit., 64.

48. United States v. Behrman, 258 U.S. 280 (1922); Lindesmith,
    op. cit., 64-65.

49. Linder v. United States, 268 U.S. 5 (1925); Lindesmith,
    op. cit., 66-67.

50. Strader v. United States, 72 F. 2nd 589 (10th Cir., 1934);
    United States v. Anthony, 15 F. Supp. 533 (1936); Carey v.
    United States, 86 F. 2nd 461 (9th Cir., 1936); Lindesmith,
    op. cit., 69.

51. Rochin v. California, 342 U.S. 165 (1952); Lindesmith,
    op. cit., 71.

52. Blackford v. United States, 247 F. 2nd 745 (9th Cir., 1957);
    Lindesmith, op. cit., 71.

53. Sherman v. United States, 356 U.S. 369 (1958); Edwin Schur,
    Crimes Without Victims: Deviant Behavior and Public Policy,
    New Jersey: Prentice-Hall, 1965, 136.

54. Robinson v. California, 370 U.S. 660 (1962); Brecher, op. cit.,
    59-60; Herbert Bloch and Gilbert Geis, Man, Crime, and Society,
    New York: Random House, 1970, 339.

55. Brecher, op. cit.; Task Force Report: Narcotic and Drug Abuse,
    op. cit.; The Challenge of Crime in a Free Society, op. cit.;
    Reasons, op. cit.

56. Ibid.

57. Ibid.

58. Brecher, op. cit., 78.

59. Marshall Clinard, Sociology of Deviant Behavior, New York:
    Holt, Rinehart and Winston 1974, 384.

60. 1977/78 U.S. Government Manual, Washington, DC: US Government
    Printing Office, 1977, 261-262.

61. Ibid., 350-351.

62. President's Commission on Law Enforcement and Administration
    of Justice, Task Force Report: Organized Crime, Washington,
    DC: US Government Printing Office, 1967, 1-2.

63. Proceedings, White House Conference on Narcotic and Drug Abuse,
    Washington, DC: US Government Printing Office, 1962.

64. Final Report, President's Advisory Commission on Narcotic and
    Drug Abuse, Washington, DC: US Government Printing Office, 1963.

65. Task Force Report: Narcotic and Drug Abuse, op. cit.

66. National Commission on Marihuana and Drug Abuse, Marihuana: A Signal of Misunderstanding, Washington, DC: US Government Printing Office, 1972; Technical papers, volumes 1-2; National Commission on Marihuana and Drug Abuse, Drug Use in America: Problem in Perspective, Washington, DC: US Government Printing Office, 1973, Technical papers, volumes 1-4.

67. American Bar Association and American Medical Association, Joint Committee on Narcotic Drugs, Drug Addiction: Crime or Disease?, Bloomington, Indiana: Indiana University Press, 1961.

68. The Challenge of Crime in a Free Society, op. cit., 230-231.

69. Health Research Council of New York City, New York State Narcotic Addiction Control Commission, and National Association for the Prevention of Addiction, Proceedings of the First National Conference on Methadone Treatment, New York, 1968.

70. Brecher, op. cit., 120; Shur, op. cit., 153-154; Schur, Narcotic Addiction in Britain and America: The Impact of Public Policy, Bloomington, Indiana: Indiana University Press, 1962; Schur, British Narcotics Policies, Journal of Criminal Law and Criminology, 51 (1961), 619-624; Schur, Drug Addiction Under British Policy, Social Problems, 9 (1961), 156-166; Alfred Lindesmith, The British System of Narcotics Control, Law and Contemporary Problems, 22 (1957), 138-154.

71. Brecher, op. cit., 121.

72. Ministry of Health, Interdepartmental Committee on Drug Addiction, Report, London: Her Majesty's Stationery Office, 1961.

73. Brecher, op. cit., 125.

74. Robert Pursley, Introduction to Criminal Justice, Encino, California: Glencoe Press, 1978, 106.

75. Brecher, op. cit., 48.

76. Ibid., 22, 468.

77. Henry Black, Black's Law Dictionary, St. Paul, Minnesota: West Publishing Company, 1968, 587.

78. Ibid., 59.

79. Henry Fairchild (ed.), Dictionary of Sociology, Paterson, New Jersey: Littlefield, Adams and Company, 1962, 99.

80. The Dushkin Publishing Group, Encyclopedia of Sociology, Guilford, Connecticut: Dushkin Inc., 1974, 85-86.

81. Expert Committee on Addiction-Producing Drugs, Seventh Report, World Health Organization Technical Report Series, Geneva, Switzerland: W.H.O. of the United Nations, 1957, in Drug Use in America, op. cit., 124.

82. Drug Use in America, op. cit., 136-140.

83. Ibid., 9.

84. Ibid., 28.

85. Ibid., 37-38.

86. Ibid., 9, 11, 13.

87. Ibid., 16-17.

88. Ibid., 18.

89. Ibid., 19.

90. District of Columbia Code, Annotated, Washington, DC: US Government Printing Office, 2, 1973, 33-401, 2158.

91. Ibid., 33-402, 2159.

92. Ibid., 33-416a, 2171.

93. Ibid.

94. Ibid., 33-417, 2175.

95. Ibid., 33-420, 2175.

96. Ibid., 33-423, 2176.

97. Ibid., 33-701, 2177.

98. Ibid., 33-702, 2178-2179.

99. Ibid.

100. Ibid.

101. Ibid., 33-703, 2179-2180.

102. Ibid., 33-704, 2180.

103. ibid., 33-708, 2181.

104. Ibid., 33-711, 2182.

105. Uniform Crime Reports of the F.B.I., Crime in the United States-1976, Washington, DC: US Government Printing Office, 1977, 184.

106. Ibid., 217.

107. Haskell and Yablonsky, op. cit., 319.

108. Drug Use in America, op. cit., 154-155.

109. Schur, Crimes Without Victims, op. cit., 120-122; Isidor Chein et al., The Road to H: Narcotics, Delinquency and Social Policy, New York: Basic Books, 1964; David Musto, op. cit.; Geis, op. cit.; Cantor, op. cit.; Duster, op. cit.; Terry and Pellens, op. cit.; Eldridge, op. cit.; Lindesmith, op. cit.; Lindesmith, Dopefiend Mythology, Journal of Criminal Law and Criminology, 31 (1940), 199-208; Lindesmith, The Drug Addict as a Psychopath, American Sociological Review, 5 (1940), 914-920; Reasons, op. cit.; Reasons, Images of Crime and the Criminal: The Dope Fiend Mythology, Journal of Research in Crime and Delinquency, (1976), 133-144.

110. Marihuana: A Signal of Misunderstanding, op. cit., 424-477.

111. Drug Use in America, op. cit., 157, 160.

112. Ibid., 160-161.

113. Ibid., 161-163.

114. Ibid., 163.

115. Ibid., 165.

116. Ibid., 156; Clinard, op. cit., 422-423; Schur, Crimes Without Victims, op. cit., 138-141; Haskell and Yablonsky, op. cit., 319-322; Don Gibbons, Society, Crime, and Criminal Careers, New Jersey: Prentice-Hall, 1973, 426-430.

117. Clinard, op. cit., 401; Kolb and DuMez, op. cit.; Task Force Report: Narcotic and Drug Abuse, op. cit.; Drug Use in America, op. cit., 174-175; Arthur D. Little Inc., Drug Abuse and Law Enforcement, A Report to the President's Commission on Law Enforcement and Administration of Justice, op. cit.; Edward Preble and John Casey, Taking Care of Business— The Heroin User's Life on the Street, International Journal of the Addictions, 4 (1969), 1-24; Brecher, op. cit., 90-100.

118. Clinard, op. cit., 463; Drug Use in America, op. cit., 174-175.

119. Drug Use in America, op. cit., 175-176; Brecher, op. cit., 475-481.

120. Brecher, op. cit., 90-100; Donald Cressey, Theft of the Nation: The Structure and Operations of Organized Crime in America, New York: Harper and Row, 1969, 91-95, 161, 278, 287; Task Force Report: Organized Crime, op. cit., 3-4.

121. The Challenge of Crime in a Free Society, op. cit., 216-221; Brecher, op. cit., 90-100.

122. Brecher, op. cit., 473-498; Robert Bell, Social Deviance, Homewood, Illinois: Dorsey Press, 1971, 219-224; Erich Goode, The Marijuana Smokers, New York: Basic Books, 1970; Marihuana: A Signal of Misunderstanding, op. cit.; Drug Use in America, op. cit.; Lester Grinspoon and James Bakalar, Cocaine: A Drug and Its Social Evolution, New York: Basic Books, 1976; Grinspoon and Peter Hedblom, The Speed Culture, Cambridge, Massachusetts: Harvard University Press, 1975.

123. Schur, Crimes Without Victims, op. cit., 134-138; Brecher, op. cit., 304-305; Interview with Captain Donald Randall, Special Investigations Branch, Metropolitan Police Department of the District of Columbia, 1977.

124. Clinard, op. cit., 388-392; Drug Use in America, op. cit., 42-43; Herbert Abelson and Ronald Atkinson, Public Experience with Psychoactive Substances, Princeton, New Jersey: Response Analysis Corp., 1975; Abelson and Patricia Fishburne, Nonmedical Use of Psychoactive Substances, Princeton, New Jersey: Response Analysis Corp., 1976.

125. Clinard, op. cit., 388-392, 400-404; Drug Use in America, op. cit., 63-69.

126. Drug Use in America, op. cit., 167-170; Gibbons, op. cit., 430-435; Clinard, op. cit., 404-408.

204

127. Ibid.

128. Clinard, op. cit., 406-407; Richard Hessler, Junkies in White:
     Drug Addiction among Physicians, in Bryant (ed.), Deviant
     Behavior, Chicago: Rand McNally, 1974, 146-153; Charles
     Winick, Physician Narcotic Addicts, Social Problems, 9
     (1961), 174-186; J.D. Fox, Narcotic Addiction Among Physicians,
     Journal of Michigan Medical Society, 56 (1957), 214-217;
     Charles Jones, Narcotic Addiction of Physicians, Journal of
     the Medical Association of the State of Alabama, 37 (1968),
     816-827; Solomon Garb, Drug Addiction in Physicians,
     Anasthesia and Analgesia- Current Researches, 48 (1969),
     129-133; William Quinn, Narcotic Addiction: Medical and Legal
     Problems with Physicians, California Medicine, 94 (1961),
     214-217.

129. Drug Use in America, op. cit., 305-306.

130. Ibid., 308-309.

131. Ibid., 309-310; Brecher, op. cit., 69-71; John O'Donnell,
     Narcotic Addicts in Kentucky, Washington, DC: US Government
     Printing Office, US Public Health Service, NIMH, 1969;
     The Challenge of Crime in a Free Society, op. cit., 225-226.

132. Drug Use in America, op. cit., 310; Brecher, op. cit., 72-75.

133. Brecher, op. cit., 72-77; The Challenge of Crime in a Free
     Society, op. cit., 228.

134. Drug Use in America, op. cit., 310.

135. Ibid., 311; Brecher, op. cit., 71-72, 77-78; The Challenge
     of Crime in a Free Society, op. cit., 226-227.

136. The Challenge of Crime in a Free Society, op. cit., 228-229;
     Brecher, op. cit., 78; Drug Use in Society, op. cit., 312-314.

137. The Challenge of Crime in a Free Society, op. cit., 227;
     Brecher, op. cit., 78-79; Drug Use in America, op. cit., 311;
     Lewis Yablonsky, Synanon: The Tunnel Back, New York:
     Macmillan, 1965.

138. Brecher, op. cit., 135-182; The Challenge of Crime in a Free
     Society, op. cit., 227; Drug Use in America, op. cit., 311-312.

139. Brecher, op. cit., 79-81.

140. Schur, _Crimes Without Victims_, op. cit., 159–163; Harry
     Anslinger and W. Tompkins, _The Traffic in Narcotics_, New
     York: Funk and Wagnalls, 1953; Anslinger and Will Oursler,
     The Murderers, New York: Farrar, Straus and Company, 1961.

141. _Drug Use in America_, op. cit.; Brecher, op. cit.

142. Brecher, op. cit., 56–89.

143. Clinard, op. cit., 430–432.

144. Lindesmith, op. cit.; Reasons, op. cit.; Geis, op. cit.;
     Schur, op. cit.; President's Commission, op. cit.; National
     Commission, op. cit.; Joint Committee of AMA–ABA on
     Narcotic Drugs, op. cit.; Pursley, op. cit., 107–110.

145. Brecher, op. cit., 521–527.

146. Anslinger, op. cit.; Clinard, op. cit., 434 (concerning
     President Nixon); James Eastland, Chairman, _Marihuana-Hashish
     Epidemic and its Impact on United States Security_, U.S. Senate,
     Washington, DC: US Government Printing Office, 1974;
     Kefauver Committee, op. cit.; McClellan Subcommittee, op. cit.;
     Carl Chambers et al., Toward Understanding and Managing
     Nonnarcotic Drug Abusers, _Federal Probation_, 36 (1972);
     Richard Schroeder, The Politics of Drugs, Washington, DC:
     Congressional Quarterly, 1975; Philip Baridon, _Addiction,
     Crime and Social Policy_, Lexington, Massachusetts: D.C.
     Heath and Company, 1976; Lindesmith, _The Addict and the Law_,
     op. cit.; Duster, op. cit.; Schur, _Narcotic Addiction in
     Britain and America_, op. cit.

XIV

MENTAL DISORDERS

Legal History

The Common Law of England indicates from earliest times (i.e., after 1226) that a person under age seven is not liable for criminal responsibility or intent (i.e., mens rea) since he does not know right from wrong; between seven and fourteen the individual is also not criminally liable if he does not know right from wrong. If an individual above age fourteen does not appear to be able to function at least to that mental age, he is deemed mentally incompetent and termed a lunatic under the Common Law. This doctrine applied to violent crimes such as murder with malice aforethought where the offender could plead lunacy as a defense and be pardoned by the crown.[1]

By 1536 under Henry VIII the first law was passed placing the poor insane under the care of the local governments. This practice was expanded under the law of Elizabeth I in 1601 whereby the crown took responsibility for the destitute insane. Thus a policy evolved in England by the seventeenth century allowing violent criminals to plead lunacy in order to avoid criminal prosecution while non-criminal lunatics who happened to be poor were placed in the work-houses and jails along with alcoholics, vagrants, and the unemployed poor. Thus during the American colonial period and well into the nineteenth century in the United States the insane were treated in the same manner as other social deviants who were jailed.[2]

It was not until 1843 that a legal test was accepted for dealing with the criminally insane. This was the M'Naghten case and the rule derived from this case states that a defendant who knows the difference between right and wrong is legally sane.[3] In an 1868 Iowa case, the irresistible impulse or wild beast test was stated. An offender who knows that his criminal act was wrong but was driven to it by an uncontrollable and irresistible impulse arising from his insanity could not be held responsible for his actions.[4] A third rule was developed in two New Hampshire cases in 1869 and 1871. The test stated that insanity was a valid defense to a crime if the defendant suffered from a mental disease (i.e., was mentally ill). Thus all tests of mental disease were questions of legal fact to be decided by juries. This test allowed for the introduction of testimony by psychiatrists.[5] In 1890 the New York state legislature passed a statute making provision for hospitals and the care for the legally insane.[6] The first psychopathy law enacted in the United States was the Briggs Act of Massachusetts in 1911, and dealt with so-called defective delinquents.[7]

The first statute authorizing the sterilization of criminals, the insane, feebleminded, and epileptics was passed in Indiana in 1907. The law was declared unconstitutional in 1921 since it denied due process of law to the offender.[8] Another similar statute was passed in Indiana in 1927.[9] The same year the U.S. Supreme Court ruled that a feebleminded Virginia girl could be sterilized on order of the superintendent of a state mental hospital in her best interest and that of society.[10] The first sexual psychopath statute was passed by Michigan in 1937.[11]

The Supreme Court in 1942 rejected an Oklahoma statute that required sterilization of habitual criminals.[12] The National Mental Health Act of 1946 passed by Congress established the National Institute of Mental Health which was to assist states and community mental health facilities develop their programs, encourage and fund research into the prevention, causes, and treatment of mental illness.[13] In 1954, the Durham rule was the result of a federal court case and stated that an offender is not criminally responsible if his crime was the product of mental disease or defect.[14] In 1959 Parliament passed the Mental Health Act which provides for the detention of the mentally ill under certain circumstances.[15]

The Joint Commission on Mental Illness and Health reported its findings on American mental hospitals and made its recommendations in 1961.[16] The Model Penal Code of 1962 proposed a test of insanity that dealt with mental disease or defect, incompetency, or unsoundness of mind. In particular the test states that an individual is not responsible for criminal conduct if at the time he commits a crime such conduct is due to mental disease or defect and that the offender does not have the capacity to either appreciate the criminality of his conduct or conform to the requirements of the criminal law.[17]

The Community Mental Health Centers Act was passed by Congress in 1963 which funded the construction and staffing of community centers that offered inpatient, outpatient, and emergency care in addition to counseling and education programs.[18] In 1970 the Supreme Court upheld a Nebraska statute permitting sterilization as a condition for release from a mental hospital but this was a situation involving voluntary sterilization of a mental patient.[19] In 1972 the federal courts rejected the Durham rule and accepted the Model Penal Code test in its place.[20] Also the same year the Supreme Court ruled that both the due process and equal protection clauses of the Constitution require that a defendant who is found incompetent to stand trial must receive procedural civil requirements; involuntary civil commitment standards must be met before one can be subjected to prolonged commitment; and the defendant must be released when no longer meeting civil commitment standards.[21]

Finally in 1973 the federal courts ruled that the sexual psychopath
laws are unconstitutional since they do not protect the procedural
safeguards of the defendant.[22]

Legal Definitions

As Clinard points out, there are many problems in attempting
to define mental illness or disorder.[23] Since this discussion
deals with crimes without victims, we will examine the legal
definition of insanity rather than the medical (i.e., psychiatric)
definition. This is an extremely difficult task since medical
jurisprudence plays a key role in the legal determination of
criminality.

Black defines insanity as unsoundness of mind, madness, mental
alienation or derangement, a morbid psychic condition. Insanity
also involves the intellect, the emotions, the will, and the moral
sense.[24] In criminal law, the term means such a perverted and
deranged condition of the mental and moral faculties as to render
the individual incapable of distinguishing right from wrong, or to
render one at the time unconscious to the nature of the act one is
committing, or if conscious of the act in terms of right and wrong
unable to control oneself to prevent the commission of the crime.
Thus an insane individual is so mentally deranged or incompetent
that he cannot be charged with criminal intent since he cannot
control his will in order to avoid perpetrating a crime.[25]

Other terms synonymous with insanity are derangement, lunacy,
and non compos mentis. Derangement is all the forms of mental
unsoundness except idiocy.[26] Lunacy is the common law term for one
who has completely lost his memory and understanding. The term is
a general description of all forms of derangement or mental
unsoundness.[27] Non compos mentis is a term applicable to all insane
individuals of whatever type of insanity.[28]

Legal insanity refers to a disorder of the intellect (i.e., a
disease of the brain rendering one incapable of distinguishing right
from wrong with respect to the crime committed).[29] Moral insanity
is a morbid perversion of the feelings, affections, or propensities
but without any illusions or derangement of the intellectual
faculties. It is the irresistable impulse or incapacity to differentiate between what is moral and immoral. Moral insanity is not
usually an acceptable defense to a crime.[30] A psychopath or sociopath (i.e., sociopathic personality) is one having mental disorders
not amounting to insanity but characterized by a defect of basic
personality character (i.e., social-self), eccentricity, emotional
instability, inadequacy or perversity of conduct, suspiciousness,
lack of social feeling, lack of self-control, or lack of truth-
fulness.[31]

Delirium tremens or settled insanity is a legal form of insanity and may be of such nature or intensity as to render the individual incapable of committing a crime. It is produced by alcoholism over a long period of time so that the habitual drunk cannot abstain from drinking or else suffer a nervous disorder that cannot be easily treated. The term is distinguished from temporary insanity or drunkenness which directly results from too much liquor at a particular time.[32]

Paranoia is the delusionary insanity of an individual who is rational mentally except in certain circumstances (i.e., a particular delusion causes the person to react in an insane manner).[33] Mania is a form of insanity where the individual is subject to hallucinations and illusions that are accompanied by a high state of excitement that may amount to complete loss of control.[34] Homicidal mania is the irresistable impulse to murder another person brought about by an insane delusion (i.e., self-defense, revenge, or the instrument of justice).[35] Kleptomania is the inability to stop from stealing.[36] Dipsomania or toxicomania is the irresistible impulse to excessive use of alcohol, opiates, cocaine, or other drugs.[37] Pyromania is the irresistible urge to set fires to property.[38]

Statutes and Enforcement Policy

The D.C. Code defines mental illness as a psychosis or other disease which substantially impairs the mental health of a person. A mentally ill person is defined as one who has mental illness but does not include a person committed to a private or public hospital by order of a court in a criminal proceeding.[39]

Any person may apply to a public or private hospital for admission as a voluntary patient for the purposes of observation, diagnosis, and treatment of a mental illness. Upon the request of any person over eighteen years of age or in the case of a person under eighteen with consent of his spouse, parent, or legal guardian, he or she shall be examined by the admitting psychiatrist to determine whether the individual should be admitted or not.[40] A voluntary patient admitted to a hospital shall be released within forty-eight hours after making a written request to leave if he is over eighteen years of age. A voluntary patient under eighteen may be released if his spouse, parent, or guardian mades the written request. A voluntary patient may be released by the chief of service if he determines that the patient has recovered and continued hospitalization would no longer be useful.[41]

A friend or relative of one believed to be suffering from a mental illness may apply on behalf of that person to the admitting psychiatrist of a hospital by presenting the person together with a reference from a practicing doctor. The admitting psychiatrist

shall admit the alleged mentally ill patient if he feels the need
for examination and treatment is indicated. The patient must state
in writing that he does not object to hospitalization.[42] A police
officer or a physician of the person in question who has reason to
believe that the person is mentally ill and because of the illness
is likely to injure himself or others if he is not immediately
detained may without a warrent take the person into custody,
transport him to a private or public hospital, and make application
for his admission thereto for purposes of emergency observation
and diagnosis. The application shall reveal the circumstances under
which the person was taken into custody and the reasons therefor.[43]

A police officer may apprehend and detain a person whom he
believes to be a mentally ill person and found under suspicious
circumstances. Said apprehended person shall be brought before a
United States commissioner for a hearing and if said commissioner
is not available to be taken to St. Elizabeths Hospital where the
superintendent may detain the person pending a hearing before a
United States commissioner. The hearing shall be within seventy-
two hours of detention. The hearing can be at St. Elizabeths
Hospital if it is medically determined that the person should not
be moved as a health or safety factor.[44] The superintendent shall
promptly examine a person committed and if not found to be mentally
ill shall discharge him, or if found to be mentally ill shall return
him to the state of his residence or to his relatives, if practi-
cable.[45]

The term sexual psychopath means a person, not insane, who by
a course of repeated misconduct in sexual matters has evidenced
such lack of power to control his sexual impulses as to be dangerous
to other persons because he is likely to attack or otherwise inflict
injury, loss, pain, or other evil on the objects of his desire.[46]
Other statutes dealing with sexual psychopaths deal with examination
by psychiatrists, hearing-commitment to St. Elizabeths Hospital,
parole-discharge, and stay of criminal proceedings.[47]

In all states and the District of Columbia commitment of the
mentally ill is a civil procedure. Thus the police are prohibited
by statute from taking a suspected mentally ill person to jail. In
many states the commitment laws specify that the mentally ill do not
have to be dangerous, just in need of care and treatment for involuntary commitment. Some states even make the welfare and needs of
persons other than the prospective patient (i.e., family members) a
sufficient criterion for involuntary commitment. Only a minority
of states continue to use the term "dangerous" or require the
likelihood of injury to self or others in order for the police to
bring the person to a hospital for involuntary commitment.[48]

The mentally ill are not the only individuals that the police deal with in terms of commitment to a public or private hospital for psychiatric observation and diagnosis. The police are also authorized in thirty-seven states to deal with mentally defective or deficient individuals (i.e., idiots and imbeciles). The same number of states also allow alcoholics to be committed; thirty-four states deal with drug addicts and abusers in the same manner; and a few states even subject epileptics to confinement in mental hospitals.[49]

Finally the criminal justice system also has to deal with those criminals who are adjudicated criminally insane. Thus individuals who are deemed incompetent to stand trial or enter a plea of guilty, defendants found guilty by reason of insanity, individuals found guilty of violation of certain statutes like sexual psychopath or defective delinquent laws, convicted and sentenced offenders who become mentally ill while in prison or jail, and the mentally ill who pose a danger to medical personnel in the course of their diagnosis and treatment are all sent to special institutions for the criminally insane. There are presently seventy-three such institutions in America today.[50]

Description of Specific Deviance

NIMH estimates for 1970 states that approximately three million Americans are treated for mental disorders of which approximately six hundred thousand are institutionalized.[51] There were more than four hundred thousand admissions to state and county mental hospitals in 1972 of which forty percent were involuntary. There are 501 mental hospitals in the United States of which 312 are state and county institutions, 39 are Veterans Administration neuropsychiatric hospitals, and 150 are private hospitals. There are also an estimated thirteen hundred general hospitals that contain psychiatric treatment facilities. There are also approximately 2100 outpatient clinics throughout the country that deal with mental health problems.[52] This is in addition to the 73 correctional institutions for the criminally insane, already noted elsewhere.

It is estimated that the medical treatment, incarceration, and loss of work costs due to mental illness exceeds twenty billion dollars per year in the United States.[53] If one considers all the social stresses that most Americans are subjected to every year and the resulting deviant solutions to these stresses (i.e., drug addiction and abuse, alcoholism, over-eating, child and spouse abuse, suicide, and violent criminal acts), the costs of mental illness are truly astronomical.

Weinberg's review of several urban studies of mental disorders shows that the overall rates of psychoses and of schizophrenia are highest near the central business districts and transitional areas of inner cities and decline as one moves outward toward the suburbs where the rates of neurosis increases significantly.[54] Social mobility appears to be related to mental illness (i.e., both upward and downward).[55] There also appears to be a positive correlation between social class and mental illness (i.e., lower class persons tend to be psychotic and middle/upper class people tend to be neurotic).[56]

There appears to be little difference in the prevalence of mental illness among males and females in society. Rates of mental disorders tend to increase as the typical individual goes through the life cycle with neuroses occuring most frequently before middle age and psychoses occuring most often during middle age or early old age although schizophrenia occurs most often before middle age.[57] Jews tend to be more neurotic while Catholics tend to be more psychotic but these findings are quite tentative. The rate of mental illness is higher for whites than for nonwhites although Blacks, Mexican-Americans, and American Indians do suffer a disproportionate amount of mental problems. Finally rates of mental disorders are higher for the divorced and separated than for those who are married.[58]

The Hospital of St. Mary of Bethlehem in London was used after 1400 as an insane asylum.[59] In 1776 Virginia became the first state to open an asylum. It was not until 1890 that the New York legislature passed a statute establishing hospitals that offered specialized care for the legally insane.[60] Up to 1960 almost ninety percent of those in mental hospitals and institutions for the criminally insane were involuntarily committed.[61] Until the early 1970's, most individuals were kept in an institution whether public or private, punitive or rehabilitative for several years.[62] The practice is currently for outpatient services except for the most difficult cases. These services include a whole range of activities from counseling, individual and group therapy, and medical treatment by both professionals (i.e., psychiatrists, psychologists, social workers) and volunteers of concerned nonprofessionals. There are also halfway houses for ex-mental patients and social organizations like Recovery Incorporated that help ex-mental patients meet others with similar backgrounds in order to discuss and overcome common problems in adjusting to the community. Sometimes nursing and foster homes are utilized as alternatives to hospitalization for the elderly mentally ill as well as the juvenile mental patient.[63]

Decriminalization

As Halleck notes, there is a problem in the diagnosing of mental illness by psychiatrists. Yet these medical experts are utilized by the criminal court to determine whether the offender meets the legal test of insanity or not. Psychiatrists are also used to determine whether the offender should be committed before trial or even if he should have a trial at all. Thus the criminal justice system allows the psychiatrist and his knowledge of medical jurisprudence to determine whether the criminal offender goes to trial at all, whether he is legally sane or insane (i.e., psychiatric testimony usually determines which way the jury votes in most instances), whether the offender should be diverted to a court clinic, hospital for the criminally insane, operate programs for sexual psychopaths, diagnostic reception centers, alcoholic rehabilitation centers, narcotics hospitals, operate programs for juvenile delinquents in training schools, and serve as parttime staff at state prisons for the general inmate population. It must be apparent to the average person who comes in contact with anyone dealing with mental health or the criminal justice system that the word of the psychiatrist is almost law (i.e., the so-called medical model which has been proposed by psychiatrists has been accepted by state legislatures in creating statutes dealing with the mentally ill, the mentally defective or deficient, the criminally insane, and sexual psychopaths). Thus we live in the age of the therapeutic state where medical science and social science team up to creat a new type of social control over our daily existence which can be used to benefit the average person as well as take away his constitutional rights in the name of psychiatric therapy.[65]

As already mentioned, the criminally insane and the mentally ill are not the only individuals who are involuntarily committed to a mental hospital or special institution for the insane criminal. There are special institutions for juvenile delinquents who are known as "defective delinquents" like the Patuxent Institution in Maryland, the narcotics hospital like the federal institutions in Kentucky and Texas, the institutions that deal with alcoholics, and the state and county hospitals that care for the mentally defective and deficient.

All states have statutes governing the individual who seeks voluntary commitment to a mental hospital. The major problem deals with the laws that govern the involuntary commitment of all kinds of people who may or may not be in need of psychiatric assistance. Some states have judicial commitment procedures while others have nonjudicial proceedings (i.e., administrative or medical certification).[66]

Forty-two states have involuntary commitment procedures that are considered judicial in nature (i.e., before a judge and jury). Notice must be given to the person who is alleged to be mentally ill in twenty-six of these states. In most states a mandatory hearing

is provided but only eleven require that the defendant be present.
All forty-two states provide that the alleged ill person has the
right to be represented by an attorney but only twenty-four states
provide for the appointment of a lawyer if the mentally ill person
cannot afford one.[67]

Nonjudicial proceedings are either administrative or medical
certification. Ten states allow administrative commitment where a
board determines whether the alleged mentally ill person should
undergo treatment. Some of these administrative hearings do not
even allow the patient the opportunity to be heard. Involuntary
commitment by medical certification is accomplished on the basis of
one or more psychiatric reports being filed with the court. Thus
the psychiatrist decides the fate of an individual without his
ability to properly defend his past or present behavior in a court
of law. Thirty-one states provide medical certification proceedings
for the mentally ill and allow judicial review of the medical
certification and allow for the patient's release within a designated
time if he gives formal notice to the court that he wants to be
re-examined in order to obtain release from the mental hospital.[68]

What one finds is the indefinite involuntary commitment of
approximately forty percent of all alleged mental patients in the
United States today. Once the procedures for commitment are
initiated, most individuals usually are placed in an institution or
are labeled as social deviants who must seek treatment at an outpatient clinic under court order and thus lose their constitutional
safeguards or have limited freedoms due to the impact of the therapeutic state (i.e., psychiatrist's control of the individual adjudicated as mentally ill).[69]

Finally we must deal with those committed to special institutions for the criminally insane (i.e., sexual psychopaths, sociopaths, and those criminals who are innocent of their crimes by
reason of insanity). At one time twenty-eight states and the
District of Columbia had sexual psychopath laws. These statutes
are vague and open to misinterpretation and many states have rescinded their laws dealing with this type of social deviance. Unfortunately for individuals labelled as psychopaths, psychiatrists do
not in general know how to deal with this category of mental illness
so rehabilitation is difficult. The term sociopath is synonomous
with psychopath but some jurisdictions make a legal differentiation
between the two concepts. At any rate, an offender who is committed
to an institution for the criminally insane will probably spend
more time in jail than a criminal who commits the same offense and
accepts a jail sentence at the state penitentiary. Thus the

criminally insane are given indeterminate sentences and allowed to deteriorate mentally even further while the same type of offender who serves his time as a normal criminal will be out in society to cause the same problem again and not be stigmatized as much as the criminally insane individual by society.[70]

216

Notes

1. Michel Foucault, Madness and Civilization: A History of
   Insanity in the Age of Reason, New York: Random House, 1973;
   Albert Deustch, The Mentally Ill in America, New York:
   Columbia University Press, 1949; Samuel Brakel and Ronald Rock,
   (eds.), The Mentally Disabled and the Law, Chicago: University
   of Chicago Press, 1971; Nicholas Kittrie, The Right to be
   Different, Baltimore: The Johns Hopkins University Press,
   1971; C. Ray Jeffery, The Development of Crime in Early English
   Society, in Chambliss (ed.), Crime and the Legal Process, New
   York: McGraw-Hill, 1969, 28; Hazel Kerper, Introduction to
   the Criminal Justice System, St. Paul: West Publishing Company,
   1972, 70-73.

2. Ibid.; Robert Dreher, Origin, Development, and Present Status
   of Insanity as a Defense to Criminal Responsibility in the
   Common Law, Journal of History of Behavioral Sciences, 3
   (1967), 47-57.

3. M'Naghten's Case, 8 Eng. Rep. 718 (1843); Sue Reid, Crime and
   Criminology, Hinsdale, Illinois: The Dryden Press, 1976,
   169-170; Lawrence Friedman, A History of American Law, New
   York: Simon and Schuster, 1973, 514-515; Martin Haskell and
   Lewis Yablonsky, Criminology: Crime and Criminality, Chicago:
   Rand McNally, 1978, 42; Kerper, op. cit., 73-74.

4. State v. Felter, 25 Iowa 67, 82 (1868); Friedman, op. cit.,
   515; Kerper, op. cit., 73-74.

5. State v. Pike, 49 N.H. 399, 442 (1869); Friedman, op. cit.,
   515; State v. Jones, 50 N.H. 369, 398 (1871); Reid, op. cit.,
   170.

6. Paul Horton and Gerald Leslie, The Sociology of Social Problems,
   New Jersey: Prentice-Hall, 1974, 526.

7. Kittrie, op. cit., 65; Harry Allen and Clifford Simonsen,
   Corrections in America: An Introduction, Beverly Hills,
   California: Glencoe Press, 1975, 347.

8. Reid, op. cit., 166; Williams v. Smith, 131 N.E. 2 (1921).

9. Burns Indiana Statutes, Annotated, 16-13-13-1 (22-1601).

10. Buck v. Bell, 274 U.S. 200, 207 (1927); Reid, op. cit., 166-167.

217

11. Edwin Sutherland, The Diffusion of Sexual Psychopath Laws, in Chambliss (ed.), op. cit., 74; Allen and Simonsen, op. cit., 347-349.

12. Skinner v. Oklahoma, 316 U.S. 535, 539, 541 (1942); Reid, op. cit., 167.

13. Horton and Leslie, op. cit., 526.

14. Durham v. United States, 214 F.2d 862, 871 (1954); Reid, op. cit., 170; Haskell and Yablonsky, op. cit., 42; Kerper, op. cit., 74.

15. P.J. Fitzgerald, Criminal Law and Punishment, London: Oxford University Press, 1962, 131.

16. Joint Commission on Mental Illness and Health, Action For Mental Health, Final Report, New York: Basic Books, 1961.

17. Model Penal Code, sections 4.01, 4.02, 1962; Kerper, op. cit., 75-77; Haskell and Yablonsky, op. cit., 43; Reid, op. cit., 170.

18. Horton and Leslie, op. cit., 526-527; Clinard, op. cit., 619; President's Commission on Law Enforcement and the Administration of Justice, Challenge of Crime in a Free Society, Washington, D.C: US Government Printing Office, 228-229.

19. State v. Cavitt, 157 N.W. 2d 171 (1968); 396 U.S. 996 (1970); Reid, op. cit., 167-168.

20. United States v. Browner, 471 F.2d 969 (1972); Reid, op. cit., 170.

21. Jackson v. Indiana, June 7, 1972 (number 70-5009).

22. Davy v. Sullivan, 354 F. Supp. 1320.

23. Clinard, op. cit., 587-597.

24. Henry Black, Black's Law Dictionary, St. Paul, Minnesota: West Publishing Company, 1968, 929.

25. Ibid., 935.

26. Ibid., 930.

27. Ibid.

28. Ibid., 931.

29. Ibid., 932.

30. Ibid.

31. Ibid., 1392.

32. Ibid., 931, 933.

33. Ibid., 931.

34. Ibid., 934.

35. Ibid.

36. Ibid., 1011.

37. Ibid., 933, 935.

38. Ibid., 935.

39. District of Columbia Code, Annotated, Washington, DC: US Government Printing Office, 2, 1973, 21-501, 1287.

40. Ibid., 21-511, 1289.

41. Ibid., 21-512, 1289-1290.

42. Ibid., 21-513, 1290.

43. Ibid., 21-521, 1290.

44. Ibid., 21-903, 1315.

45. Ibid., 21-905, 1315.

46. Ibid., 22-3503, 1571.

47. Ibid., 22-3506 to 22-3510.

48. Brackel and Rock, op. cit., 36; Egon Bittner, Police Discretion in Apprehending the Mentally Ill, Social Problems, 14 (1967), 278-292.

49. Brackel and Rock, op. cit., 37.

50. Allen and Simonsen, op. cit., 345.

51. National Institute of Mental Health, Mental Illness and Its Treatment, U.S. Public Health Service, Washington, DC: US Government Printing Office, 1970.

219

52. Alan Stone, Mental Health and the Law, NIMH Crime and Delinquency Issues, U.S. Public Health Service, Washington, DC: US Government Printing Office, 1976, 43.

53. Mental Illness and its Treatment, op. cit.

54. Kirson Weinberg (ed.), The Sociology of Mental Disorders, Chicago: Aldine Publishing Company, 1967; Thomas Scheff (ed.), Mental Illness and Social Process, New York: Harper and Row, 1967; E.G. Jaco, The Social Epidemiology of Mental Disorders, New York: Russell Sage Foundation, 1960; H.W. Dunham, Community and Schizophrenia: An Epidemiological Analysis, Detroit: Wayne State University Press, 1965.

55. Robert Faris and Warren Dunham, Mental Disorders in Urban Areas, Chicago: University of Chicago Press, 1939; August Hollingshead and Frederick Redlich, Social Class and Mental Illness, New York: John Wiley, 1958; Hollingshead et al., Social Mobility and Mental Illness, in Weinberg, op. cit., 48-53; Leo Srole and Thomas Langner, Socioeconomic Status Groups: Their Mental Health Composition, in Weinberg, op. cit., 33-47; Langner and Stanley Michael, Life Stress and Mental Health, New York: Free Press, 1963; James Rinehart, Mobility Aspirations-Achievement Discrepancies and Mental Illness, Social Problems, 15 (1968), 478-488.

56. Faris and Dunham, op. cit., 23-81, 143-150; Hollingshead and Redlich, op. cit., 220-302, 186-213; Dunham, op. cit., 86-198; Leo Srole et al., Mental Health in the Metropolis, in Silverstein (ed.), The Social Control of Mental Illness, New York: Thomas Y. Crowell, 1968; Frank Riessman et al., Mental Health of the Poor, New York: Free Press, 1964; Jaco, op. cit., 125-173.

57. Faris and Dunham, op. cit., 38-81; Jaco, op. cit., 32-39; Langner and Michael, op. cit., 77; Riessman, op. cit., 33-34; Stephen Spitzer and Norman Denzin (eds.), The Mental Patients: Studies in the Sociology of Deviance, New York: McGraw-Hill, 1968.

58. Langner and Michael, op. cit., 77-79; Jaco, op. cit., 40-59, 109-124; Spitzer and Denzin, op. cit., 121-147.

59. Black, op. cit., 196; Horton and Leslie, op. cit., 526.

60. Horton and Leslie, op. cit., 526.

61. Deutsch, op. cit., 425; Kittrie, op. cit., 55; U.S. Congress, Senate Committee on the Judiciary, Subcommittee on Constitutional Rights, Hearings On Constitutional Rights of the Mentally Ill, 87th Congress, 1st Session, Washington, DC: US Government Printing Office, 1961, 43.

62. David Mechanic, Mental Health and Social Policy, N.J.: Prentice-Hall, 1969; Brackel Rock, op. cit., 36-45; Kittrie, op. cit., 79; Challenge of Crime in a Free Society, op. cit., 228-229.

63. Clinard, op. cit., 618-624; M. Greenblatt and B. Simon (eds.), Rehabilitating of the Mentally Ill, Washington, DC: American Association for the Advancement of Science, 1969; Shirley Angrist et al., Women After Treatment: A Study of Former Mental Patients and Their Normal Neighbors, New York: Appleton-Century-Crofts, 1968; David Landy and Sara Singer, The Social Organization and Culture of a Club for Former Mental Patients, in Spitzer and Denzin, op. cit., 449-476; Francine Sobey, The Nonprofessional Revolution in Mental Health, New York: Columbia University Press, 1970; William Henry et al., The Fifth Profession, San Francisco: Jossy-Bass, 1971; Harry Gottesfeld (ed.), The Critical Issues in Community Mental Health, New York: Behavioral Publications, 1972; Arthur Bindman and Allen Spiegel (eds.), Perspectives in Community Mental Health, Chicago: Aldine, 1969.

64. Seymour Halleck, Psychiatry and the Dilemmas of Crime: A Study of Causes, Punishment, and Treatment, New York: Harper and Row, 1967, 205-318; Karl Menninger, The Crime of Punishment, New York: Viking Press, 1968; Kittrie, op. cit.; Thomas Szasz, The Myth of Mental Illness: Foundations of a Theory of Personal Conduct, New York: Harper and Row, 1961.

65. Ibid.; Charles McCaghy, Deviant Behavior: Crime, Conflict, and Interest Groups, New York: Macmillan Publishing Company, 1976, 330-340; Thomas Szasz, Law, Liberty and Psychiatry: An Inquiry into the Social Uses of Mental Health Practices, New York: Macmillan, 1963; Szasz, Ideology and Insanity: Essays on the Psychiatric Dehumanization of Man, Garden City, New York: Doubleday, 1970; Thomas Scheff, Being Mentally Ill: A Sociological Theory, Chicago: Aldine, 1966; Seymour Halleck, The Politics of Therapy, New York: Science House, 1971.

66. Clinard, op. cit., 608-611; Brackel and Rock, op. cit., 37, 53-59; McCaghy, op. cit., 333-337.

67. Brackel and Rock, op. cit., 53-59.

68. Ibid.

69. Thomas Scheff, The Societal Reaction to Deviance: Ascriptive
Elements in the Psychiatric Screening of Mental Patients in a
Midwestern State, Social Problems, 11 (1964), 401-413; Scheff,
Social Conditions for Rationality: How Urban and Rural Courts
Deal with the Mentally Ill, American Behavioral Scientist, 8
(1964), 21-24; Dorothy Miller and Michael Schwartz, County
Lunacy Commission Hearings: Some Observations of Commitments
to a State Mental Hospital, Social Problems, 14 (1966), 26-35;
L. Kutner, The Illusion of Due Process in Commitment Proceedings,
Northwestern University Law Review, 57 (1962), 383-399; Sara
Fein and Kent Miller, Legal Processes and Adjudication in
Mental Incompetency Proceedings, Social Problems, 20 (1972),
57-64; James Greenley, Alternative Views of the Psychiatrist's
Role, Social Problems, 20 (1972), 252-262; Henry Steadman, The
Psychiatrist as a Conservative Agent of Social Control, Social
Problems, 20 (1972), 263-271; The Administration of Psychiatric
Justice: Theory and Practice in Arizona, Arizona Law Review,
13 (1971); D.L. Rosenhan, On Being Sane in Insane Places,
Science, 179 (1973), 250-258; Judith Rabkin, Public Attitudes
Toward Mental Illness: A Review of the Literature, Schizophre-
nia Bulletin, 10 (1974), 9-33; Bruce Ennis, Prisoners of
Psychiatry: Mental Patients, Psychiatrists, and the Law, New
York: Harcourt, Brace Jovanovich, 1972.

70. Haskell and Yablonsky, op. cit., 373-380, 381-401; McCaghy,
op. cit., 337-340; Sutherland, op. cit.; Alan Swanson, Sexual
Psychopath Statutes: Summary and Analysis: Journal of
Criminal Law and Criminology, 51 (1970), 215-218; Ralph
Brancale, Psychiatric and Psychological Investigation of
Convicted Sex Offenders, American Journal of Psychiatry, 109
(1952), 17-21; Halleck, op. cit.; Kittrie, op. cit.; William
and Joan McCord, The Psychopath, New York: Van Nostrand
Company, 1964; Harvey Cleckley, The Mask of Sanity, St. Louis:
C.V. Mosby, 1941; Gordon Trasler, The Explanation of Criminality,
London: Routledge and Kegan Paul, 1962; Harrison Gough, A
Sociological Theory of Psychopathy, American Journal of
Sociology, 53 (1948), 365; Albert Rabin, Psychopathic (Socio-
pathic Personality), in Toch (ed.), Legal and Criminal
Psychology, New York: Holt, Rinehart and Winston, 1961; Harry
Allen et al., Hostile and Simple Sociopaths: An Empirical
Typology, Criminology, 9 (1971), 27-47.

XV

SUICIDE

Legal History

Suicide was a crime at Common Law in England. The deceased's body was treated with disrespect as it was allowed to be mutilated by the public, dragged through the streets, and exhibited in public as a warning to others not to commit suicide. The offender's corpse was denied Christian burial by the church and what remained of the mutilated corpse was denied burial in hallowed ground. The property of the suicide was confiscated by the king. This was apparently the situation by the time of King William in the eleventh century since by the time of Henry II in the twelfth century suicide was a felony and attempted suicide was a misdemeanor punishable by fine and possible imprisonment.[1]

Over the centuries in England, the suicide was given an ignominious burial in the crossroads of the public highway with a stake driven through the body and lost all his personal and real property to the crown.[2] The colony of Massachusetts followed the Common law and in 1660 passed a statute requiring suicides be buried by a highway under a load of stones so that all could see the infamous grave. The colony of North Carolina in 1715 accepted the same practice.[3]

Upon independence from England and the passage of the United States Constitution after 1789, the states stopped dealing with suicides in terms of ignominious burial and forfeiture of estates as punishment for the crime.[4] Massachusetts repealed its statute of 1660 in 1823 but most states still carried criminal laws against suicide attempts.[5] In 1824 Parliament passed an Act stopping the centuries old practice of burying suicides in the highway with a stake through the body and provided for burial in churchyards but without religious ceremony and only at night between nine p.m. and midnight.[6] Attempted suicide was a crime in England from 1854 until 1961 (i.e., a misdemeanor punishable initially by a short jail sentence and up to six months for a second attempt).[7] In 1870 Parliament repealed the statute confiscating the property of suicides.[8] In 1882 Parliament passed an act allowing suicides normal burial with religious rites.[9]

In the United States during the late nineteenth and early twentieth centuries, a number of states began examining their statutes concerning suicide and attempted suicide. As early as 1877 Massachusetts stated that suicide was a crime (i.e., malum in se) though not punishable if self-murder is accomplished. Similar conclusions were reached by the state courts in Alabama, New Jersey, and South Carolina.[10] New York and Illinois recognized suicide as a grave public wrong but did not consider it a crime.[11] Several states like Iowa, Indiana, and Texas have no common law crimes so suicide could not be considered a criminal act.[12] Massachusetts in 1816 ruled that one who aids and abets another in, or is accessory before the fact to, self-murder is also a criminal.[13] Alabama and Tennessee cases concluded that two parties who agree to kill themselves together and only one succeeds in dying, the other can be charged with the crime of murder.[14] South Carolina ruled that an individual who attempts to commit suicide but accidently kills another is guilty of a crime.[15] Until recently in New Jersey, and South Dakota, attempted suicide was a crime.[16]

The Suicide Act of 1961 passed by Parliament rescinded the law in England that made suicide a crime and thus attempted suicide could no longer be considered criminal either. But the Act did make it a crime to aid, abet, counsel, or procure the suicide of another individual.[17]

Legal Definitions

Black defines suicide as the deliberate termination of one's life while in possession and enjoyment of one's mental faculties (i.e., self-destruction).[18] Other definitions state that suicide is the intentional act of voluntarily taking your own life.[19] Durkheim defined suicide as "all cases of death resulting directly or indirectly from a positive or negative act of the victim himself, which he knows will produce the result".[20] Cavan defines suicide as either "the intentional taking of one's life or the failure when possible to save oneself when death threatens" (i.e., self-murder).[21]

Statutes and Enforcement Policy

At present there are no statutes making suicide or attempted suicide a crime in the United States.[22] In the state of South Dakota, it is a crime to willfully in any manner, advise, willfully furnish another individual with any deadly weapon or poisonous drug knowing that such person intends to use the same in taking his own life, and in the case such person thereafter uses the same in taking his own life, one is guilty of aiding suicide and punishable by imprisonment for not less than seven years.[23] Anyone who willfully aids another in the attempt to take his own life in any manner but does not succeed in actually taking his own life is guilty of a felony punishable by imprisonment not to exceed two years or by fine not to exceed one thousand dollars, or both.[24] It is no defense to a person who aides a suicide or attempts to aid a suicide who is unsuccessful in the attempt that the individual committing suicide or attempting to commit suicide was not capable of committing the crime himself.[25] These statutes are similar to the English Suicide Act of 1961

According to Captain Clark and Lieutenant Morris of the
Metropolitan Police Department (District of Columbia), there are a
number of problems that the police have to deal with where suicides
or attempted suicides are concerned. The police have to consider
whether the individual acted alone while in complete control of his
faculties, whether the individual was under the influence of
alcohol, narcotics, other dangerous drugs, or whether the situation
involved other individuals (i.e., homicide-suicide).[26]

The police officer has to take into consideration the nature
of the suicide attempt in order to best deal with the individual.
Thus the officer is faced with a dilemma of whether to approach the
potential suicide with compassion and in an attempt to help or to
interpret the situation as potentially prone to violence and take
appropriate protective measures. If the potential suicide is not
in possession of his mental faculties, the officer can take him
into protective custody as mentally ill and dangerous and deliver
the person to a public hospital for diagnosis and observation.[27]
If the potential suicide is under the influence of alcohol, drugs,
or both, the officer is in potential danger for his life and the
life of others around the vicinity of the suicidal person. Thus
the person could have a hand gun or rifle and be shooting aimlessly
so as to draw attention to himself, or be trying to jump off a
bridge or building, or driving a vehicle in a reckless manner. The
officer has a real problem in dealing with this type of potential
suicide since many innocent bystanders as well as the officer could
be injured or possibly killed in the attempt to stop the potential
suicide from completing his act of self-destruction.

The individual who has committed a homicide and then kills
himself before the police can respond to the scene poses no additional threat to third parties or the police. Unfortunately all too
often there are individuals who kill another and then wait for the
police to respond to the incident. These anomic murderers want the
police to shoot them and in reality are using the police as the
mechanism for completing the suicide act since this type individual
must kill someone else in order to force himself into a confrontation
with the police where they will hopefully kill him in a shoot-out.[28]

A considerable number of murder-suicide offenders usually have
a close relationship with those whom they murder (i.e., parent
killing a child, mercy killings, death pacts, and accidental deaths
initiated from family quarrels). Individuals who become this type
of criminal tend to have violent personalities and are also self-
destructive. Murder-suicide offenders tend to have very close ties
with nuclear family members and are usually forced by circumstance
to commit suicide rather than planning to end their lives without
harming others.[29]

Police officers have a suicide rate approximately six times greater than that of the general population. Many officers find that dealing with criminals and other social deviants on a daily basis causes problems for them and members of their families when they are off-duty. Officers find that they must protect themselves psychically from the realities of their work and they become too cynical, serious, emotionally withdrawn from immediate family members, cold, and authoritarian. The fact that officers must carry their guns while off-duty and are technically on-call if the need arises makes it hard to relax away from work. This job-related problem coupled with the fact that the enforcement bureaucracy is somewhat authoritarian (i.e., officers must accept orders and shift changes without question) creates a need in the officer to find a way to escape the tensions of his job. Some officers become alcoholics, others become drug abusers, and some take out their frustrations on wives and children. All these deviant solutions which are caused by the demands of police work leave the officer a prime candidate for suicide if the pressures reach the breaking point. Thus police officers become susceptable to suicide before retirement, when his marriage is breaking up, if his children are a major source of anxiety, or if he becomes sick (i.e., physically or emotionally).[30]

Description of Specific Deviance

The current estimated suicide rate for the United States is eleven per one hundred thousand population.[31] It is estimated that this figure is probably underreported by as much as forty percent. Of those who commit suicide approximately one-third had attempted suicide. Thus there are approximately twenty-five thousand suicides each year and probably a ratio of 8 to 1 in terms of attempted suicide to completed suicide during the same twelve month period.[32]

Males tend to have a high rate of suicide while females have a low rate of suicide but make more attempts at suicide than men.[33] More older people (i.e., age cohorts 55-64 and 75 and older) tend to commit suicide than younger.[34] More whites and American Indians commit suicide than Blacks and other minorities.[35] Divorced individuals have a higher rate of suicide than married people.[36] Protestants have a higher suicide rate than either Catholics or Jews.[37] Individuals of both high and low social status tend to commit suicide more often than people of average social status. Also individuals who are downwardly mobile socially are more apt to commit suicide than either those who are socially stable or upwardly mobile.[38] Supposedly there is some correlation between mental health and suicide but the data appears to be inconclusive. The most one can conclude is that individuals who are depressed over long periods of time tend to be more suicidal than those who are not. There also appears to be a link between alcoholism and drug abuse and suicide.[39] Both the West and Central parts of America have more suicides than the

North and South. Central city residents tend to be more suicidal than surburban residents.[40]

The first organization to become concerned about suicides was the Royal Humane Society in 1774 in England.[41] The National Save-a-Life league was founded in the United States in 1906. The first of the Suicide Prevention Centers to appear in recent years in this country was founded in 1958 in Los Angeles. Today there are a variety of formal organization and voluntary associations that deal with suicide prevention (i.e., Suicide Prevention Service, Call-for-Help Clinics, Crisis Call Centers, Rescue, Inc., Dial-a-Friend, and Suicides Anonymous).[42] The District of Columbia operated a suicide hotline until 1977 but transferred the service to the emergency mental health admitting office at D.C. General Hospital.[43]

The Center For Studies of Suicide Prevention was established by the National Institute of Mental Health in 1967 and also began publication of the Bulletin of Suicidology. The Institute conducts and supports research on the various aspects of suicide prevention and provides support to public and private organizations that deal with this topic.[44]

Decriminalization

Since it is not a crime to commit suicide in the United States, little can be said concerning the decriminalization of this practice. The practice of suicide is still considered by many as immoral and reprehensible. Thus most of the concern with this form of social deviance is with suicide prevention.

Those who attempt suicide can endanger others by the method utilized (i.e., using a vehicle as a means to killing oneself, attempting suicide via use of gas, jumping off high places, and lying down on railroad or subway tracks). There are also those individuals who try to involve others consciously or subconsciously in the act of suicide (i.e., force another person to deliberately kill them or murder someone else in order to be forced into the act of self-destruction). Our present criminal statutes dealing with homicide supposedly deal with murder-suicide cases and suicide pacts, but are somewhat confusing as to how to deal with the particular circumstances of suicide cases.[45]

Thus the criminal justice system must develop some way of dealing with suicide prevention cases other than processing these individuals as offenders except in the cases of murder-suicide attempts. There should be better coordination of police with mental health personnel. General orders should be developed to aid law enforcement personnel deal with the variety of types of potential suicides. Finally since a high percentage of police officers are themselves potential suicides, there should be specialized personnel in each department (i.e., psychologist or psychiatrist) to counsel officers who appear to be in need of help.

The federal government which already operates The Center For Studies of Suicide Prevention should actively work with both professional and volunteer groups on the county and municipal levels to educate the public on this social problem. The stigma attached to the individual who attempts suicide should be handled in a similar manner to that of Alcoholics Anonymous so that the individual will not be forced into another attempt that may succeed in his or her self-destruction. Thus the mass media should be involved along with various educational and social service institutions in an effort to prevent suicide and suicide-homicides in our society.[46]

1. C. Ray Jeffery, The Development of Crime in Early English
   Society, in Chambliss (ed.), Crime and the Legal Process,
   New York: McGraw-Hill, 1969, 23-28; Leon Radzinowicz, A
   History of English Criminal Law, London: Macmillan, 1948-53.

2. Norman St. John-Stevas, Life, Death and the Law, Bloomington,
   Indiana: Indiana University Press, 1961; Louis Dublin, Suicide:
   A Sociological and Statistical Study, New York: Ronald Press,
   1963; Jack Gibbs (ed.), Suicide, New York: Harper and Row,
   1968; Erwin Stengel, Suicide and Attempted Suicide, Middlesex,
   England: Pelican Books, 1969; G.L. Williams, The Sanctity of
   Life and the Criminal Law, New York: Alfred A. Knopf, 1957;
   William Lecky, A History of European Morals, New York:
   Appleton-Century-Crofts, 1906; Edmund Cahn, The Moral Decision,
   Bloomington, Indiana: Indiana University Press, 1959; Crime
   of Suicide, The Economist, 196 (1960), 871-872; Kenneth
   Robinson, Suicide and the Law, The Spectator, March 4, 1958,
   317.

3. Ibid.

4. American and English Encyclopedia of Law and Practice, volume
   24, section II, 490-491; Corpus Juris Secundum, 1953, 871-785;
   American Jurisprudence, 1968, section 583.

5. Marshall Clinard, Sociology of Deviant Behavior, New York:
   Holt, Rinehart and Winston, 1974, 630; Robert Bell, Social
   Deviance, Homewood, Illinois: Dorsey Press, 1976, 211; Gibbs,
   op. cit., 53.

6. 4 George IV, c. 52, s. 1.

7. Williams, op. cit., 280.

8. Herbert Bloch and Gilbert Geis, Man, Crime and Society, New
   York: Random House, 1970, 64.

9. Ibid.

10. Commonwealth v. Mink, 123 Mass. 422; State v. Carney, 69 N.J.
    Law 478, 55A. 44; Southern Life and Health Ins. Co. v. Wynn,
    29 Ala. App. 207, 194 So. 421; State v. Levelle, 13 S.E. 314,
    34 S.C. 120.

11. Hundert v. Commercial Travelers' Mut. Acc. Ass'n. of America, 244 App. Div. 459, 279, N.Y.S. 555, 556; Burnett v. People of State of Illinois, 204 Ill 208, 68 N.E. 505, 510.

12. State v. Campbell, 217 Iowa 848, 251 N.W. 717, 92 A.L.R. 1176; Prudential Ins. Co. of America v. Rice, 52 N.E. 2nd 624, 222 Ind. 231; Grace v. State, 69 S.W. 529 Texas.

13. Commonwealth v. Bowen, 13 Mass. 356.

14. McMahan v. State, 968 Ala. 70, 53 So. 89; Turner v. State, 119 Tenn. 663, 108 S.W. 1139, 15 L.R.A., N.S.

15. State v. Levelle, op. cit.

16. Williams, op. cit., 283.

17. Clinard, op. cit., 632; Bloch and Geis, op. cit., 65-66; Crime of Suicide, op. cit.

18. Henry Black, Black's Law Dictionary, St. Paul, Minnesota: West Publishing Company, 1968, 1602.

19. Henry Fairchild (ed.), Dictionary of Sociology, Paterson, New Jersey: Littlefield, Adams and Company, 1962, 312; The Dushkin Publishing Group, Encyclopedia of Sociology, Guilford, Connecticut: Dushkin Publishing Inc., 1974, 289.

20. Emile Durkheim, Suicide, New York: Free Press, 1951, 44.

21. Ruth Cavan, Suicide, Chicago: University of Chicago Press, 1928, 3.

22. Williams, op. cit., 283.

23. American Jurisprudence, op. cit., 22-16-37.

24. Ibid., 22-16-38.

25. Ibid., 22-16-39.

26. Interviews with Captain Clayton Clark and Lieutenant Anthony Morris, Metropolitan Police Department, Washington, D.C., 1977.

27. General Order number 308.4, Metropolitan Police Department, Washington, D.C.

28. Marvin Wolfgang, Patterns in Criminal Homicide, Philadelphia: University of Pennsylvania Press, 1958, 274; Donald West, Murder Followed by Suicide, Cambridge, Massachusetts: Harvard University Press, 1966; Stengel, op. cit.; Andrew Henry and James Short, Suicide and Homicide, New York: Free Press, 1965; Manfred Guttmacher, The Mind of the Murderer, New York: Farrar, Straus, 1960; T. Dorpat, Suicide in Murderers, Psychiatry Digest (1966), 51-55.

29. West, op. cit., 145-146.

30. Edward Shev, Good Cop/Bad Cops: Memoirs of a Police Psychiatrist, Los Angeles: S.F. Book Company, 1977; Interviews with Captain Clark and Lt. Morris, op. cit.

31. Department of Health, Education, and Welfare, Statistical Abstracts of the United States, Washington, DC: US Government Printing Office, 1972, 59.

32. Bell, op. cit., 213; Gibbs, op. cit., 53, 61-63; James Wilkins, Suicidal Behavior, American Sociological Review, 32 (1967), 286-298.

33. Gibbs, op. cit., 57-73; Dublin, op. cit., 22-29; Ronald Maris, Social Forces in Urban Suicide, Homewood, Illinois: Dorsey Press, 1969, 91-98, 107-108; Calvin Schmid and Maurice Van Arsdol, Completed and Attempted Suicides: a Comparative Analysis, American Sociological Review, 20 (1955), 273-283.

34. Ibid.; Suicide Among Youth, Special Supplement, Bulletin of Suicidology, 1971, 2, 19, 37.

35. Warren Breed, The Negro and Fatalistic Suicide, Pacific Sociological Review, 13 (1970), 156-162; Maris, op. cit., 100-107; Gibbs, op. cit., 64-67; Dublin, op. cit., 30-35.

36. Maris, op. cit., 91-98; Dublin, op. cit., 22-29; Gibbs, op. cit., 63-66, 227-245.

37. Maris, op. cit., 101-102; Gibbs, op. cit., 64-67; Dublin, op. cit., 74-79.

38. Maris, op. cit., 122-123; Warren Breed, Occupational Mobility and Suicide Among White Males, American Sociological Review, 28 (1963), 179-188; Gibbs, op. cit., 68-69; Dublin, op. cit., 61-66.

39. Bell, op. cit., 218; Stengel, op. cit.; Jack Douglas, The
    Social Meaning of Suicide, Princeton, New Jersey: Princeton,
    University Press 1967; Douglas, Deviance and Respectability,
    New York: Basic Books, 1970, 192-228; Edwin Schneidman and
    Norman Farberow (eds.), Clues to Suicide, New York: McGraw-
    Hill, 1957.

40. Dublin, op. cit., 49-55, 223-225; Gibbs, op. cit., 66; Maris,
    op. cit., 136, 156; Schmid and Van Arsdol, op. cit., 276.

41. James Coleman, Abnormal Psychology and Modern Life, Glenview,
    Illinois: Scott, Foresman and Company, 1972, 347-348.

42. Clinard, op. cit., 654.

43. Interview with Doris Loughlin, Chief of Mental Health Services,
    D.C. General Hospital, Washington, D.C., 1977.

44. Clinard, op. cit., 654.

45. District of Columbia Code, Annotated, Washington, D.C.: U.S.
    Government Printing Office, 2, 1973, 22-2401 to 22-2405,
    1463-1488.

46. Norman Farberow and Edwin Schneidman,The Cry for Help, New
    York: McGraw-Hill, 1961; Schneidman and Farberow, op. cit.;
    Stengel, op. cit.; Donald McCormick, The Unseen Killer: A
    Study of Suicide, its History, Causes, and Cures, London:
    Chapman and Hall, 1955; Jack Douglas, op. cit.; Albert Cain,
    Survivors of Suicide, Springfield, Illinois: Charles C. Thomas,
    1972; David Lester, Why People Kill Themselves: A Summary of
    Research Findings on Suicidal Behavior, Springfield: Charles
    C. Thomas, 1972; Jack Zusman and David Davidson, Organizing
    the Community to Prevent Suicide, Springfield: Charles C.
    Thomas, 1972.

INDEX